Second Language Identities

BLOOMSBURY CLASSICS IN LINGUISTICS

Multimodal Teaching and Learning, *Gunther Kress,
Carey Jewitt, Jon Ogborn and Charalampos Tsatsarelis*
Opposition in Discourse, *Lesley Jeffries*
Second Language Identities, *David Block*
Worlds of Written Discourse, *Vijay Bhatia*

More titles coming soon!

Second Language Identities

DAVID BLOCK

BLOOMSBURY
LONDON • NEW DELHI • NEW YORK • SYDNEY

Bloomsbury Academic

An imprint of Bloomsbury Publishing Plc

50 Bedford Square
London
WC1B 3DP
UK

1385 Broadway
New York
NY 10018
USA

www.bloomsbury.com

Bloomsbury is a registered trade mark of Bloomsbury Publishing Plc

First published 2007 by Continuum International Publishing Group

Paperback edition 2009

Bloomsbury Classics in Linguistics edition first published
in 2014 by Bloomsbury Academic

© David Block 2007, 2014

David Block has asserted his right under the Copyright, Designs and
Patents Act, 1988, to be identified as the Author of this work.

British Library Cataloguing-in-Publication Data

A catalogue record for this book is available from the British Library.

ISBN: PB: 978-1-4725-2604-5
ePDF: 978-1-4725-7102-1
ePub: 978-1-4725-7103-8

Library of Congress Cataloging-in-Publication Data

A catalog record for this book is available from the Library of Congress.

Typeset by Deanta Global Publishing Services, Chennai, India
Printed and bound in Great Britain

Contents

Acknowledgements

During the process of writing the book, I have benefited from different kinds of help from different people. I would like to thank Bethan Benwell, Jan Blommaert, Anna Jones, Celeste Kinginger, Claudia Lapping, Masuko Miyahara, Liz Stokoe and (especially) Amos Paran, for reading and commenting on draft chapters. At the Institute of Education, I would like to thank MA students attending sessions on the module *Second Language Learning Experience* and research students and staff attending the fortnightly *Culture, Identity and Language* seminars. It is in such fora that my ideas about identity in second language learning are continually shaped and reshaped. At Continuum, I would like to thank Jennifer Lovel for having faith in this book and Rebecca Simmonds and Joanna Taylor for taking care of editorial matters. Finally, as always, I am grateful to Adrià and Vicky for the kinds of distractions that keep me centred.

List of abbreviations

FL	foreign language
EFL	English as a foreign language
ESL	English as a second language
SA	study abroad
SLL	second language learning
SLLG	second language learning group
SLA	second language acquisition
SSL	Spanish-speaking Latinos
TL	target language
TLG	target language group

1

Introduction

> It is surprisingly easy for someone to steal your identity – all it takes is a discarded bank statement or utility to get into the wrong hands. Criminals can use your personal details to open bank accounts and get credit cards, loans, passports or driving licences in your name. (Letter from the author's bank, December 2005)

> SLA [Second Language Acquisition] theorists have not developed a comprehensive theory of social identity that integrates the language learner and the language learning context. (Norton, 1995: 12)

This book is about how identity is a key construct in different ways in different second language learning contexts. I have chosen the above three quotations to open it because they represent three very different perspectives on identity. The first quotation is taken from a letter that I received from my bank in December 2005. It tells me that I am in danger of losing my identity if I am not careful about where I leave documents that contain my personal details, such as my address, phone number and credit card account numbers. Who and what I am will be harmed – or in any case, economically damaged – if someone else is able to claim to be me by using such documents. Here identity is about how individuals are defined, contained and enabled by documents as opposed to the actions they take.

The second quotation offers a very different view of identity, one that is as open-ended and unstable as my bank's is fixed and deterministic. It is taken from 'Crush with Eyeliner', a song by the American rock band REM about obsessive and perhaps unrequited love. In the quotation, singer Michael Stipe provides the listener with a paean of sorts to the heady times of self-creation in the 1990s. 'Imbibed', 'infatuated' and 'smitten', he considers different positions he might 'wear' to win over the object of his passion. There is an ambiguity here between being 'the real thing' and being 'invented', which will have to remain unresolved (for lack of further data!). Suffice it to say that the song captures common themes in current discussions of identity, such as authenticity and the extent to which identity is a self-conscious and ongoing project.

In the third quotation, identity is invoked as an academic concept. Bonny Norton laments how as recently as ten years ago, second language learning (SLL) researchers had not worked out how to adopt a more socially sensitive perspective in their work. Specifically, before the 1990s there was little or no work examining how language learners position themselves and are positioned by others depending on where they are, who they are with and what they are doing.

The starting point of this book is that matters have changed considerably since Norton first began making calls like the one reproduced above and a long list of publications featuring identity as a central construct attests to this change (e.g. Norton, 2000; Pavlenko, Blackledge, Piller and Teutsch-Dwyer, 2001; Pavlenko and Blackledge, 2004). However, this rise has not come about because applied linguistics suddenly began to talk about identity in the 1990s. Rather, it has been the result of systematic and extensive borrowing from contiguous social science fields of inquiry. Thus, in her early attempt to develop a theory of social identity in second language learning (SLL), Norton (1995) drew heavily on the work of the social theorist Chris Weedon (1987) and the sociologist Pierre Bourdieu (1977). In more recent work, second language researchers look for inspiration from and cite considerably longer lists of scholars who are social theorists, sociologists and anthropologists. The rise of identity in SLL has, therefore, been a question of catching up with developments in other social sciences. But where did all of this talk about identity come from?

Authors who have explored the history of identity (e.g. Taylor, 1989; Holstein and Gubrium, 2000; Woodward, 2002; Hall, 2004; Benwell and Stokoe, 2006) go back to the Western European enlightenment to find the roots of the current obsession with identity, citing a long line of renowned scholars such as Machiavelli, Descartes, Locke, Kant and Hegel. Elsewhere, Bendle (2002) discusses why identity is currently such a popular concept among many social scientists. First, he cites the late nineteenth century and early twentieth century psychology and the psychiatry of William James (e.g. 1890) and Sigmund Freud (e.g. 1923), respectively. For the first time scholars put the self at the centre of research, as something worthy of empirical study that required expert knowledge. Second, Bendle argues that during the nineteenth and twentieth centuries there was a long process of secularization in the industrializing world. This secularization led to a greater valuing of life on earth and self-fulfilment via worldly activity as opposed to other-worldly activity, namely religion. Bendle's third reason for the rise of identity relates to human rights advances in the advanced industrialized nations of the world in the twentieth century. These advances took place concurrently with the rise of secularism, which meant the eroding of traditional institutions blocking social mobility across social class, racial, ethnic and gender lines. Finally, as a long line of social theorists such as Giddens (1991) and Beck (1992) and Bauman (1992) began to make clear some 15 years ago, life in the late modern/postmodern age of globalization is different from life in previous ages and so too is the very ontology that social scientists frame and study. That ontology is a world full of daytime television talk shows and reality shows, sections upon sections of self-help literature in bookshops and a series of technological developments (PCs, mobile telephones, ipods) that have all combined to make the present first and foremost about individuals: their pasts, presents and futures; their trials and tribulations and their aspirations; and in short, who they are. In the work of many social scientists, there has been a movement away from a preoccupation with stability, function and structure to a priming of individual agency and a shift from fixed *essentialized* versions of demographic categories such as race, ethnicity, gender and age to a generally constructivist perspective which sees these categories as more fluid and unstable.

This final point is where I begin this book, presenting in Chapter 2 the broadly poststructuralist view of identity that has become popular among many social theorists, sociologists, anthropologists and sociolinguists, and which has been the general view of identity taken up by a growing number of SLL researchers. I begin by examining the key constructs that arise in current discussions of identity in the aforementioned areas of inquiry, before moving on to consider seven key perspectives on identity which, to varying degrees, have been present in theories and research on identity: race, ethnicity, nationality, migration, gender, social class and language. The discussion of identity in this chapter sets the stage for the remainder of the book in which I examine how some second language researchers, in the past and in the present, have incorporated identity into their work.

Identity as an issue in past SLL research is the focus of Chapter 3. In this chapter I examine key studies carried out in the 1960s, 1970s and 1980s. My aim is to provide a view of how identity was dealt with before second language learning (SLL) researchers began to catch up with the emergent interest in identity in contiguous areas of the social sciences. The time frame is not arbitrary as it represents the years when second language learning research was taking off as an academic discipline in its own right (Block, 2003), up until the recent point in time – the 1990s – when researchers first began to turn their attention to identity in a more explicit and self-conscious way.

My analytical approach in this chapter, as well as the remainder of the book, is borrowed in part from Larry Selinker (1992). At the beginning of his book *Rediscovering Interlanguage*, Selinker sets up his historical account of the concept of interlanguage in second language learning research by stating that he intends to engage in the 'purposeful misreading of founding texts' (Selinker, 1992: 3). Here I see myself doing something along these lines as I examine in detail a selection of past and present second language learning studies in which identity has been an issue. As I discuss these studies, the reader should bear in mind that I am deliberately misreading them, as I frame findings according to my own purposes and intentions.

In Chapters 4 to 6, I move to the recent past and present, examining how research in the 1990s and 2000s has examined identity issues in three distinct SLL contexts. By context, I mean the physical location of language learning as well as the sociohistorical and sociocultural conditions that accompany that physical location.[1] Thus, when I focus on adult migrant contexts in Chapter 4, I am interested, on the one hand, in how the countries, cities and communities that are hosts to migrants are factors in the SLL of these migrants. However, I am also interested in specific social conditions in these host settings that shape the development of second-language-mediated identities. When I focus on foreign language (FL) contexts in Chapter 5, I am interested in how the institutional classroom setting is the most significant mediator of second language activity. However, I am also interested in how such institutional classroom settings will vary due to the sociohistory and socioculture of the educational contexts in which they are embedded and the idiosyncrasies of all of the individuals involved, from teachers to fellow students to stakeholders who never set foot in the classroom. Finally, when I examine study abroad contexts in Chapter 6, I am interested in the combination of an institutional classroom and a naturalistic setting as a backdrop to all second language activity. However, I am also interested in the sociohistorical and sociocultural particularities of both.

In Chapter 4, I frame the adult migrant context as the SLL context of millions of people in the world today who have moved to a new cultural and linguistic environment in search of work, political asylum or even a better quality of life. The cases of interest in this book are those where individuals are long-term sojourners or immigrants, aged 18 or over, who must make a new life mediated by a new culture and language. I argue that it is in this context, more than other contexts, that one's identity and sense of self are put on the line, not least because most factors that are familiar to the individual – sociohistorically, socioculturally, sociolinguistically and linguistically – have disappeared and been replaced by new ones. In this situation, individuals must reconstruct and redefine themselves if they are to adapt to their new circumstances. However, the processes of reconstruction and redefinition do not take place in predictable manners simply because one is classified as an adult migrant. For example, the extent to which such migrants have access to local people, culture and language varies considerably. The oft-cited immersion in the target language (TL), which is assumed to come with a naturalistic setting, therefore, is not always an option.

In Chapter 5, I focus on FL contexts, defined as 'the context of millions of primary school, secondary school, university and further education students around the world who rely on their time in classrooms to learn a language which is not the typical language of communication in their surrounding environment' (Block, 2003: 48). Such contexts vary considerably as regards a long list of variables that include:

- the ratio of teachers to students;
- the relative preparation and professional experience of teachers;
- the number of hours of instruction per week, month, term or year;
- the state of accommodation (size of classroom, condition of furniture, number of windows and so on);
- availability and quality of information technology available;
- quality and quantity of teaching materials.

In addition, there are factors related to local language ideologies, such as:

- the relative importance of learning an FL;
- the relative importance of learning the particular FL in question.

Finally, there are an infinite number of sociohistorical and sociocultural factors away from the classroom that impinge on and shape what goes on in a given context.

In this chapter, I focus on studies of adult FL learners, 18 years of age and older. I make the point that most of the FL learner's activity is mediated not by the TL, but by the local languages, and not by speakers of the TL but by communities of practice emergent locally, inside and outside classrooms. As a result, it is fairly difficult for individuals in FL contexts to experience the kinds of identity transformations associated with the naturalistic contexts of adult migrants discussed in Chapter 4. Nevertheless, I conclude with a discussion of how a focus on imagined and aspired-to international subject positions and the incorporation of internet-mediated activity can open up the prospect of emergent new subject positions in and through the TL in FL contexts.

In Chapter 6, I focus on study abroad (SA) contexts, seen here as involving university-level FL students in stays of one month to two years in length in countries where the FL is the primary mediator of day-to-day activity. In many ways, study abroad contexts represent a mix of the adult migrant and FL classroom contexts, discussed in Chapters 4 and 5. I say this because they combine the institutional and formal classroom of the FL context with an immersion in the trials and tribulations of 'being there' that comes with taking on adult migrant subject positions in a new environment. However, seeing study abroad as a fusion of adult migrant and FL contexts does have its limitations. For example, the migrant subject positions of study abroad students are, from the outset, different from those of adult migrants. Among other things, study abroad students are generally middle-class university students from wealthy countries, aged 19–22, who contrast markedly with adult migrants who are from a broad range of socioeconomic backgrounds (poor, working class, middle class, wealthy), countries (both rich and poor) and age groups (anywhere from 18 to 60). The connection with FL contexts is also potentially problematic as the classroom part of study abroad is different from that experienced by students back home. Thus, while some programmes incorporate teaching by staff from the home university, this teaching is embedded in the new host environment and is therefore different from teaching back home. In addition, when participants attend classes at local universities, they find that the experience is very different from what they have been accustomed to back home and that they are learning not only about the content of their course but also about local educational and socializing processes.

In Chapter 6, I also examine several subject positions arising in study abroad research. I make the point that while study abroad contexts seem to hold great potential for the emergence of intercultural competence and even TL-mediated subject positions, they often become the site of intense comparisons of the home culture with the host culture that often lead individuals to a heightened and reinforced sense of national identity.

Following the discussion of second language identities in the three contexts in Chapters 4–6, I close the book with Chapter 7, which has two distinct aims. First, I provide a brief summary of what has been discussed in previous chapters. Second, I discuss five directions for future research on second language identities.

I am all too aware that in choosing to focus exclusively on three fairly narrow contexts in Chapters 4–6, I am opening myself up to accusations of ignoring a great deal of literature that links SLL with identity issues. One context that is noteworthy by its absence here is that of minority language children in mainstream education in a variety of contexts around the world. I have chosen to omit this particular context from my discussion because I believe it has been dealt with sufficiently elsewhere. Books focusing wholly or in part on this area of inquiry include Cummins (1996, 2000), Toohey (2000), Mohan, Leung and Davison (2001), Day (2002), Miller (2003), Bayley and Schechter (2003), Kanno (2003), Creese (2005) and Hadi-Tabussum (2006).

Another context noteworthy by its absence is that of postcolonial settings, where there has been an increase in the number of publications available internationally in recent years. These publications tend to focus on language ideologies, language policies and language practices, but they include specific references to the interaction of language learning and identity. Three examples suffice to make this point. First, there is Tope Omoniyi's (2004) thorough discussion of the interrelationship between language and identity on the border of Nigeria and Benin. Omoniyi examines how different forms of ex-colonial English and French interact with forms of Yoruba and how language practices are shaped by national identity and local ethnic identity. Elsewhere, Vaidehi Ramanathan (2005) examines the positioning of English vis-à-vis the 15 nationally recognized languages in modern-day

India and how nationalism, language ideologies, social class, caste and gender all impact on how Indians develop language-mediated senses of who they are. Finally, there is John Joseph's (2004) book on the interaction of nationalism, ethnicity and religion with language and identity. Joseph includes two case studies of postcolonial contexts. In case 1, he discusses the emergent identities at the crossroads of Cantonese and English in a post-1997 Hong Kong which is reshaping and reorienting itself to China and the rest of the world. In case 2, he examines how in Lebanon, French, English and Arabic serve to shape how Lebanese people position both themselves and others according to religion and ethnicity.

I am also aware of a bias at work here involving the inclusion of studies published in English and the exclusion of studies published in other languages, although this bias has not resulted from a lack of concern or effort on my part. Indeed, in some cases I have carried out extensive and exhaustive searches for relevant publications in languages other than English, only to end up frustrated, as these searches have been fruitless on the whole. One problem might be that there simply is not a significant amount of work published in other languages that examines the kinds of identity-related issues that I am interested in here. Indeed, the view of identity dominant in this book, presented in great detail in Chapter 2, is a version of the construct very much of the English-speaking world. From this perspective, it is not surprising that the research I have sought to analyse in Chapters 3–6 is all published in English. In the end, however, it is perhaps best (and safest) to say that I have tried to use a select number of studies to help me think about second language identities and my aim is that the resulting discussion will resonate to different variations on these contexts – mediated, to be sure, by different languages – around the world.

For some readers, the terminology used in this book might be confusing, starting with the very title on its cover: *Second Language Identities*. The term 'second' is extremely problematic when talking about language learning, not least because it is often used to refer to a variety of contexts. In this book, 'second' should be understood as an all-purpose term to refer to what might otherwise be called 'additional' or 'other' (see Block, 2003, for a discussion). Still, I do not always use the term 'second language' to refer to a language being learned, preferring 'target language' (TL) on some occasions. This is particularly the case when the context involves students in formal education.

Throughout the book, I consistently use 'Second Language Learning' (SLL) to refer to the field of study that focuses on the learning of additional/other/second languages in different contexts. In Block (2003), I referred to the field of inquiry in question as 'Second Language Acquisition' (SLA), even including this name in the title. However, at present there seems to be a division of sorts between those who use one name or the other. Thus while there is Doughty and Long's (2003) *Handbook of Second Language Acquisition*, there is also Mitchell and Myles's (2004) *Second Language Learning Theories*. In this book, I have opted for 'Second Language Learning' because I see it as a simpler alternative, using 'learning' more in its prosaic sense than in any kind of technical sense, such as in Stephen Krashen's (1981) acquisition/learning distinction.[2]

Finally, I provide a note about transcriptions. In Chapters 3–5, I have reproduced examples of speech data taken from some of the publications that I discuss. For the sake of consistency in presentation, I have adapted these examples of speech data so that they conform to the same transcription conventions. These conventions, based on Jennifer Coates (2003), look as follows:

- X means an unidentified speaker

- A slash / shows the end of a chunk of talk

- A hyphen - illustrates an incomplete word or utterance

- A question mark ? indicates question intonation

- Pauses of less than one second are shown with a full stop inside brackets (.)

- Pauses of one second and longer are timed to the nearest second and the number of seconds is put in brackets (3)

- [square brackets on top of each other indicates the point where[speakers overlap

- An equals sign = at the end of one utterance and the start of the next speaker's utterance shows that there was no audible gap between speakers

- Double brackets around a word or phrase shows that there is ((doubt about the transcription))
- Double brackets around x's ((xxx)) shows that the speaker's utterance is inaudible or can't be made out
- <phrases or words in angled brackets> is an additional comment by the transcriber on what is happening at the time or the way in which something is said
- WORDS or Syllables in CAPital letters are spoken with extra emphasis
- %words% or phrases enclosed by percentage symbols are spoken very quietly, almost like an aside
- : means an elongated vowel (e.g. no:o)

I have also reproduced interview data from the publications I discuss. All such interview excerpts are presented with standardized spelling and punctuation. Suspension points (i.e. . . .) mean either a pause or that a part of the reproduced excerpt has been removed to aid readability. Comments about paralanguage or other relevant additional information appear in brackets as follows: (laughing). Words inserted by the author to add coherence are in brackets as follows: [in the]. Capital letters are used to indicate that the person has raised his/her voice suddenly.

Notes

1 See Siegel (2003) and Ellis (2007) for more detailed discussions of context in SLL research.
2 For Krashen, there are two ways of developing knowledge of a second language. The first, what he calls 'acquisition', is a subconscious and incidental process that leads to the development of tacit linguistic knowledge. The second, what he calls 'learning', is a conscious and intentional process that leads to the development of explicit linguistic knowledge.

2

Identity in the social sciences today

Introduction

> Identity becomes an issue when the self ceases to be taken for granted. . . . Today, identity has become an issue because the reference points for the self have become unstuck: the capacity for autonomy is no longer held in check by rigid structures, such as class, gender, national ethnicity. The self can be invented in many ways. The contemporary understanding of the self is that of a social self formed in relations of difference rather than of unity and coherence. Identity becomes a problem when the self is constituted in the recognition of difference rather than sameness.
> (Delanty, 2003: 135)

In this quotation, Gerard Delanty succinctly sums up identity as a construct for social scientists who subscribe to a generally poststructuralist view of the world. Over the past 15 to 20 years, in publications ranging from Anthony Giddens's (1991) *Modernity and Self-identity* to Zygmunt Bauman's (2005) *Liquid Life*, this generally poststructuralist view has emerged and become influential in the social sciences. Its rise to some (though by no means, total) prominence has come in part as a response to approaches to research which in broad terms take either biology or social structure as determinant of identity. According to a strong form of biological determinism, individuals are what their genes make them. Traditionally, this has meant basic physical characteristics, such as skin colour, biological sex, facial features, body size and so on. However, apart from indexing these more obviously genetically transferred characteristics, the biological argument often bleeds into the very large area of human behaviour. Thus, biological determinists such as Simon Baron-Cohen (2003) explain both the characteristics and behaviour of human beings as directly linked to genes and the evolutionary advantages of their existence. On a lay level, biological determinism manifests itself in many ways that pass unnoticed in day-to-day discourse. In a family context, a child's actions are explained by saying, for example, that 'she is just like her father'. At a broader level, the biological bleeding into the behavioural is manifested when entire groups of people, defined by the above-cited biological characteristics, are associated with particular behaviours. This would be the case of relating someone's behaviour to his/her skin colour or biological sex.

A social structuralist approach to identity is understood here to involve the search for universal laws or rules of human behaviour. It is the default approach to identity which arose in the sociology of Emile Durkheim ([1895] 1964) over 100 years ago and over the decades passed through the functionalism of Talcott Parsons (1937) and the anthropology of Claude Levi-Strauss (1972). The self is seen as the product of the social conditions in and under which it has developed. Traditionally, this has meant that individuals are determined by their membership in social categories based on social class, religion, education, family, peer groups and so on. In a broader sense, it has also meant that they are shaped and formed by their 'culture', understood to be the relatively fixed worldview, modes of behaviour and artefacts of a particular group of people. This environmental argument has often been put forth as more progressive in outlook than the previously cited biological one, not least because environmental factors can be tinkered with. In this case, one can make a better society and therefore produce better individuals, an option which an extreme biological argument would not admit. Nevertheless, both arguments share one key characteristic and that is the belief that individuals are formed and shaped – in a word, determined – by formations which precede them, be these biological or social in nature.

Both the biological determinism and social structuralist approaches to identity are formulated as forms of what is known as essentialism. Essentialism is defined by Mary Bucholtz as:

> the position that the attributes and behavior of socially defined groups can be determined and explained by reference to cultural and/or biological characteristics believed to be inherent to the group. As an ideology, essentialism rests on two assumptions: (1) that groups can be clearly delimited; and (2) that group members are more or less alike. (Bucholtz, 2003: 400)

In recent years, the essentialist position – that human beings are determined by either biology or environment – has come to be questioned by many social theorists. These theorists have been influenced by the generally poststructuralist approach to the study of social phenomena mentioned above. Poststructuralism is at best a vague term, as witnessed by the fact that many authors who use it never actually formulate a straightforward definition of it. However, in simple terms, it means the surpassing of structuralism, defined as the search for 'universal and invariant laws of humanity that are operative at all level of human life – at the most primitive and the most advanced' (Ekeh, 1982: 128; cited in Ritzer, 1992: 498).

In current social science literature, poststructuralism is about moving beyond the search for such 'universal and invariant laws of humanity' to more nuanced, multilevelled and ultimately, complicated framings of the world around us. Specifically, as Smart (1999) notes, poststructuralists show a 'critical concern' with a multitude of issues, such as:

> (i) the crisis of representation and associated instability of meaning; (ii) the absence of secure foundations for knowledge; (iii) the analytic centrality of language, discourses and texts; and (iv) the inappropriateness of the Enlightenment assumption of the rational autonomous subject and a counter, contrasting concentration on the ways in which individuals are constituted as subjects. (Smart, 1999: 38)

A survey of recent publications focusing on topics such as language learning, language socialization and multilingual language practices reveals how this poststructuralist approach to identity has taken hold, to varying degrees, as a common way of conceptualizing identity in applied linguistics. Thus, if I visit the applied linguistics section of the Institute of Education library, I can find a good number of recent books in which authors adopt a partial or completely poststructuralist take on identity. These books include Norton's (2000) study of immigrant women in Canada; Pavlenko, Blackledge, Piller and Teutsch-Dwyer's (2001) edited collection on language learning and gender; Schechter and Bayley's (2002) study of the language practices and language affiliations of Mexican American families in the US; J. K. Hall's (2002) textbook on culture and research; Bayley and Schechter's (2003) collection of papers on language socialization and multilingualism; Kanno's (2003) study of the life stories of Japanese returnees; Miller's (2003) account of the language and socialization processes of immigrant children in Australia; Pavlenko and Blackledge's (2004) collection of papers on the negotiation of identities in different language, cultural and political contexts; Omoniyi's (2004) study of the relationship between sociolinguistic variables such as language choice, language mixing and attitudes towards language and the ongoing construction of identities on the Nigerian/Benin border; Benson and Nunan's (2005) collection of papers on second language learners' accounts of their experiences; and finally, my own discussion of multilingual identities in London (Block, 2006a).

My aim in this chapter is to lay out for the reader a general approach to identity, strongly influenced by notions related to poststructuralism, which, as I suggested above, has become popular among many social scientists today. This approach is in no way unitary; nor is it consistent. Indeed, as will become clear as I proceed, what theorists and researchers mean by identity seems to veer back and forth between structuralism and poststructuralism. In effect, the different authors I cite engage in the balancing act of trying to maintain those structuralist bits that they like, such as Marxism-inspired sociology, whilst taking on board more purely poststructuralist concepts, such as 'the crisis of representation and associated instability of meaning' (Smart, 1999: 38).

I begin by taking the reader on a journey through the key constructs associated with this poststructuralism-inflected approach to identity. Most of the constructs and authors I cite work in the areas of social theory, sociology and anthropology; however, along the way, I also cite authors from applied linguistics who have contributed to this view of identity. Having discussed these key constructs, I move to consider seven key perspectives on identity which to varying degrees have been present in theories and research on identity: race, ethnicity, nationality, migration, gender, social class and language. The discussion of identity in this chapter sets the stage for the remainder of the book in which I examine the past and present of second language research which has had identity at its centre.

Subjectivity, discursive construction and discourse

Chris Weedon (1987, 1997) is often cited as a foundational theorist in poststructuralist discussions of identity, despite the fact that she hardly uses the term, preferring instead to focus on 'subjectivities'. Weedon takes the latter term from the work of the French psychoanalyst Jacques Lacan, although, as Taylor (1989) and Hall (2004) note, there is a longer historical lineage dating back to Hegel ([1806] 1977) and his theorization of self-consciousness as vital to an understanding of the development of individual freedom. Weedon uses 'subjectivity' to refer to 'the conscious and unconscious thoughts and emotions of the individual, her sense of herself and her ways of understanding her relation in the world' (Weedon, 1997: 32). In contrast to the structuralist view of identity, Weedon proposes 'a subjectivity which is precarious, contradictory and in process, constantly reconstituted in discourse each time we think or speak' (Weedon, 1997: 32).

One thing one sees very often is that identity is 'discursively constructed' and Weedon here makes reference to subjectivities being 'reconstituted in discourse'. What exactly does this mean? In order to answer this question, one must first examine what is meant by discourse. On one level, discourse has a more linguistic definition, one which associates the term with the fine-grained study of texts, be these oral or written (e.g. Widdowson, 1978). Among other things, discourse in this sense is about aspects of spoken language such as the use of fillers and turn taking and in written texts, the use of hedges and cohesion. However, in the social sciences in the past 20 years there has been a move among many scholars to adopt an interpretation of discourse which is not just about the nuts and bolts of written or spoken text. Paul du Gay (1996) defines 'discourse' as follows:

> By the term 'discourse' . . . [theorists] refer to a group of statements which provide a language for talking about a topic and a way of producing a particular kind of knowledge about a topic. Thus the term refers both to the production of knowledge through language and representation and the way that knowledge is institutionalized, shaping social practices and setting new practices into play. (du Gay, 1996: 43)

This view of discourse as simultaneously a language and a process of knowledge production is echoed by Derek Layder, who offers the following definition:

> Discourse refers to what is known and can be talked about in relation to a particular topic or area – anything from modern medicine to sports car engines, and thus there can be discourses encompassing any particular body of knowledge. (Layder, 1997: 45)

Elsewhere, James Paul Gee (1996) provides an even broader inter-pretation of the term, including more explicitly than du Gay and Layder non-linguistic dimensions, such as bodily movement and clothes. He refers to Discourses (with capital 'D' and in plural form) as opposed to discourse in the following oft-cited definition:

> Discourses are ways of being in the world, or forms of life which integrate words, acts, values, beliefs, attitudes and social identities, as well as gestures, glances, body positions, and clothes. A Discourse is a sort of identity kit which comes complete with the appropriate costume and instructions on how to act, talk and often write so as to take on a particular social role that others will recognize. (Gee, 1996: 127)

This more amplified view of discourse has been expanded on more recently in Gee's later work (Gee, 2004) and it is the main focus of a recent book-length account of the construct by Jan Blommaert (2005).

For Blommaert, '[d]iscourse . . . comprises all forms of meaningful semiotic human activity seen in connection with social, cultural, and historical patterns and developments of use' (Blommaert, 2005: 3). Blommaert's emphasis on the centrality of semiotics in his definition is in line with current work on multimodality where 'multimodal' refers to 'the use of several semiotic modes in the design of a semiotic product or event, together with the particular way in which these modes are combined' (Kress and van Leeuwen, 2001: 20).

Along with Gee and Blommaert, Weedon draws heavily on the work of Michel Foucault (1981, 1986, 1988), who used the term 'discursive fields' to refer to the 'competing ways of giving meaning to the world and of organizing social institutions and processes' (Weedon 1997: 34). For Weedon, there can be harmony in the ongoing adoption of subject positions across a lifetime. However, the process becomes conflictive when full identification with the discourses on offer does not exist:

> Where there is a space between the position of the subject offered by a discourse and individual interest, a resistance to that subject position is produced. Such resistances are a frequent feature, for example of women's writing in patriarchal societies. The discursive constitution of subjects, both compliant and resistant, is part of wider social play for power. (Weedon, 1997: 109)

Combining Weedon, du Gay, Layder, Gee and Blommaert, discursive activity means any semiotic behaviour on the part of an individual which counts as the expression of a subject position (or subjectivity), the latter originating in a particular discursive field or what Gee calls a Discourse. In this sense, D/discourses may be seen as resources of identity construction. Weedon also describes subjectivities as 'constantly reconstituted' and here her views echo those of Judith Butler (1990, 1999, 2004) and her performative theory of gender.

Performativity and presentation of self

Drawing on J. L. Austin's (1962) earlier work on utterances as instances of 'doing things with words' as opposed to reflections of a true and verifiable reality, Butler argues that gendered selves are determined neither by nature nor nurture. Rather, they are the effects of day-to-day 'acting' in ways normatively defined as masculine or feminine. Through interaction with societal norms – rewards and restrictions – individuals continually stylize their physical appearance (i.e. clothing, make-up, tattoos, etc.) as well as their language and bodily movements as they 'do' being women or men. As Butler puts it:

> Gender ought not to be construed as a stable identity or locus of agency from which various acts follow; rather, gender is an identity tenuously constituted in time, instituted in an exterior space through *stylized repetition of acts.* The effect of gender is produced through stylization of the body and, hence, must be understood as the mundane way in which body gestures, movements, and styles of various kinds constitute the illusion of an abiding gendered self. The formulation moves the conception of gender off the ground as a substantial model of identity to one that requires a conception of gender as a constituted *social temporality.* Significantly, if gender is instituted through acts which are internally discontinuous, then the *appearance of substance* is precisely that, a constructed identity, a performative accomplishment which the mundane social audience, including the actors themselves, come to believe and to perform in the mode of belief. (Butler 1999: 179)

If Butler's views on gender are expanded so that they refer to identity in general, then it is easy to see identities and subject positions as performances, that is bodily and linguistic enactments of discourses at particular times and in particular places.

Although Butler does not cite him directly, Erving Goffman had, some 30 years earlier, drawn on dramaturgical metaphors to make sense of how individuals do identity in different contexts. In *The Presentation of Self in Everyday Life* (Goffman, 1959), there is an explicit focus on how individuals self-consciously present themselves in different social contexts, that is, the impression that they 'give'. However, for Goffman there is also a more symptomatic side to performance in the form of what individuals 'give off', that is, what the audience might imagine that is not contained in the observed performance. Much observed activity described by researchers as 'identity work' is about individuals seeking to align and make as consistent as possible what they 'give' and 'give off', in short, to control the reception of the subject positions they choose to adopt.

In his later work, Goffman took a decidedly more sociolinguistic orientation. First, he began to focus more explicitly and in detail on face-to-face interactions mediated by language and other forms of semiotic behaviour, such as 'assessment of reception through visual back-channelled cues . . . the paralinguistic function of gesticulation . . . the synchrony of gaze shift . . . the provision of evidence of attention (as in the middle-distance look) . . . the assessment of engrossment through evidence of side involvements and facial expressions' (Goffman, 1981: 130). In this work, he introduced the notion of 'footing', a term he used to refer to the 'change[s] in alignment we take up to ourselves and the others present as expressed in the way we manage the production or reception of an utterance' (Goffman, 1981: 128). Such alignments are about three different notions of 'the speaker'. First, a speaker might be seen as an 'animator', that is, a 'talking machine, a body negated in acoustic activity, or . . . an individual active in the role of utterance production' (Goffman, 1981: 144). Or, he/she might be seen as an 'author', that is, 'someone who has selected the sentiments that are being expressed and the words in which they are encoded' (Goffman, 1981: 144). Finally, a speaker might be seen as a 'principal', that is, 'someone whose position is established by the words that are spoken, someone whose beliefs have been told, someone who is committed to what the words say' (Goffman, 1981: 144). In simpler terms, the footing of 'animator' is about speaking other people's words (and beyond words, enacting their multimodality); the footing of 'author' is about speaking one's own words (and enacting one's own multimodality); and the footing of 'principal' is about speaking from an institutional position (and enacting a multimodality associated with that institution).

Goffman's work has been very influential in the social sciences over the past 30 years. However, not all theorists and researchers interested in discourse and identity have found it useful. As I noted above, Judith Butler does not mention Goffman in her work, despite developing a dramaturgical metaphor, 'performativity', which superficially looks similar to Goffman's notion of 'footing'. Elsewhere, Bronwyn Davies and Rom Harré (1999) are rather dismissive of Goffman's work, stating that his approach 'takes for granted that alignments exist prior to speaking and shape it, rather than that alignments are actual relations jointly produced in the very act of conversing' (Davies and Harré, 1999: 45). These authors see Harré's positioning theory as a far more appropriate way to capture the ongoing and emergent nature of the multiple subject positions adopted in the course of communication.

Positioning

According to Harré and others, '[p]ositioning is the discursive process whereby people are located in conversations as observably and subjectively coherent participants in jointly produced storylines' (Davies and Harré, 1999: 37). The 'discursive process' in question is the ongoing engagement with others as individuals participate in their day-to-day activities. As was observed above, this involves not only the use of language but also other forms of semiotic activity such as dress and body movement. Important in this view of identity are the physical metaphors of position and location. For Davies and Harré, individuals both situate themselves through their discursive practices and at the same time, they are situated by others. In both cases, there is a sense of what constitutes a coherent subject position, within a particular activity, transpiring in a particular place at a particular time. In other words, all actors will position themselves and others according to their sense of what constitutes a coherent narrative for the particular activity, time and place.

The importance of activity, time and place in positioning can be understood by looking at a simple example. If I position myself and am positioned by others as a specialist in language behaviour in the context of a seminar at my place of work, then my words and overall behaviour may be taken as authoritative and appropriate by all present. However, if I were to act in the same way during a dinner party with friends, then my being positioned as friend would make my seminar-like behaviour seem arrogant and probably boring. Drawing on Austin's (1962) speech act framework, van Langenhove and Harré

(1999) frame these differences, in terms of illocutionary acts – the functional meaning of utterances (e.g. relating one's thoughts on a matter) and the perlocutionary force – the effect of the speech act. Thus in the above example, I am holding forth on academic matters, both at work and with friends, and hence the illocutionary force of what I say is more or less the same. The difference is in the perlocutionary force: while in the context of the seminar the effect on all present may be favourable (I am doing my job), in the context of the dinner party, the perlocutionary force may be to put off friends who do not wish to be lectured.

Van Langenhove and Harré (1999) suggest that a conversation can be framed as a mutually determining triad with each pole impacting on the other two (see Figure 2.1). The positions taken by or assigned to an individual have an effect on the speech acts produced and the story that emerges in the interaction. Similarly, the story line developing will have an effect on how interlocutors position themselves and are positioned, as well as the specific speech acts that occur. Finally, the speech acts produced will have an effect on interlocutor positions and the story line.

It is worth noting that positioning takes place along a time scale ranging from past to present to future. Thus, speaking in the present, the individual's ongoing story line may be about events and experiences in the past, present or future. Regarding the future, a growing number of identity and language learning researchers (e.g. Norton, 2001; Kinginger, 2004; Murphey, Jin and Li-Chi, 2005; Piller and Takahashi, 2006) have recently turned their attention to how in their talk about language learning, language learners often adopt 'imagined' subject positions in 'imagined' communities of speakers

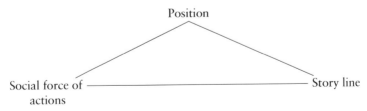

FIGURE 2.1 *Mutually determining triad (Van Langenhove and Harré, 1999: 18).*

of the language they are learning. Exploring such subject positions, projected into the future, these researchers draw on Wenger's (1998) discussions of imagination as an integral part of ongoing identity work. For Wenger:

> The concept of imagination refers to a process of expanding our self by transcending our time and space and creating new images of the world and ourselves. Imagination in this sense is looking at an apple and seed and seeing a tree. (Wenger, 1998: 176)[1]

It is also worth noting, as Weedon (1997) observes, that the adoption of subject positions, that is performances and positioning, do not take place in a vacuum and all of the authors cited thus far, in one form or another, make reference to the inherently conflictive nature of our ongoing identity work. In a sense, the ongoing push and pull and give and take of discursive activity translates into the constant positioning and repositioning and the constant definition and redefinition of who one is.

Ambivalence and hybridity

Another form of conflict – one that is more obvious and profound – arises when individuals move across geographical and sociocultural borders. In such situations individuals often find that any feelings they might have of a stable self are upset and that they enter a period of struggle to reach a balance. At this stage it is easy to conceive of identity as contested in nature as the new and varied input provided to the individual serves to disturb taken-for-granted points of reference. Elsewhere (Block, 2002a), I have used the term 'critical experiences' to refer to such periods in one's life. Echoing Delanty's (2003) quote at the beginning of this chapter, as well as Zygmunt Bauman's claim that: 'No thoughts are given to identity when "belonging" comes naturally' (Bauman, 1999: xxx) and Kobena Mercer's suggestion that 'identity only becomes an issue when it is in crisis, when something assumed to be fixed, coherent and stable is displaced by the experience of doubt and uncertainty' (Mercer, 1990: 43), I define this construct as follows:

> By critical experiences, I mean periods of time during which prolonged contact with an L2 and a new and different cultural setting causes irreversible destabilization of the individual's sense of self. There is, in a sense, an element of before and after in critical experiences as the individual's sociohistorical, cultural and linguistic environment, once well defined and delimited, becomes relatively ill defined and open-ended. (Block, 2002a: 4)

In such cases, the ensuing and ongoing struggle is not, however, a question of adding the new to the old. Nor is it a half-and-half proposition whereby the individual becomes half of what he/she was and half of what he/she has been exposed to. Rather the result is what has come to be known variably as 'hybrid' and 'third place' identities (Bhabha 1994; S. Hall, 1996; Papastergiadis, 2000, Nederveen Pieterse, 2004). The former term, with its roots in agriculture and animal breeding, may be seen to communicate the very notion that I have just denied, namely, that mixing A with B leads to a biological and essential 'hybrid' that is 50 per cent A and 50 per cent B. However, as Jan Nederveen Pieterse (2004) notes, hybridity has been reconstructed by social theorists to refer to a variety of *melange* in three distinct areas of social activity, which he outlines as follows:

> Leisure – music, the visual arts, fashion, literature and cuisine
>
> Institutional – religious fusions, mixed finance initiatives (e.g. private-public initiatives); mixed government (traditional governments, ONGs, lobbies), mixed management styles in industry; new academic disciplines, and so on
>
> Human – cross-ethnic/racial/nationalism

Hybridity has thus come to be seen less in agricultural and breeding terms and more in terms of creolization, that is the mixing of languages which yields a linguistic system which clearly draws on different contributions but contains characteristics that would not have been predictable by simply summing up these contributions.[2] It is in part because of this lack of predictability that Nikolas Papastergiadis sees hybridity as the 'negotiation of difference' in 'the presence of fissures, gaps and contradictions' during which the past and the present 'encounter and transform each other' (Papastergiadis, 2000: 170).

Resulting from the 'negotiation of difference' and the consequent 'fissures, gaps and contradictions' is a key concept in any discussion of identity as hybrid in nature, and that is ambivalence. Ambivalence is the uncertainty of feeling a part and feeling apart. It is the mutually conflicting feelings of love and hate. And it is the simultaneous affirmation and negation of such feelings. For Anthony Elliot, 'the *ambivalence of identity* . . . [is] the tension between self and other, desire and lack, life and death, consciousness and unconsciousness' (Elliot, 1996: 8). For Bauman, it is a 'language specific disorder' (albeit a natural one), 'the main symptom of . . . [which] is the acute discomfort we feel when we are unable to read the situation properly and choose between alternative actions' (Bauman, 1991: 1). Papastergiadis (2000) relates ambivalence to the notions of 'nearness' and 'farness' put forward by Simmel (1950) in his discussion of the 'stranger', that is the state of being intimate with one's surroundings while remaining, metaphorically, outside them.[3]

Ambivalence, it would seem, is the state of human beings who are forced by their individual life trajectories to make choices where choices are not easy to make. However, it is not a desirable state and in studies based on life narratives, individuals generally attempt to resolve the conflicts that underlie their ambivalence. Such attempts to resolve ambivalent feelings tie in with Giddens's view of self-identity as an ongoing narrative in search of 'ontological security', that is the possession of '"answers" to fundamental questions which all human life in some way addresses' (Giddens, 1991: 47).

The idea that individuals strive for a coherent life narrative, seeking to resolve conflicts and assuage their ambivalent feelings, raises the issue of consciousness. To what extent is identity a self-conscious, reflexive project of individual agency, created and maintained by individuals? Surely, in the work of some scholars, there is an element of individuals making choices, in other words an emphasis on individual agency? Giddens, for example, has suggested that even in the most extreme of life conditions, there is some space for individual choice and the 'reflexive constitution of self-identity' (Giddens, 1991: 86). Elsewhere, the cultural anthropologist, Gordon Mathews (2000), argues that identities are not entities into which one is 'raised'; rather, one 'assumes' an identity and then works on it. Identity is thus seen to develop in what Mathews (2000) calls the *cultural supermarket*: just as the modern supermarket offers foods from all over the world, in all shapes and sizes, so the international media and advanced technology together make available to individuals around the world a range of identities to be assumed. However, the cultural supermarket is not a completely free market where any self-identity under the sun can be assumed; nor is it a reality in an equal way for all of the inhabitants of this planet. In the former case, there are social structures within which individuals exist (be these state governments, peer groups or educational systems) which constrain the amount and scope of choice available to individuals. In the latter case, there are individuals living within social structures that do not allow them to make as many choices (e.g. societies where the roles of men and women are circumscribed by tradition).

In the context of his discussion of language and minority rights, Stephen May (2001), argues that much of the work around the concept of hybridity and third places is 'overstatement' and '[i]f taken to an extreme, for example, all choices become possible; a position represented by the methodological individualism of rational choice theory' (May, 2001: 39). In making his criticism, May echoes the views of social theorists such as Derek Layder (1993, 1997) who defend the notion that social constructs such as ethnic affiliation, while not fixed for life, do nevertheless provide a grounding for much of our day-to-day activity. What May writes is also in line with current discussions on the role of consciousness in the construction of subjectivities in cultural anthropology, where scholars such as Sherry Ortner take the following stance:

> At the individual level, I will assume, with Giddens, that actors are always at least partially 'knowing subjects', that they have some degree of reflexivity about themselves and their desires, and that they have some 'penetration' into the ways in which they are formed by circumstances. They are, in short, conscious in the conventional psychological sense, something that needs to be emphasized as a complement to, though not a replacement of, Bourdieu's insistence on the inaccessibility to actors of the underlying logic of their practices. (Ortner, 2005: 34)

Despite his concern about the limits of agency, May does accept some degree of instability in social constructs such as ethnicity in the form of ongoing negotiation (as argued by Papastergiadis), but, in agreement with Layder and Ortner, he does not want to throw away all notions of structure which condition our lives. May explains his position as follows:

> Negotiation is a key element here to the ongoing construction of ethnicity, but there are limits to it. Individual and collective choices are circumscribed by the ethnic categories available at any given time and place. These categories are, in turn, socially and politically defined and have varying degrees of advantage or stigma attached to them . . . Moreover, the range of choices available to particular individuals and groups varies widely. (May 2001: 40)

The importance of structure in studies where identity is a key construct has in fact been accepted by most applied linguists (e.g. Norton, 2000; Kanno, 2003; Block 2006a), even if they have not always explicitly acknowledged this acceptance. This is particularly the case where questions of power come into play in institutional and other social contexts (more on this below). However, attention to structure in the world of these authors has not meant that constructs such as hybridity and third places, as defined by authors such as Hall and Papastergiadis, have been sidelined. Indeed, the broadly poststructuralist approach to identity that has been borrowed from the social sciences by applied linguists has been poststructuralist in its embrace of hybridity and third place, but it has also included and retained structure.

Most social theorists, sociologists and applied linguists today engage with May's argument that it is probably wrong to take concepts such as hybridity, third places and choice to the extreme of arguing that social phenomena such as ethnic affiliation cease to have any meaning. For example, in current discussion and debates about gender (e.g. Alsop, Fitzsimons and Lennon, 2002; Eckert and McConnell-Ginet, 2003; Holmes and Meyerhoff, 2003), there is disagreement about whether or not poststructuralism, associated with arguments against fixed and 'essentialized' notions of femininity and masculinity, offers a way forward, or simply serves to drain debate of any foundation from which to argue. As authors such as Gayatri Spivak (1990) have observed, there may be strategic reasons for engaging in essentialized community politics, in particular the need to make claims about a stable group membership so as to have more political clout and get things done. However, it might be argued that what Spivak has in mind takes place at the level of people's day-to-day activities, and that while essentializing group and cultural traits and practices might work at this level, as a tool to get things done, it is not a good strategy to adopt when working as a researcher, trying to construct understandings and explanations of social phenomena. Indeed, in my own work (e.g. Block, 2002a, 2006a), I have found that constructs such as hybridity and third places work far better than essentialized notions of identity when it comes to making sense of the cases of individuals who have moved between and among qualitatively different sociocultural contexts (e.g. the cases of French, Japanese and Latin American migrants living in London).

Communities of practice

One way to take on board May's concerns about abandoning structure in favour of agency is to frame identity work in terms of individual participation in 'communities of practice' (e.g. Lave and Wenger, 1991; Eckert and McConnell-Ginet, 1992; Wenger, 1998). Penelope Eckert and Sally McConnell-Ginet define a community of practice as 'an aggregate of people who come together around mutual engagement in an endeavour' (Eckert and McConnell-Ginet, 1992: 464). Emerging from this mutual engagement in an endeavour are '[w]ays of doing things, ways of thinking, ways of talking, beliefs, values, power relations – in short practices' (Eckert and McConnell-Ginet, 1992: 464). Such a framework starts with the assumption that learning is situated 'in the context of our lived experience of participation in the world . . . [and] is a fundamentally social phenomenon, reflecting our own deeply social nature as human beings capable of knowing' (Wenger, 1998: 3).

In Wenger's discussion, the relationship between social partic-ipation and communities of practice is essential. Social participation refers 'not just to local events of engagement in certain activities with certain people, but to a more encompassing process of being active participants in the *practices* of social communities and constructing *identities* in relationship to these communities' (*ibid.*: 4). Communities of practice correspond to the different subject positions individuals adopt on a moment-to-moment and day-to-day basis, and indeed throughout their lifetimes, depending on who they are with (examples cited by Wenger include the family, colleagues at work, social groups at schools). However, communities of practice are not just collections of individuals engaging in particular practices, which all people can join at all times. It is, therefore, worthwhile to consider the rules of entry.

In a welcoming context, the individual gains entry by means of 'legitimate peripheral participation'. This peripheral participation is achieved via exposure to 'mutual engagement with other members, to their actions and their negotiation of the enterprise, and to their repertoire in use' (Wenger, 1998: 100). However, as Wenger points out, '[i]n order to be on an inbound trajectory, newcomers must be granted enough legitimacy to be treated as potential members' (Wenger, 1998: 101). Participation thus must always begin peripherally and if the individual is not deemed legitimate, or the individual chooses not to participate as a reflective form of resistance, then it might not begin at all. Thus, in order to participate in particular communities of practice, the individual needs to have acquired or accumulated sufficient and appropriate *cultural capital* (Bourdieu, 1977, 1984), that is, the educational resources and assets, necessary to be a fully functioning participant in a particular community of practice. These resources and assets exist as behavioural patterns (e.g. accent and attitude), as an association with particular artefacts (e.g. books and qualifications) and as a connection to certain institutions (e.g. university and professional associations). I will have more to say about Bourdieu and his capital metaphors when I discuss social class below.

The upshot of May's and Lave and Wenger's work is that while identity is conditioned by social interaction and social structure, it at the same time conditions social interaction and social structure. It is, in short, constitutive of and constituted by the social environment. This is the two-way action commonly described in the work of sociologists such as Bourdieu (e.g. 1977) and Giddens (1991). These authors do not accept that structure can ever be a 100 per cent determinant of behaviour and thought, but at the same time, they do not wish to portray identity as merely a matter of individual agency. Thus, individuals do not carve out an identity from the inside out or from the outside in, as it were; rather, their environments impose constraints whilst they act on that same environment, continuously altering and recreating it.

Power and recognition

These constraints are often wrapped up in the different power relations between and among individuals. Following Foucault (1981, 1986, 1988), power is seen to exist at all levels of human activity and practice, from the level of international corporations or the governments of nation states down to micro-level interactions between individuals on a moment-to-moment basis. It may be conceived of as positive when it enables and empowers individuals to act as members of communities of practice, thus creating subjects, and as negative when it constrains and weakens the capacity to act. In the latter case, the issue of resistance arises, that is the active and intellectualized opposition to oppressive power and its passive acceptance and the development of rival power and the formulation of an alternative form of action to combat it (Canagarajah, 1999).

Another issue key to current approaches to identity is the recognition that identity is neither contained solely inside the individuals nor does it depend exclusively on how others define the individual. Rather, one needs to consider both self-generated subject positionings as well as subject positionings that are imposed on individuals by others. Jan Blommaert makes the following call to those interested in the study of identity in sociolinguistics:

> Whenever we talk about identity, we need to differentiate between 'achieved' or 'inhabited' identity – the identity people themselves articulate or claim – and 'ascribed' or 'attributed' identity – the identity given to someone by someone else. (Blommaert, 2006: 238)

Identity is also about what Butler (2004) calls 'norms of recognition', norms that make it possible for us to be 'intelligible' to others so that they can ascribe to us a particular identity or subject position.

Of course, these norms of recognition change over time and therefore the interface between self-construction and intelligibility to others does as well. Creating such an intelligibility, so that others can 'recognize' us, is about achieving what Bucholtz (2003) calls 'authentication', that is 'the assertion of one's own or another's identity as genuine or credible' (Bucholtz, 2003: 408). Authentication is when fellow members of a community of practice accept the symbolic behaviour of an individual as appropriate and 'real', in short as the way of behaviour constitutive of membership in the community of practice in question.

Identity in a nutshell

In the previous sections, I have discussed what I see as the key constructs associated with the broadly poststructuralist approach to identity that in recent years has been adopted by many social scientists, including applied linguists. In a nutshell, these social scientists frame identities as socially constructed, self-conscious, ongoing narratives that individuals perform, interpret and project in dress, bodily movements, actions and language. Identity work occurs in the company of others – either face-to-face or in an electronically mediated mode – with whom to varying degrees individuals share beliefs, motives, values, activities and practices. Identities are about negotiating new subject positions at the crossroads of the past, present and future. Individuals are shaped by their sociohistories but they also shape their sociohistories as life goes on. The entire process is conflictive as opposed to harmonious and individuals often feel ambivalent. There are unequal power relations to deal with, around the different capitals – economic, cultural and social – that both facilitate and constrain interactions with others in the different communities of practice with which individuals engage in their lifetimes. Finally, identities are related to different traditionally demographic categories such as ethnicity, race, nationality, migration, gender, social class and language.

As I have made clear thus far, identity is a complex and multilayered construct. It is also a construct that has tended to be examined from particular perspectives by theorists and researchers. In the sections that follow, I examine what I consider to be the seven most common perspectives taken. I begin with a discussion of race and ethnicity together, as these two constructs are often conflated both in lay and academic discourses. I then consider, in separate sections, national identity, migrant identity, gender identity, social class identity and language identity.

Ethnicity and race

As May (2001) notes, most researchers who focus on ethnicity do not usually say what they mean by the term. In such cases, one is generally left to wonder if ethnicity is about culture, or if it is a polite way to talk about race. In the former case, ethnicity may be seen to be more about 'common descent and . . . a cultural heritage shared because of common descent' (Joseph, 2004: 162). Elsewhere, Puri (2004) echoes Joseph's cultural view of ethnicity as follows:

> Ethnicity is . . . a form of collective identity based on shared cultural beliefs and practices, such as language, history, descent, and religion. Even though ethnicities often allude to enduring kin-based and blood ties, it is widely recognized that they are cultural, not biological, ties. (Puri, 2004: 174)

Such cultural-minded definitions certainly make sense and they clearly differentiate ethnicity from national identity and race. Nevertheless, this kind of clarity is certainly not the norm in public discourse, where the term is sometimes conflated with nationality and quite often conflated with skin colour. There is perhaps no better example of this tendency to conflate than the 2001 England and Wales population census question: 'What is your ethnic group?', which I reproduce in Table 2.1.

As I explain elsewhere (Block, 2006a), this census question is extremely problematic, as it constantly mixes race and nationality with ethnicity. Thus, under the first category, 'White', the respondent is given choices that are about nationality: Irish and British. However, under Mixed, the choices may be about skin colour mixed with geographical regions (Caribbean African, Asian). Categories c, d and e show similar patterns mixing nationality, geographical region and skin colour.

Table 2.1 'What is your ethnic group?'

What is your ethnic group?
(a) White: British ( ), Irish ( ), Any other White background ( )
(b) Mixed: White and Black Caribbean ( ), White and Black African ( ), White and Asian ( ), Any other Mixed background ( )
(c) Asian or Asian British: Indian ( ), Pakistani ( ), Bangladeshi ( ), Any other Asian background ( )
(d) Black or Black British: Caribbean ( ), African ( ), Any other Black background ( )
(e) Chinese or other ethnic group: Chinese ( ), Other ethnic group ( )

This kind of mixing, not surprisingly, is questioned by researchers exploring race and ethnicity. On this matter, Pilkington has the following to say about keeping the two terms separate:

> Race and ethnicity both involve drawing boundaries between people. A conceptual distinction can, however, be made between race and ethnicity. While racial boundaries are drawn on the basis of physical markers, ethnic boundaries are drawn on the basis of cultural markers. (Pilkington, 2003: 27)

Elsewhere, MacMaster (2001) expresses a view held by many who have focused on race (e.g. Gilroy, 2000, 2004; Solomos, 2003; Ali, 2004) stating that '[r]acial categories cannot be explained through a scientific system of classification based on biological/genetic methods, but are ideological constructs, forms of boundary definition between groups that have evolved within specific historical and social contexts' (MacMaster, 2001: 1). Perhaps in recognition of the inherent instability of social constructs and the kind of conceptual bleeding and slippage that commonly goes on in the world (both lay and academic), Pilkington concludes his discussion of the differences between race and ethnicity, saying that 'the two may empirically overlap, with people defined as a race becoming over time an ethnic group' (Pilkington, 2003: 27).

National identity

Examining the concept of national identity historically, Anthony Smith argues that: 'the quest for national identity . . . began in earnest in the late eighteenth century . . . [and] was part and parcel of the wider Romantic yearning for *authenticity*, which became a key nationalist aspiration' (Smith, 2004: 247). National identities have always been forged, or instilled in individuals growing up in particular places and times, as 'a complex of common or similar *beliefs or opinions* internalized in the course of socialization . . . and of common or similar *emotional attitudes* as well as common or similar *behavioural dispositions*' (Wodak, de Cillia, Reisigl and Liebhart, 1999: 28), all relating directly to a particular nation state. For Wodak *et al*, national identity is, in effect, a kind of Bourdieu-ian *habitus,* that is an 'acquired system of generative schemas objectively adjusted to the particular conditions in which it is constituted' (Bourdieu, 1977: 95). However, while the discussion of 'similar beliefs and opinions' might suggest stability and indeed perhaps a deterministic attitude towards the construction of self identity, Wodak *et al* are careful to distinguish between structure as emergent in individual and collective agency and structure as determinant of individual and collective agency. They make the point that 'national identities are generated and reproduced through discourse' and that 'there is no such thing as one national identity in an essentialist sense, but rather that different identities are discursively constructed according to . . . the degree of public exposure of a given utterance, the setting, the topic addressed, the audience to which it is addressed, and so on' (Wodak *et al*; 1999: 186–7).

The views expressed by Wodak *et al* are consistent with those espoused by other authors who have written extensively about national identity such as Gellner (1983), Hobsbaum (1990), B. Anderson (1983, 1991), Smith (1991), Billig (1995), Reicher and Hopkins (2001) and Puri (2004). Drawing on B. Anderson's (1983) view of nations as 'imagined communities' and Renan's ([1882] 1990) suggestion that nations depend on their ongoing construction by individuals who have opted to see themselves as forming part of a larger group, these authors all make more or less the same point, namely that individuals position themselves, via their discourse, as nationals of a particular stripe, and that nation identity is neither an objective nor a stable construct. National identity thus is not fixed at birth and tied to one's birthplace; rather, it is an ongoing project, recreated daily via actions such as flag waving and the invocation of historical events to explain present day phenomena (Billig, 1995). Thus even in the cases of individuals who are born, raised and educated in a particular locality of a particular nation state, their sense of national identity is an ongoing project that must be nurtured by any number of symbols and activities.

Migrant identity

In the current global age, people are on the move as they have never been before. This movement has led not only to re-evaluations by social scientists of what it means to have a national identity, but also to a more overt interest in how to conceptualize the movement of peoples around the world – migration – and new ways of doing being a migrant. And while there are obviously many people in the world today who do not merit the label 'migrant', there is a growing tendency for such individuals to position themselves in contrast to migrants. For example, Australian passport holders may position themselves as Australian nationals by highlighting the fact they are not migrants, but 'real' Australians. There is, therefore, space in this discussion of perspectives on identity for what I will call a migrant identity, an attempt to capture the subject positions of the millions who have, over the years, crossed geographical borders in their lifetimes.

Migration may be defined as 'the movement of people across borders, both by choice and under economic and political forces, which involves stays of over a year' (Jordan and Düvell, 2003: 5). There is a long history of migration in the world, dealt with in different ways by authors such as Castles and Miller (2003), Cohen (1997), Held *et al* (1999), Papastergiadis (2000), Faist (2000) and Jordan and Düvell (2003). Space does not allow a careful consideration of the work of all of these authors (see Block, 2006a); suffice it to say that paralleling many other fields of inquiry in the social sciences, migration theorists have moved away from more static, deterministic models to more open-ended, dynamic ones. For many years, the two main competing models of migration were what Papastergiadis (2000) calls the 'voluntarist push-pull model' and the 'structuralist centre-periphery model'. The former model sees rational choice and individual agency as the driving forces behind migration. According to this model, people move from one place to another in order to improve their economic lot. By contrast, the structuralist centre-periphery model draws on Marxist economic theory. It sees world capitalism as the driving force behind migration, which serves the function of providing an everlasting supply of cheap and dispensable labour to the developed economies of the world, helping them through the ups and downs of ongoing expansion and contraction.

For most migration theorists today, these two models are both too simple and incomplete. Faist (2000) and Castles and Miller (2003) discuss as an alternative theory of migration, what they call the multi-level migration systems theory. According to this theory, migration can be conceptualized as a series of overlapping and interacting systems working at three levels: macro, micro and meso. At the macro level, there is a consideration of the kinds of global forces discussed by the globalization theorists cited above: global politics, global markets, global ideologies, global media and so on. All of these macro-level factors impact on the flow of individuals between and among countries. At the micro level, the human element is introduced in the form of the individual values and expectations such as the desire to improve one's standard of living or gain political autonomy. The meso level refers to the various networks that intercede between the macro and micro levels. These networks include social ties (be these family or occupational), symbolic ties (belonging to a particular ethnic, national, political or religious group) and transactional ties (e.g. reciprocity, solidarity, access to resources). Faist (2000) understands these networks in terms derived from the work of Bourdieu (1991), making reference to cultural capital (the educational resources migrants bring with them; the know-how and ability necessary if one is to migrate) and social capital (the safety net of already established relationships among previous migrants, family and organized assistance).

In discussions of migration as multi-level, complex phenomenon, David's Harvey's (1989) concept of 'time-space compression' is often invoked, either explicitly or implicitly. Time-space compression means that via advanced technology and transportation, people can be in either physical or virtual contact with one another much faster and more effectively and efficiently than has ever been the case in the past. As Perlmutter (1991) notes, the impact of this time-space compression has meant that the world is coming to be organized less vertically, along nation-state lines, and more horizontally, according to communities of shared interests and experiences. Thus there are progressively more and more communities which transcend nation-state boundaries and individuals who in much of their lives feel more allegiance and affinity to these communities than they do to the national states in which they reside. These communities are based on a long list of shared experiences and orientations, such as: tastes in fashion, music, cinema, literature and so on; beliefs and opinions; and lifestyle options.

Given its effect on relatively stable populations, it is not surprising that time-space compression should have a great impact on migration processes. Indeed, once they have settled in a particular nation-state, today's migrants are progressively forming part of what are termed transnational social spaces as opposed to (or even in addition to) classical immigrant or expatriate subject positions. Classical immigrants are understood to be individuals who settle in a new country – socially, economically and politically – with little or no expectation or prospect of returning to their country of origin. As a rule, classical immigrants assimilate to the ways of their adopted homes as they, in turn, impact on these ways. Inside most classical immigrants, there is a tug of war going on, between cultural maintenance and fitting into the new environment. In marked contrast to classical immigrants, expatriates are individuals who have chosen to live abroad for an extended period of time. They know that whenever they want, they can return to their home country, and indeed, they embark on their migrant experience with the expectation that they will return to their country of origin. The period of time they live abroad may vary from months to years and this time period may be divided up into shorter sojourns or it may be one long extended stay.

While classical immigration and the expatriate experience are still options for migrants today, there is a progressive tendency towards transnationalism and the development of what are known as transnational social spaces. According to migration specialists (e.g. Glick

Schiller, Basch and Blanc-Szanton, 1992; Basch, Glick Schiller and Blanc-Szanton, 1994; Portes, Guarnizo and Landolt, 1999; Faist, 2000; Foner, 2001; Jordan and Düvell, 2003), transnational social spaces emerge at the crossroads of migration-facilitating institutionalized and informal networks (see Faist's meso-level constructs above). Jordan and Düvell (2003) describe transnational social spaces as sites where groups, defined by ethnicity (e.g. Latino), religion (e.g. Muslim), nationality (e.g. Turkish) or geographical region (e.g. North African), have settled in nation states, but have nevertheless 'retained and developed their cultural and economic links with their homelands, including (in some cases) their political loyalties and commitments' (Jordan and Düvell, 2003: 76). Such groups behave differently from traditional immigrants in that they have not made a firm commitment as regards personal and cultural loyalties to the host society. For Jordan and Düvell, the transnational existence of these groups

> defies notions of assimilation and acculturation to the national 'core', and goes beyond the ethnic pluralism of multicultural membership. It suggests that dual or multiple forms of nationality and citizenship might better reflect and recognize the realities of these socio-economic systems. (Jordan and Düvell, 2003: 76–7)

The agents who inhabit these transnational spaces, known as 'transmigrants', act as follows:

> [They] do more than stay in touch with family members left behind. They organize daily economic, familial, religious, and social relations within networks that extend across the borders of two nation-states. Transnational connection takes many forms, all of which go beyond immigrant nostalgia in which a person who is removed from his or her ancestral land tries to recreate on the new land a sense of the old, through foods, music and storytelling. (Fouron and Glick Schiller, 2001: 60)

Thus, migration today opens up new and different adaptation options for migrants. Whereas in the past, immigration, with the connotation of 'staying for life', was the dominant option, today migrants can live, as it were, straddling geographical, social and psychological borders.

Gender

Apart from identity framed in terms of ethnicity, race, nationality and migration, there has been a growing interest in recent years with gender identities, especially as these relate to language. According to authors such as Deborah Cameron (1995, 1996, 2005), from a feminist linguistics perspective, there have been four approaches to language and gender over the past 30 years, each of which frames gender identities in very different ways. However, all four have in common their rejection of biological determinism whereby individuals are born sexed – either male or female – and then proceed to live their lives determined by this distinction.

The first approach, known as the *deficit* model, frames women as disadvantaged speakers and communicators, particularly in professional settings. This disadvantage is said to arise from their upbringing and socialization as females (Lakoff, 1975) and the way forward for women is to align their speech to male-dominant norms. Career-orienting advice is typically the lay public face of this line of enquiry, an excellent example being a book by Janice Ellig and William Morin entitled *What Every Successful Woman Knows* (2001). This book aims to provide professional women with effective strategies which will allow them to get ahead in the male-dominated business world. Ellig and Morin very clearly align themselves with *deficit*, framing women as inept communicators in the world of business which requires confidence and assertiveness. According to the authors, these skills are learnt by boys in a natural way early in their lives, but

> women have been trained since childhood to be less direct . . . [Y]oung girls were traditionally taught to believe that they would get more through coyness than through directness. . . . Women simply gather and process information differently from men. In fact they approach the whole process of communication in a different way. (Ellig and Morin, 2001: 109–110)

The suggestion is that if women are to compete with men and be successful in this world, they have to adopt the characteristics of men when communicating, or in any case imitate their behaviour.

The view of gender is highly essentialized in that it is about having certain characteristics which are determined by the environment and which are stable throughout one's lifetime. And although the notion that women can adopt male speech and behaviour norms affords some space for individual agency, the *deficit* model is conservative in that it encourages women to follow modes of behaviour laid down by men, as opposed to challenging them.[4]

A second approach, the *cultural difference* model, is also about different socialization patterns, namely that men and women belong to separate but equal cultures (Tannen, 1990). Unlike the deficit model, the *cultural difference model* does not see difference in a negative light; rather, it adopts the socially liberal position that men and women are different but equal: women's speech and communication styles are not inferior to men's; rather the relationship between the two are problematic at least in part due to the clashing of cultures. If Lakoff's *deficit* work has spawned an overtly popularized literature, primarily in the business sector, the *cultural difference* model has produced a wide variety of publications. While some of these publications are addressed exclusively to women (e.g. 'how to talk to men' pieces in magazines such as *Cosmopolitan* or *Marie Claire*), others are addressed to both men and women. The most notable example from the latter category is John Gray's seemingly never-ending series of books about men being from Mars and women being from Venus (e.g. Gray, 1992). The general aim of such publications is for men and women to improve their communication skills and, as a result, the state of communication in their heterosexual relationships. Interestingly, as Cameron (1996) points out, in those cases where books are written for both men and women (e.g. Gray's series), they are disproportionately read by women. This phenomenon somewhat undermines the ethos of the cultural difference model in that it points to the prospect that it is women who are doing the bulk of the bridging work necessary for a more harmonious existence between men and women.

A third approach to language and gender is the *dominance* model. In this model women are seen to perform their femininities in patriarchal societies in which they negotiate, as best they can, their position of relative powerlessness vis-à-vis men (Fishman, 1980; West, 1984). Whereas the politics of the *deficit* and *cultural difference* models are more mainstream to North American society, the *dominance* model is more overtly socialist. In effect, it challenges the foundations of socio-economic hierarchies in different societies around the world, proposing not just the adjustment of individuals' ways of speaking, but the dismantling of the entire social structure edified over centuries which has given men the upper hand over women. Given its more radical political agenda, it is perhaps not surprising that this approach to language and gender has not led to a corresponding popularized literature. After all, the international publishers of lifestyle magazines and self-help books are not likely to support calls for the overthrow of international capitalism!

Nevertheless, the *dominance* model does share with the *deficit* and *cultural difference* approaches one very important characteristic, namely that it too is an essentialized, structuralist approach to social phenomena where, among other things, notions of clear boundaries, social stability and determinism are manifest. In this sense, like the *deficit* and *cultural difference* approaches, it is not powerful enough to represent adequately and explain with sufficient sophistication the increasing complexity of language and gender in late modernity (Giddens, 1991). Thus, what has emerged in recent years is a less unified, poststructuralist approach to gender. This poststructuralist approach to gender has been derived from the work of feminist theorists such as Judith Butler (1990, 1993) and Chris Weedon (1997) and is captured well by many of the contributors to Holmes and Meyerhoff's (2003) *Handbook of Language and Gender.* Notwithstanding their differences, most poststructuralist gender specialists share several key views.

First, there is a consensus that gender is about doing as opposed to having or being. This relates to Butler's concept of performativity and gender identities as 'constituted in time [and] instituted in an exterior space through *stylized repetition of acts'* (Butler, 1999: 179). Second, gender is the outcome of engagement in social practices mediated by language and other forms of semiotic behaviour as opposed to the predecessor and causant of such engagement. In short, gender identities emerge in and from activity and interaction and do not precede or cause them. This is not to deny that individuals do their gender work drawing on established gender-related discourses; however it is to emphasize the gender is an emergent phenomenon, as opposed to a determined one. Third, gender work is done by all human beings, not just those classified as female. For a long time, it seems that work on gender was associated almost exclusively with feminism and women. However, in recent years progressively more theorizing and research has focused on masculinities (e.g. Johnson and Meinhof, 1997; Benwell, 2003; Coates, 2003), and there is now a greater balance in gender studies. Finally, adopting a poststructuralist approach also means that gender cannot be studied in isolation from other perspectives on identity, such as ethnicity, race, nationality and social class.

In addition, in recent years there has been an increased interest in sexual identity and the notion that sexual identity is inextricably linked to gender identity (e.g. Cameron and Kulick, 2003; Bucholtz and Hall, 2004; Cameron and Kulick, 2005; Cameron, 2005). In a review article focusing on the place of identity of language and sexuality research, Mary Bucholtz and Kira Hall (2004: 470) define sexuality as 'the systems of mutually constituted ideologies, practices, and identities that give sociopolitical meaning to the body as an eroticized and or reproductive site'. Sexual identity, understood narrowly, is about the labelling of individuals according to their sexual orientation: straight, gay, lesbian, bisexual and so on. However, if the broadly post-structuralist framework for identity is taken seriously, then sexual identity must be seen as discursively constructed, that is, emergent in the multimodal activities (speaking, writing, bodily movement, dress and so on), related to erotic desires and practices, that individuals engage in.

According to Deborah Cameron, sexual identity research has developed along two lines: 'one in which the focus is on non-mainstream, liminal, or "queer" sexual identities, and one in which heterosexual identities become an explicit object of attention' (Cameron, 2005: 494). The former category includes not only the identity work of gays and lesbians, but also what Cameron calls 'traditional non-western categories' such as *hijra*, mainly male transvestites in India who self-identify as hermaphrodites (Hall, 1997), or Brazilian *travestis* (Kulick, 1998). The focus on heterosexual identities is often about heteronormativity, that is, the 'structures, institutions, relations and actions that promote and produce heterosexuality as natural, self-evident, desirable, privileged and necessary' (Cameron, and Kulick,

2003: 55). However, as Cameron notes, it is almost impossible to focus on one particular type of sexual identity without involving others. Thus, the multimodal practices of male transvestites draw on what might be understood as 'heterosexual' resources, including the dress, movement and manner of speech of stereotypical 'sexy' female icons such as Marylyn Monroe. Likewise, as children adolescents are socialized into what Eckert (1989) calls the 'heterosexual market', they engage in identity work related to homosocial (same sex but non-sexual) relationships, such as a group of boys making misogynist comments, and they learn about taste and hierarchies with regard to heterosexual activity. Perhaps more importantly, they explicitly contrast their heterosexuality, adopted as the norm, and (often stereotypified) gay and lesbian subject positions.

Social class

Social class has traditionally served as a label in the social sciences for any one, some or all of the following variables: wealth, occupation, education and symbolic behaviour (e.g. language, clothing, pastimes). However, as a perusal of recent books on topics such as globalization, migration and sociolinguistics reveals, social class was, for a time, assigned very little space by some social scientists discussing identity. This was due, in part, to a fairly generalized interpretation of Marxism as a framework that primes the material over the cultural and the collective over the individual, and in so doing, adopts a deterministic and predominantly economic view of human activity and development. While this interpretation is no doubt partial and somewhat overstated, it is nonetheless common and it is not always refuted with very much enthusiasm by scholars discussing Marxism (e.g. Antonio, 2000). In addition, social class is considered by some as a kind of screen that prevents researchers from seeing other important elements that are factors in human interaction, such as nationality, race, ethnicity and gender. Thus, a Brazilian woman of European and African heritage, who migrates to London to work as a cleaner, can be positioned in her new home as an exploited member of the new economic underclass. However, this classification will only capture a part of a larger picture in which racial phenotype, cultural habitus, and language identity as a Portuguese speaker and available gendered subject positions loom as perhaps more important.

Nevertheless, as Beverley Skeggs (1997, 2004) argues, social class has never gone away as a powerful identity marker, even if this is not acknowledged by social science researchers or informants in ethnographic studies. In her detailed discussions of class, Skeggs (1997, 2004) draws on Bourdieu's (1977, 1984, 1991) array of 'capital' metaphors to provide a framework which she believes can work in today's postmodern world. First, there is economic capital, plainly and simply the financial wealth and income of an individual, as well as his/her acquired property and assets. Second, there is cultural capital. As I noted above, cultural capital is about having the right cultural resources and assets, which exist as behavioural patterns (e.g. accent and attitude), as an association with particular artefacts (e.g. books and qualifications) and as a connection to certain institutions (e.g. university and professional associations). Social capital, Bourdieu's third metaphor, relates directly to these institutional contacts. Social capital is above all about connections to and relationships with less, equally or more powerful others: the greater the cultural capital of these others, the greater the social capital accrued by knowing them. Fourth and finally, there is symbolic capital, which is 'commonly called prestige, reputation, fame, etc. [and] . . . is the form assumed by [the] . . . different kinds of capital when they are perceived and recognized as legitimate' (Bourdieu, 1991: 230). Social class understood in terms of these capitals, as a composite of wealth, occupation, education and symbolic behaviour, is useful if one wishes to develop a complete understanding of identity.

A complement to seeing social class in terms of Bourdieu's capitals is to see it in terms of occupation, whereby people have traditionally been categorized as belonging to three general classes – upper, middle and working class. However, the structures of economies around the world have changed over the past thirty years and so have the characteristics of occupations. As authors such as Gee, Hull and Lankshear (1996) have suggested, the 1980s and 1990s saw the rise of a 'new work order'. This new work order grew out of phenomena such as the globalization of finance and the rise of 'footloose' capital; the growth of the service based economy, which went hand in hand with the demise of the industrial economy; and the deregulation of labour, which included the dismantling of organized labour and the rise of more precarious work conditions and reduced long-term career prospects. As result of these changes to economies, traditional upper, middle and working class categories no longer seemed to capture the realities of working populations.

Among other things, the traditional middle class has divided, with a minority moving into higher income brackets and the majority finding their existence far more precarious, in terms of both pay and job security, than was previously the case. There is now, in effect, a new three-part division of the labour marker into what Reich (1991) calls *in-person servers, routine producers* and *symbolic analysts*. *In-person servers*, such as sales staff at department stores, secretaries, hairdressers, bus drivers and teachers, are involved in repetitive tasks (controlled ultimately by *symbolic analysts*) which are carried out in the presence of those consuming their products. *Routine producers* are blue- and white-collar workers who have in common the routine nature of their work (in this sense they are similar to *in-person servers*) and the fact that it is not carried out in the presence of those who will ultimately consume its products (in this sense they are different from *in-person servers*). In the category of *routine producers*, there are those who work in manufacturing contexts (both assembly line workers and managers) as well as the growing number of individuals working in data and information processing of different types (for example, those who enter information about clients onto computer databases). *Symbolic analysts* are the problem identifiers and solvers, a superclass of highly educated and skilled individuals who are becoming progressively less dependent on traditional local organizations and frameworks and more integrated with a developing international socioeconomic and intellectual elite.

Language identity

A final perspective on identity often invoked in poststructuralist literature, and one most relevant to the research discussed in this book, is what most sociolinguists would call ethnolinguistic identity,[5] but which I will here call language identity. Language identity may be understood as the assumed and/or attributed relationship between one's sense of self and a means of communication which might be known as a language (e.g. English) a dialect (Geordie) or a sociolect (e.g. football-speak). A language identity is generally about three types of relationship with such means of communication, what Leung, Harris and Rampton (1997) call *language expertise, language affiliation* and *language inheritance* (see also Rampton, 1990). Expertise is about how proficient a person is in a language, dialect or sociolect, that is, if he/she can talk a particular talk in such a way that he/she is accepted by other users of the language, dialect or sociolect in question. Affiliation is about the individual's attitudes towards and affective connection to a language, dialect or sociolect. In effect, it is the extent to which a person identifies with and feels attached to a particular form of communication. Finally, inheritance is a matter of being born into a family or community setting that is associated with a particular language or dialect. Importantly, this birthright says nothing about one's expertise in the putative language or dialect. Nor does it guarantee any degree of positive affiliation. One can inherit a language or dialect, but feel no affiliation towards it nor have expertise in it. As is the case with other types of identity, language identities can shift dramatically during one's lifetime. Thus, one can be born into a language community – a question of inheritance and possibly expertise – but then later in life develop a strong affiliation to and expertise in another language community.

In addition, language identity is understood in terms of what Le Page and Tabouret-Keller (1985) call 'acts of identity'. For these researchers, all utterances can be interpreted as an index of the speaker's identity. In addition, this process of indexing is not just two-dimensional, as was the case for early sociolinguistic work which focused on associations such as accent-social class (e.g. Labov, 1966); rather it is multidimensional. This multidimensionality means that emerging from all human utterances, framed as acts of identity, is the enactment of different dimensions of identity, such as ethnicity, nationality, gender and social class. In addition, this multi-dimensionality occurs simultaneously, that is, utterances index ethnicity, nationality, social class, gender and other dimensions of identity at the same time.

Following Silverstein (1998; cited in Blommaert, 2006), one might also consider language identity with regard to 'language' and 'speech' communities. The former are 'groups professing adherence to the

normatively constructed ideologically articulated "standard" language . . . and the latter are groups characterized by the actual use of
specific language forms' (Blommaert, 2006: 243). Thus the language
expertise, language affiliation and language inheritance of individuals
might relate to allegiances to notions of a standard form of language
or it might relate to the same orientations with regard to language
in use. In addition, the acts of identity discussed by LePage and
Tabouret-Keller can be linked directly to speech communities, given
the exclusive concern with language and not meta level allegiances to
standard norms. Elsewhere, Blommaert (2005) makes the point that
membership in a language community is often an ascribed identity
that perhaps has little to do with the achieved or inhabited identity
arising from language use in the different speech communities with
the different communities of practice to which the individual belongs
and with which the individual is engaged, respectively. Indeed, in
discussions of language identities, there needs to be a great focus on
the achieved or inhabited subject positions around language use and
semiotic behaviour in communities of practice as opposed to subject
positions presumed by outsiders (e.g. researchers) to be important
and real to individuals.

This question of semiotic behaviour leads to a fourth view of
language identity, one that, in effect, moves beyond language to
multimodality. As was observed above, multimodality is about 'the
use of several semiotic modes in the design of a semiotic product
or event, together with the particular way in which these modes
are combined' (Kress and van Leeuwen, 2001: 20). While 'semiotic
product' may be understood to be an artefact such as a television
advertisement or traffic sign, I understand that it can also refer to the
momentary and ongoing achievements of particular subject positions
by individuals (Scollon, 2001; Scollon and Scollon, 2003) In this way, I
attempt to frame communication as more than the various linguistic
means which can be drawn on to mediate self-expression (accent,
pronunciation, lexical choice, syntax, morphology). Communication
is also about a range of multi-sensory accompaniments to the
linguistic, such as hairstyle, clothing, facial expressions, gait and so
on. Effectively, there is an argument here in favour of a *multimodal
identity,* not so much *in addition to* language identity, but perhaps as
a replacement for it.

Finally, a second language identity is about degrees of audibility in the second language. Audibility is superficially about being heard, but as invoked by Jennifer Miller (2003) in her research on immigrant children in Australia, it is about a combination of the right accent as well as the right social and cultural capital to be an accepted member of a community of practice. Audibility thus may be linked to intelligibility (Butler, 2004) and authentication (Bucholtz, 2003), as discussed above, as well as notions taken from the work of Bourdieu (1977) such as 'right to speech' and the 'power to impose reception'. Adding a multimodal layer, and therefore stretching the construct substantially, audibility is about developing an identity in an additional language not only in terms of linguistic features, but also dress, expressions, movement, behaviour and other forms of semiotic behaviour. Audibility may thus be seen as corresponding to the extent to which the individual can 'do' the multimodal package required by a particular community of practice. It should be noted, however, that due to aspects of physical appearance, such as racial phenotype or relative conformity to local notions of what constitutes beauty, the individual cannot always control reception of his/her audibility. Indeed, for many immigrants and children of immigrants in countries where immigration is a relatively new phenomenon, there is the grating experience of presenting an acceptable multimodal package (accent, cultural capital, dress, movement, etc.) but still being positioned as 'foreign' by those who conform to the default assumed racial phenotype and overall physical appearance of the host community. Thus the daughter of Black Ghanaian immigrants, born and raised in Barcelona, might elicit expressions of amazement from 'pure', white Catalans when she speaks *their* language (Catalan), which also happens to be the language through which she was educated and a language through which she has always socialized with others outside her family.

Conclusion

In Table 2.2, I summarize the different perspectives on identity discussed thus far. This table, I believe, requires several qualifications and clarifications. First, all of the identities listed and glossed in the

Table 2.2 Individual/collective identity types

Ascription/affiliation	Based on
Ethnic identity	shared history, descent, belief systems, practices, language and religion, all associated with a cultural group
Racial identity	biological/genetic make-up, i.e. racial phenotype.
National identity	shared history, descent, belief systems, practices, language and religion associated with a nation state
Migrant identity	Ways of living in a new country, on a scale ranging from classic immigrant to transmigrant
Gender identity	nature of conformity to socially constructed notions of femininities and masculinities, as well as orientations to sexuality and sexual activity
Social Class identity	income level, occupation, education and symbolic behaviour
Language identity	relationship between one's sense of self and different means of communication, understood in terms of language, a dialect or sociolect, as well as multimodality.

table are about positionings by others and self-positionings, about ascriptions from without and affiliations from within. The different identity types are, therefore, co-constructed and, furthermore, simultaneously individual and collective in nature. Importantly, they are manifestly social in nature, generally having nothing to say about the inner self or the psyche of individuals. I will have more to say about a more psychological and psychoanalytical perspective on identity in the final chapter of this book.

Second, although I list and gloss these different identity types separately, I in no way wish to suggest that they stand independent of one another in the larger general identity of a person. As I point out above, when discussing race, ethnicity, nationality, migrant positions, gender, social class and language, it is indeed difficult to discuss one type of identity without mentioning others. Thus, masculinities and femininities must be understood in terms of language positioning (Pavlenko *et al*, 2001; Holmes and Meyerhoff, 2003; Eckert and McConnnell-Ginet, 2003); race and ethnicity are interrelated in many people's minds (Pilkington, 2003; Ali, 2004); language and social class have often been seen as interrelated by sociolinguists (e.g. Labov, 1966, 2001; Eckert, 2000; Rampton, 2006; Harris, 2006); migration is a classed, gendered and racialized process (Miller, 2003; Block, 2006a); and so on.

Third and finally, there are obviously ways to conceptualize identity not listed here as perspectives in their own right. For example, there are what are variably known as 'consumer identities' (du Gay, 1997) or 'commodified identities' (Benwell and Stokoe, 2006). According to the latter two authors, this perspective on identity takes into account phenomena ranging from the aspirational – *'we consume according to who we are and who we want to be'* (Benwell and Stokoe, 2006: 167; italics in the original) – to the objectified – '[n]ot only do bodies, through their aesthetic and sexualized presentation, sell commodities and services by association, they are themselves an object of consumption' (Benwell and Stokoe, 2006: 172). As consumerism is one of the pillars of globalization (see Held *et al*, 1999) and life in late modernity (Bauman, 2005), it is not surprising that it has come to be seen as a chief mediator of identity work.

Elsewhere, under the general rubric of ethnic identity, there is perhaps space for what could be termed 'religious identity'. Indeed, there is a growing interest in identity defined in terms of religious practices (e.g. Smith, 2003; Sardar, 2004; Fetzer and Soper, 2005; Modood, 2005) as well as how collective and national identities emerge at the crossroads of religion and language (Joseph, 2004). Of particular interest is how authors such as Tariq Modood suggest that Muslims the world over orient far more to their religion as a mediator of their group and individual identity, than they do to nation, skin colour or social class.

Finally, as I explained in the previous section, the entire concept of language has been questioned in recent years with the rise of multimodality as a way of viewing communication (e.g. Kress and van Leeuwen, 2001; Scollon, 2001; Scollon and Scollon, 2003). Taking multimodality seriously raises the prospect that progressively more and more researchers will come to see that language as but one semiotic mediator among many in communication and the ongoing construction of identity. Subsumed under multimodality is the recent interest in spatial and place identity, that is, how ongoing identity work is inextricably linked to our access to and occupation of physical locations and how we are situated within these locations as regards proximity to others, landmarks and moving objects (Scollon and Scollon, 2003; Collins and Slembrouck, 2005; Benwell and Stokoe, 2006). Clearly, where and how one is physically situated is a big part of who one is.

In this chapter, I have discussed the key elements of an approach to identity that has become influential in the social sciences in recent years and – relevant to this book – applied linguistics, sociolinguistics and SLL research. The different constructs I have introduced here appear in different combinations with different emphases in the work of different researchers. Thus, notions of power might be prominent in one researcher's work (e.g. Goldstein, 1996), but be relatively absent from another's (e.g. Schechter and Bayley, 2002). Ambivalence might figure as a key concept (e.g. Block, 2006a) or hardly be mentioned (e.g. Norton, 2000). A framework like 'communities of practice' might figure fairly prominently (e.g. Kanno, 2003) or not at all (Omoniyi, 2004).

As I stated in the introduction to this chapter, my discussion of this general approach to identity sets the scene for the remainder of the book in which I examine the past and present of second language research which has had identity at its centre. As I go through research carried out over the past 50 years, I will return to the key constructs and perspectives on identity outlined here again and again. In my journey through this research, my first stop, in Chapter 3, is early SLL research carried out in the 1960s, 1970s and early 1980s.

Notes

1 Though not acknowledged by Wenger or any of the applied linguists who have taken up the concept of imagination in their work, the idea of 'expanding our self by transcending our time and space and creating new images of the world and ourselves' (Wenger, 1998: 176) resonates with H. R. Fuchs Ebaugh's (1988) earlier work on 'anticipatory socialization'. According to Fuchs Ebaugh, '[b]y identifying with a group that one hopes to join, the person begins to be like members of the group in value orientation and normative expectations before actually entering the new role' (Fuchs Ebaugh, 1988: 7)

2 But see Harris and Rampton (2002) on the appropriacy of the creole analogy and Hutnyk (2005) for a critical discussion of the adoption of hybridity in the social sciences. Harris and Rampton point out that creoles have traditionally been framed by sociolinguists as relatively stable and systematic, which leads them to question the appropriacy of the construct as a metaphor for current social phenomena, framed as heterogeneous, unstable and fissiparous. Meanwhile, Hutnyk takes on what he sees as the over-optimistic way that hybridity is used to frame diversity in the world today, arguing that it passes over more pressing and serious political issues such as inequality and urban overcrowding.

3 As Simmel explains:

> [The stranger] is not radically committed to the unique ingredients and peculiar tendencies of the group, and therefore approaches them with the specific attitude of 'objectivity'. But objectivity does not simply involve passivity and detachment; it is a particular structure composed of distance and nearness, indifference and involvement. (Simmel, 1950: 404)

4 It should be noted that Lakoff would not support these public representations of the deficit model; nor would she subscribe to the idea that rather than challenge existing power imbalances favouring men over women, the latter should simply try to become more like the former.

5 Blommaert defines ethnolinguistic identity as:

> an identity expressed through beginning to a particular language community and articulated in settlements such as 'I speak Dutch', 'I am British [*ergo* I speak English]', or 'In Dutch, we call this N'. . . . Technically, ethnolinguistic identity is a complex notion covering both linguistic and 'ethnic' features. (Blommaert, 2005: 214)

3

Revisiting the past: Identity in early SLL research

Introduction

As I noted at the start of this book, in the mid-1990s Bonny Norton identified a challenge for SLL researchers: how to develop a more social perspective on SLL, which would act as a complement to the already well-developed individual/cognitive perspective, and how to take on board identity in the study of SLL. Attempts to address this struggle have appeared in recent years in more programmatic publications such as Atkinson (2002), Block (2003), Watson-Gegeo (2004), DeWaele (2005) and Zuengler and Miller (2006), in which authors call for a greater integration of what in loose terms might be termed the social and the psychological as shapers of the language learning process. In addition, the solution that Norton proposes to the social problem – the development of 'a comprehensive theory of identity that integrates the language learner and the language learning context' (Norton, 1995: 12) – would appear to be well under way, if one is to judge by the number of publications that either mention identity in passing or put it at centre stage.

In Chapter 2, I discussed the key constructs associated with a broadly poststructuralist approach to identity in the social sciences. As is often the case when a new theorization of social phenomena is ascendant, there is a tendency among many researchers and theorists to link past research to a theoretically impoverished epistemological playing field. This was certainly the case in psychology when there was a seismic shift from behaviourism to the information-processing paradigm from the late 1950s onwards (Lachman, Lachman and Butterfield, 1979; Baars, 1986). And it has been the case among current theorists and researchers subscribing to the approach to identity outlined in Chapter 2. In much recent identity-based research, authors either imply or directly claim that older sociological and anthropological research, inspired as it was in structuralist frameworks, did not or could not take on identity as negotiated or volatile, indeed as processual as opposed to product-like. However, in older ethnographies carried out by anthropologists and sociologists, there are the seeds of poststructuralism and an approach to identity not dissimilar to that found in the work discussed in Chapter 2.

A good example of what I mean is William Foote Whyte's *Street Corner Society,* which first appeared in 1943. *Street Corner Society* is a classic sociological study in which the author presents the detailed ethnography of an Italian-American community in a large American city in the 1930s. Foote describes two groups in this community, the more upwardly mobile 'college boys' and the more socially marginalized 'corner boys'. On the surface, the almost claustrophobic atmosphere that Whyte portrays in the case of the corner boys suggests a deterministic approach to identity: leadership is in the hands of one charismatic individual named 'Doc' and other roles, such as lieutenants and the bottom men or followers, seem well defined. However, Whyte makes clear that identity within the group is neither static nor fixed for life:

> Each member of the corner gang has his own position in the gang structure. Although the positions may remain unchanged over long periods of time, they should not be conceived in static terms . . . When the pattern of interactions changes, the positions change . . . Each individual has his own characteristic way of interacting with other individuals. This is probably fixed within wide limits by his native endowment, but it develops and takes its individual form through the experience of the individual in interacting with others throughout the course of his life. (Whyte, 1943: 262–3)

Thus, despite a certain loyalty to essentialized concepts such as an individual's 'own characteristic way of interacting with other individuals' and 'native endowment', Whyte uses the term 'position' in a similar way to Harré and others (see Chapter 2), acknowledging that 'positions . . . should not be conceived in static terms' as they change according to 'the pattern of interactions'.

In a similar way, SLL research taking place from the 1960s onwards also carries in it references to the concept of identity, even if in many cases the term was never used. In this chapter, I go back in time to reconsider several high-profile and oft-cited publications and bodies of research, examining how identity was either explicitly an issue, albeit an underdeveloped one, or was, in a sense, lurking in the wings, but not explicitly invoked. I proceed from the early work on motivation, initiated by Wallace Lambert in the late 1950s, to research from the 1980s. This discussion serves as a backdrop to Chapter 4–6 in which I focus on how identity has become more central to the work of some second language researchers over the past 20 years.

Early research on motivation and French/English bilingualism

Wallace Lambert, a key figure in early SLL research, included references to identity in his research in the 1960s and 1970s. Lambert was one of the founders of a long line of research carried out in Canada examining a number of issues related to bilingualism. Individually or along with Robert Gardner and other colleagues, Lambert has published for almost 50 years on the topic of motivation, attitudes and other factors deemed relevant to the bilingual context of Quebec. For my purposes here, however, Lambert's early work, in particular an article he published in 1967 (hereafter referenced as 1972), is of interest because in his research about bilingualism, he did at times talk in terms which might be linked to current discussions of identity. For example, in the midst of an examination of the instrumental and integrative motivation[1] of Canadians learning either French or English as an additional language, Lambert states that 'to be successful in his attempts to learn another social group's language [the learner] . . . must be both able and willing to adopt various aspects of behaviour, including verbal behavior, which characterize members of the other linguistic-cultural group' (Lambert, 1972: 225).

However, for Lambert this convergent movement towards the target linguistic-cultural group is not without its consequences for the individual's sense of self. He explains:

> the more proficient one becomes in a second language the more he may find that his place in his original membership group is modified at the same time as the other linguistic-cultural group becomes something more than a reference group for him. It may in fact, become a second membership group for him. Depending upon the compatibility of the two cultures, he may experience feelings of chagrin or regret as he loses ties in one group, mixed with the fearful anticipation of entering a relatively new group. (Lambert, 1972: 225)

These feelings of chagrin and regret are then related by Lambert to Emile Durkheim's concept of *anomie*. Durkheim ([1893] 1964) originally used this term in his studies of the ever-increasing complexity which came with the rise of industrialized cities in Europe in the nineteenth century, and the effects of this complexity on individuals. The changes taking place in European cities at this time meant economic progress, but they also meant precarious living conditions for many. Above all, they meant the upsetting and overturning of stable and traditional social conditions, giving way to less stable modern social conditions. For Durkheim such rapid and drastic change stimulated in individuals feelings of 'normlessness' and 'moral chaos', what he termed *anomie*.

Lambert uses the term in a narrower manner than Durkheim, to refer to feelings of 'social uncertainty or dissatisfaction' (Lambert, 1972: 226). He focuses on a group of Anglophone students on a six-week advanced French course at McGill University in Montreal, the majority of whom were American. According to Lambert, these students 'oriented themselves mainly to the European-French rather than the American-French community' (Lambert, 1972: 227). Using attitude scales developed in previous studies carried out in Quebec, but adapted for this particular study to take into account the

European-French bias, the researchers charted the evolution of these students' attitudes towards French people, French language, French culture and so on. Lambert explains the *anomic* angle uncovered as follows:

> As the students progressed in French skill to the point that they said they 'thought' in French, and even dreamed in French, their feelings of anomie also increased markedly. At the same time, they began to seek out occasions to use English even though they had solemnly pledged to use only French for the six-week period. This pattern of results suggests that these already advanced students experienced a strong dose of anomie when they commenced to <u>really</u> master a second language. That is, when advanced students became so skilled that they began to think and feel like Frenchmen, they became so annoyed with feelings of anomie that they were prompted to develop strategies to minimize or control the annoyance. Reverting to English could be such a strategy. (Lambert, 1972: 227–8)

Notwithstanding Lambert's qualification that 'the chain of events listed needs to be much more carefully explored' (Lambert, 1972: 228), there are some remarkable claims made in this excerpt, the most striking of which is that after just six weeks of intensive study in Quebec, 'the advanced students became so skilled that they began to think and feel like Frenchmen'.

More importantly, Lambert seems on the verge here of making a statement about identity as outlined in Chapter 2. For example, his use of *anomie* reminds me of a concept that I have come to see as key to the feelings manifested by those crossing geographical, social and psychological borders, namely ambivalence. However, in this article he does not, in the end, take *anomie* forward in any way that is interesting in the context of current discussions of identity. Rather, he seems more interested in relating *anomie* back to attitude, in particular how increased proficiency in a second language affects measured attitudes towards both the first and second linguistic-cultural groups.

More promising, as regards links with identity, is a later discussion by Lambert of what he calls the 'socio-cultural tugs and pulls' that form part of the bilingual's experience. Here he talks about pressures on individuals to pledge allegiance to one community or the other, noting how accent and dialect are the markers of such allegiances. In this case, the conflict moves from inside (as was the case with *anomie*) to outside, in the form of social pressure to conform. All of this pressure is exerted on individuals, who, due to their bilingualism, are far less ethnocentric than those who are exerting the pressure.

To make his point, Lambert cites an earlier study by Irving Childs (1943) on second generation Italian-Americans living in New England in the US. The study explored the question of whether these individuals saw themselves more as Italians or as Americans. Childs grouped participants in the study into three categories: those who rejected their Italian heritage in favour of an American identity; those who rejected the pressure to become Americans to the best of their ability, holding on to their Italian heritage; and finally, those who avoided self-positioning themselves in ethnic terms. Lambert relates these findings to a later study that he carried out with Robert Gardner (no citation year provided in Lambert, 1972). In this study, Lambert and Gardner administered their attitude scales to French American adolescents in New England. Their aim was to relate participants' linguistic-cultural attitudes to their levels of proficiency in French and English. Lambert and Gardner found that there were two groups similar to Childs's first two groups: one group which embraced American culture and English over French culture and French, and another which attempted to conserve French heritage. Not surprisingly, the former group was more proficient in English than the latter and the latter more proficient in French than the former. Members of a third group, which selectively favoured one culture or the other depending on the domain of activity, were termed 'ambivalent' by Lambert and, curiously, 'retarded in their command of both languages when compared to the other groups' (Lambert, 1972: 232). A final fourth group consisted of French Americans who were 'open minded' and non-ethnocentric', who had achieved proficiency in both languages. With reference to this group, Lambert concludes:

> These young people had apparently circumvented the conflicts and developed means of being members of both cultural groups. They had, in other terms, achieved a comfortable bicultural identity. (Lambert, 1972: 232)

Here and elsewhere in his work in the 1960s and 1970s, Lambert makes reference to identity; however, his understanding and use of the term is very different from the view presented in Chapter 2. For Lambert, identity was inextricably linked to attitudes, which could be collected from individuals via structured questionnaires. There is no fieldwork here which would allow researchers to examine language practices *in situ* or operationalize questionnaire-based attitudes via interviews. Indeed, Lambert's priority is more about how such individuals might be replicated in the future in places where two distinct linguistic-cultural communities exist side by side. The goal is to move towards a more tolerant and less ethnocentric society and not to explore what it means to say that someone has a 'bicultural identity'.

Still, those were other times and it would be unfair to take Lambert to task for carrying out the research that he carried out. Thus, what I glean from this survey of Lambert's view on language, psychology and culture, *circa* 1967, is a glimpse of a research agenda that never was, or one that had to wait nearly 30 years to get up and running. Still, Lambert was not the only one who was on the cusp of a major breakthrough in our understandings of how language learning and identity interrelate. At more or less the same time, just across the Canadian-US border in Michigan, Alexander Guiora was also dealing with identity issues in language learning.

Language ego and the pronunciation of adult ESL learners

It is our contention that second-language learning in all of its dimensions exerts a very specific demand with regard to self-representation. Essentially, to learn a second language is to take on a new identity. Since pronunciation appears to be the aspect of language behaviour most resistant to change, we submit that it is therefore the most critical to self-representation. Hence, we propose that that the most sensitive index of the ability to take on a new identity, i.e. the degree of permeability of language ego boundaries, is found in the ability to achieve native-like pronunciation in a second language. (Guiora, Beit-Hallahmi, Brannon, Dull and Scovel, 1972: 422)

This quotation sums up fairly well a body of research carried out by Alexander Guiora and a long list of colleagues in the late 1960s and early 1970s (see also Guiora, Lane and Bosworth, 1967; Guiora, 1972; Guiora, Brannon and Dull, 1972; Guiora, Acton, Erard and Strickland, 1980), who put pronunciation at centre stage as the aspect of language most connected to one's 'language ego'. As Brown (1980) puts it, in his survey of this research:

> For any monolingual person the language ego involves the inter-action of the native language and ego development. Your self-identity is inextricably bound up with your language, for it is in the communicative process – the process of sending out messages and having them 'bounced' back – that such identities are confirmed, shaped, and reshaped. (Brown, 1980: 53–4)

In his use of the term 'ego', Guiora is of course drawing on Freud who elaborated the concept in work such as *The Ego and the Id* (Freud, 1923). In simple terms, the ego develops as the child becomes conscious of a world outside his/her own body, acting as a voice of reason and deliberation to control the base instincts associated with the 'id'. In Guiora's work, the language ego is relatively weak in children and therefore there is not as much at stake identity-wise when they encounter an additional language. Children are thus said to have greater language ego 'permeability': in effect, they are more open to language input they receive. For adolescents and adults, however, matters are said to be different. As Brown (1980) points out, adolescents are caught up in the whirlwind of physical and emotional changes as their personalities are being formed for adulthood. At this stage in life, individuals become more inhibited and therefore ego permeability wanes. As regards adults, the view is that because their egos are already fixed and they are comfortable with themselves as they are, ego permeability is at a minimum.

Another key concept in Guiora *et al's* work is empathy. Guiora (1972: 142) defines empathy as 'a process of comprehending in which a temporary fusion of self-object boundaries, as in the earliest pattern of object relation, permits an immediate emotional apprehension of the affective experience of another . . .'. Importantly, empathy is not passive in nature; rather it requires the individual to project his/her sense of self onto his/her perception of another's sense of self. In a sense, the individual inhabits the other so as better to understand him/her. For Guiora and colleagues, empathy is the key to language success and the penetration of the language ego: in short, the more empathetic someone is the more likely it is that he/she will be a successful language learner.

The research carried out by Guiora and associates involved attempts to relax participants using alcohol (Guiora, Beit-Hallahmi, Brannon, Dull and Scovel, 1972) and valium (Guiora, Acton, Erard and Strickland, 1980). In the former case, groups of students studying Thai at an American university were administered varying doses of alcohol (from zero to three ounces) and then asked to take a test in Thai pronunciation. The researcher found that the students who performed the best were those who had ingested alcohol in the medium range (i.e. 1.5 ounces). Those who consumed no alcohol or more than this amount did significantly worse. The conclusion was that the alcohol relaxed inhibitions, increased ego permeability and that this resulted in better pronunciation.

In Guiora *et al* (1980), valium was administered in variable doses to another group of American university students who were asked to take the same Thai pronunciation test used in the previous study. In this case, no direct correlation was found between test performance and the dose of valium. However, the authors noted that testers, whose role was limited to simply explaining the test and playing recorded pronunciation samples, somehow had an effect on test performance. According to Guiora *et al*, '[s]ubjects may . . . have been able to interpret non-verbal cues from the testers, placing them in the total context of the interaction, and reacting to them in their test behavior' (Guiora *et al*, 1980: 359). In this case, the study participants were said to be responding to good or bad 'vibes' associated with the tester.

The work of Guiora and his colleagues is reviewed in detail in Schumann (1978), Brown (1973, 1980) and Ellis (1985). Criticisms range from Brown's suggestion that pronunciation might have improved because muscles were relaxed and not because ego permeability was enhanced, to Schumann's perplexity at how in different publications Guiora could not seem to decide if he was interested exclusively in pronunciation (Guiora, Beit-Hallahmi, Brannon, Dull and Scovel, 1972) or language learning in general (Guiora, Brannon and Dull, 1972).

My concern is that Guiora, like Lambert, was too dependent on questionnaires and controlled experiments to engage in a more exploratory approach to identity. For example, attitude questionnaires might tell us about the preferred responses of respondents, but they do not go very far towards finding out how individuals construct themselves through language or indeed the kind of language practices they engage in. The pronunciation experiments might tell us something about the effects of alcohol and valium on pronunciation, but they do not show us how individuals normally interact with others. They also do not allow for individuals making choices about how they wish to sound in a second language, surely an integral part of their audibility, as discussed in Chapter 2. To conclude, although Guiora, Beit-Hallahmi, Brannon, Dull and Scovel (1972: 422) state that 'to learn a second language is to take on a new identity', they had neither the constructs nor research questions necessary to explore this claim in detail.

The labour migrant experience and the Acculturation Model

As the 1970s proceeded, there was another researcher who seemed to argue that language learning was related to one's sense of self: John Schumann. Like Lambert, Guiora and others before him, Schumann (1974, 1976a, 1976b, 1978) also relied on questionnaires, tests and structured elicitations; however, his major source of data were unplanned interviews, called 'spontaneous conversations', which were sometimes initiated by the researcher and at other times initiated by the participants. In addition, while he drew on existing theories of motivation (e.g. Gardner and Lambert, 1972) and Guiora's work, he also brought in new socially sensitive constructs that were new to SLL researchers.

Schumann's Acculturation Model began its life as the Pidginization Hypothesis (or Process). It grew out of a ten-month study of the acquisition of English by six Spanish speakers (classified as two children, two adolescents and two adults) living in the US, carried out by Courtney Cazden, Herlinda Cancino, Ellen Rosansky and Schumann in 1973 (see Cazden, Cancino, Rosansky and Schumann, 1975, for a final report). The main thrust of the project was to chart the linguistic development of the six participants in longitudinal fashion. However, in a series of publications (Schumann, 1974, 1976a, 1976b, 1978), Schumann developed a model of language learning which argued that acculturation, a macro variable comprised of a long list of social and affective variables, was the chief causal variable in language learning. The main focus of Schumann's work was a 33-year-old Costa Rican named Alberto, who showed very limited linguistic development over the ten-month period.

The starting point of Schumann's Acculturation Model was Alberto's pidginized English. A pidgin was defined by Schumann as 'a simplified and reduced form of speech used for communication between people with different languages' (Schumann, 1978: 69). Schumann claimed that Alberto's English had pidginized because it shared certain characteristics with other pidgins documented at the time. These characteristics included the use of 'no' for most negative utterances; no question inversion; and the deletion of auxiliaries and subject pronouns. The Acculturation Model was offered as an explanation for why Alberto's English had pidginized.

The first key category in Schumann's model, social distance, is related to eight questions which Schumann asked about the relationship between two groups: the Second Language Learning Group (hereafter SLLG) and the Target Language Group (hereafter TLG). The first question was about the relative power between the two groups as regards political, cultural, economic and technical status. If the SLLG has higher status than the TLG as regards these variables, then members are not likely to learn the language of their hosts. At the other extreme, if they have a lesser status, they will feel pressure to learn the language of their hosts. The intermediate position – non-dominance – means that the SLLG might opt to learn the language of the host community under relatively egalitarian conditions of mutual respect.

The second question has to do with what Schumann terms 'integration patterns'. Assimilation means that the SLLG abandons its culture to take on the culture of the TLG. Preservation, on the other hand, means that members of the SLLG attempt to conserve their culture, rejecting the TLG culture. Acculturation is the intermediate condition, whereby SLLG members adapt to the TLG culture while maintaining the SLLG culture for in-group practices. According to Schumann, a preservation pattern is likely to hinder language learning, while the assimilation pattern is likely to lead to the most successful language learning. The acculturation pattern falls somewhere in the middle. One caveat is in order when considering these different patterns, namely, that one has to consider that the two groups may not share the same goals.

The third question about social distance refers to what Schumann calls 'enclosure', that is the extent to which the two groups share social institutions such as workplaces, schools, leisure faculties, churches and so on. High enclosure means that the two groups are generally separated and this will impact negatively on the SLLG members' prospects for successful language learning.

The remaining five questions have to do with how cohesive the SLLG is (do group members tend to associate exclusively with fellow groups members, as opposed to outsiders?); how big it is relative to the TLG; how similar the two cultures are; the attitudes that members of the two groups hold towards one another; and finally, SLLG members' expected length of stay in the TLG area. The bad language learning situation is one where the SLLG is tightly knit and large, the two cultures in question are relatively dissimilar; the two groups have negative attitudes towards one another and finally, the SLLG members generally do not stay in the TLG area.

Drawing on information picked up during his fieldwork, as well as batteries of questionnaires and tests, Schumann constructed Alberto as a second language learner in a bad SLL situation. First, he belonged to a group – 'lower class Latin American worker immigrants' – which was politically, economically, technically and culturally subordinate to the dominant Anglo community. This view was held not only by members of the Anglo community but also by Alberto and other members of the Latin American community. As regards integration patterns, the Anglo community expected Alberto to assimilate; however, Schumann notes that Alberto was likely engaged in a strategy falling somewhere between acculturation and preservation. This situation had probably come about because Alberto belonged to a broader Latin American community which was both large and living in relative isolation from the dominant Anglo community. However, this segregation might have been more the result of socio-economic and socio-political forces than the Latin Americans' extreme cultural distance from the host community, since there is a shared western Christian culture between the two groups. Nevertheless, Schumann also notes that the Latinos probably represented a different economic culture to Anglos, one of poverty, which was to be kept at a distance. As regards the attitudes of the two groups towards one another and Alberto's intended length of stay, Schumann professes ignorance.

The second key category in Schumann's model is psychological distance, that is, the individual's affective state and relative predisposition towards learning the TL. Here, Schumann examines four constructs: language shock, culture shock, motivation and ego permeability. Language shock is about the feelings of stress and even shame in individuals who suddenly find that they have to communicate in a code in which they sound comical and over which they do not have a firm command. Culture shock is defined as 'the anxiety resulting from the disorientation encountered upon entering a new culture' (Schumann, 1978: 88). Motivation is discussed in the rather stark terms of integrative vs. instrumental, with Schumann arguing that integrative motivation is most likely to enhance language learning. Finally, despite the criticisms cited above, Schumann includes Guiora's concept of ego permeability in his research, with the caveat that it 'is best regarded as an essential factor in the overall ability to acquire a second language rather than simply in the ability to acquire authentic pronunciation' (Schumann, 1978: 96).

To access Alberto's psychological profile, Schumann relied on one questionnaire and this only aimed to measure Alberto's motivation and attitudes. Schumann noted that Alberto scored highly on this questionnaire, which would have indicated that he was positively predisposed towards learning English. However, he immediately questioned this finding, stating that 'Alberto tended not to like to displease and therefore his answers may reflect what he thought the experimenters wanted to hear' (Schumann, 1978: 97). Schumann explained his position as follows:

> There are several aspects of Alberto's lifestyle that appear to contradict the positive attitude and motivation expressed in the questionnaire. First of all, he made very little effort to get to

know English-speaking people. In Cambridge he stuck quite close to a small group of Spanish-speaking friends. He did not own a television, and expressed disinterest in it because he could not understand English. On the other hand, he purchased an expensive stereo set and tape deck on which he played mostly Spanish music. Also, he chose to work at night as well as in the day, rather than attend English classes which were available in Cambridge. (Schumann, 1978: 97)

Norton (2000) challenges Schumann's assessment of Alberto's social and psychological profile, suggesting that rather than blame Alberto, as Schumann appears to be doing in the above quotation, he should have looked to 'the dominant power structures within society [which] had relegated Alberto to a marginalized status . . .' (Norton, 2000: 116). Indeed, it does seem a little odd to fault an immigrant with precarious life and work conditions for not attending English classes. Schumann's assertion that Alberto 'chose' to work instead of study seems a rather ill-advised attribution of agency to an individual who quite possibly had to work day and night to make ends meet. In addition, maintaining Spanish as a social language (see references to friends and music) does not preclude a positive attitude towards English, unless one wishes to adopt the view that individuals can only live their lives in one language. Finally, Schumann's claim that Alberto 'made very little effort to get to know English speaking people' is problematic because it precludes the possibility that 'members of the dominant Anglophone community had ambivalent attitudes towards Alberto, offering him limited opportunities to practice English . . .' (Norton, 2000: 116). In short, while Norton singles Schumann out as one of the few major SLL researchers to consider social factors in his work, she finds his analysis impoverished. Indeed, she sees Schumann as unable to accept that Alberto might have been motivated to learn English but that he was relatively powerless to do so because this Anglophone community positioned him in such a way that he had little access to English.

On the whole, I agree with Norton's assessment of Schumann, but I also think it worthwhile to consider his particular sociocultural and sociohistorical context. Schumann was doing research at a time when identity was not really on the SLL agenda, as it certainly was beginning to be when Norton was writing about her research in the 1990s. In other words, Schumann's work, prescient as it was as regards its attention to social variables, was still far more linked to the research done by Lambert, Guiora and others than the research that Norton and others currently carry out, focusing on the interrelationship between SLL and identity.

Affect in SLL

As I suggest elsewhere (Block, 2003), the 1980s was the decade when SLL researchers began to feel confident enough to state clearly that an area of inquiry called SLA existed. This can be seen in the founding of the specialized journal *Studies in Second Language Acquisition* at the end of the 1970s, as well as the appearance of the first full-length texts about language learning (e.g. Brown, 1980, Ellis, 1985, McLaughlin, 1987). Language learning research in the 1980s was for the most part driven by Stephen Krashen's notions of the importance of input (e.g. Krashen, 1981), followed by Michael Long, Susan Gass and others' work on the importance of interaction (Long, 1985; Gass, 1988). However, the interest in affect continued in the work of some researchers.

H. Douglas Brown's (1980) *Principles of Language Learning and Teaching* is an early attempt to bring together and package for language teachers a wide-ranging body of knowledge about language learning which had accumulated during the period 1945–1979. Importantly, Brown begins the book with something akin to the claim that learning a second language is tied to cultural and identity issues:

> Becoming a bilingual is a way of life. Every bone and fiber of your being is affected in some way as you struggle to reach beyond the confines of your first language and into a new language, a new culture, a new way of thinking, feeling and acting. Total commitment, total involvement, and a total physical, intellectual, and emotional response are necessary to successfully send and receive messages in a second language. (Brown, 1980:1)

This opening to Brown's book is interesting in the context of this discussion because of what it says about language learning being more than the acquisition of a new linguistic system, that it is an experience interlinked with questions of culture, involving a transformation of the 'way of thinking, feeling and acting'. Brown does not mention the word 'identity' here, but what he says in these two sentences certainly sounds like something akin to identity, as described in Chapter 2. However, later in the book, when Brown compares first and second language learning, the word identity does appear during a brief discussion of Guiora's theory of language ego in first and second language learning. Brown observes:

> It would appear that the study of second language learning as the acquisition of a *second identity* might pose a fruitful and important issue in understanding not only some differences between child and adult first and second language learning, but second language learning in general. (Brown, 1980: 55)

Later, Brown examines in detail affective factors, which he divides into two categories: egocentric and transactional. Egocentric affective factors, that is 'one's view of self and its relevance to language learning' (Brown, 1980: 102), include the notions of self-esteem and inhibition. Transactional affective factors, that is, factors related to 'how the self is transacted to others' (Brown, 1980: 102–3), include empathy, extroversion and aggression. These two groups of variables are dealt with in an even-handed way, with Brown casting some doubt on any simplistic or reductionist arguments about how a good language learner would necessarily have high self-esteem, low inhibition, high empathy, high extroversion and an assertive personality, arguments which had arisen out of research on 'the good language learner' (e.g. Naiman *et al,* 1978). However, his discussion does not really deal with how additional language learning impacts on one's sense of self; rather the concern is more with how the presence or absence of certain affective factors relates to successful language learning.

Closer to the mark is Brown's discussion of what he calls 'sociocultural variables', despite the fact that Brown begins with a discussion of culture which today would be qualified as deterministic and essentialist. He sees culture as 'the ideas, customs, skills, arts, and tools which characterize a given group of people in a given period of time' (Brown, 1980: 123) and then goes on to state that: 'Culture . . . establishes for each person a context of cognitive and affective behaviour, a blueprint for personal and social existence' (Brown, 1980: 123). Having defined culture in this way, Brown moves on to consider Peter Adler's work on culture shock, defined as follows:

> Culture shock . . . is thought to be a form of anxiety that results from the loss of commonly perceived and understood signs and symbols of social intercourse. The individual undergoing culture shock reflects his anxiety and nervousness with cultural differences through any number of defence mechanisms: repression, regression, isolation and rejection. These defensive attitudes speak, in behavioural terms, of basic underlying insecurity which may encompass loneliness, anger, frustration and self-questioning of competence. With familiar props, cues, and clues of cultural understanding removed, the individual becomes disoriented, afraid of, and alienated from the things that he knows and understands. (Adler, 1972: 8; cited in Brown, 1980: 132)

Brown presents the four stages of culture shock as follows:

Stage 1   'the period of excitement and euphoria over the newness of the surroundings'

Stage 2   'culture shock emerges as the individual feels the intrusion of more and more cultural differences into his image of self and security'

Stage 3   'the person begins to accept the differences in thinking and feeling that surround him, slowly becoming more empathetic with persons in the second culture'

Stage 4   'near or full recovery, either assimilation or adaptation, acceptance of the new culture and self-confidence in the "new" person that has developed in this culture'

(Brown, 1980: 132)

This model does not in itself have much explanatory potential, as regards language learning. However, Brown draws on three strands of research which allow him to make something of it: Schumann's concept of social distance (see above), Lambert's work on *anomie* (see above) and Bill Acton's (1979) 'perceived social distance', which I will now briefly discuss.

Acton found a problem in Schumann's concept of social distance, namely its vagueness: one may more or less understand what it means, but how does one know it when one sees it? To get around this problem, Acton explored not social distance in itself, but language learners' *perceptions* of social distance. He administered his Professed Difference in Attitude Questionnaire to a group of ESL learners in the US. This questionnaire asked respondents to consider different attitudes towards concepts such as 'divorce', falling across three dimensions: (1) their views on such concepts compared to how they perceived members of their L1 culture to view them; (2) their views on such concepts compared to how they perceived members of the target L2 culture to view them; and (3) how they perceived both the L1 culture and the L2 culture to view such concepts. Acton found that the students who qualified as good learners (i.e. those who did well on proficiency tests) were those whose perceived social distance from the target culture was neither too close nor too distant. In other words, these learners were maintaining a delicate balance between retaining their L1 culture and moving towards integration in the L2 culture.

Drawing on the work of Schumann, Acton and Lambert, Brown arrives at the following conclusion about what he calls a 'cultural critical period':

> If you combine Acton's research with Lambert's a rather interesting hypothesis emerges – namely, that mastery or skilful fluency in a second language (within the second culture) occurs somewhere at the beginning of the third stage of acculturation . . . Stage 3 may provide not only the optimal *distance,* but the optimal cognitive and affective *tension* to produce the necessary *pressure* to acquire the language, yet pressure that is neither too overwhelming (such as that which may be typical of Stage 2 or culture shock) nor too weak (Stage 4). Language mastery at Stage 3, in turn, would appear to be an instrument for progressing psychologically through Stage 3 and finally into Stage 4. (Brown, 1980: 138–9)

But is this identity in language learning as it was described in Chapter 2? In my view, not exactly, as researchers were still trying to harness variables and establish clear cause and effect relationship between these variables and successful language learning. However, what is perhaps more important about Brown's book and the fact that he devotes a fair amount of space to affective and sociocultural variables, is that by the late 1970s and early 1980s, there was a cadre of scholars interested in and attracted to the social psychological perspective on language learning. Much of this work revolved around diary studies chronicling the self-reflective experiences of applied linguists.

Diary accounts of foreign language learning experiences

In a seminal paper, Kathleen Bailey (1983) reviews diary studies carried out during the late 1970s by nine language teachers/applied linguists (including Bailey herself) and two 'non teachers'. Bailey focuses on two key constructs – competitiveness and anxiety – charting how they manifest themselves in diary entries. Importantly, the research discussed by Bailey marks a shift from the studies I have examined thus far. First, there is the use of diaries as the exclusive source of data. This means a move away from the reliance on questionnaire-based correlation studies and elicited language data that characterized previous research into affective factors. Diaries are seen as a way of tapping into the learners' affective responses to their learning environments and of charting the evolution of these responses over time.

As I stated above, the key constructs in Bailey's analyses of the 11 diary studies are competitiveness and anxiety. The latter construct is one that had been floating around in social psychology for some time before Tom Scovel (1978) suggested that it might be important to language learning. Scovel distinguished between 'facilitating' and 'debilitating' anxiety, defining the former as a motivation to actively engage with the environment and the latter as a motivation to 'flee' and avoid the environment. Bailey relates these two types of anxiety to situations in which the language learner has an unsuccessful self-image but a competitive nature. According to her theory, the language learner with a negative self-image but competitive nature will feel anxiety. If he/she feels debilitating anxiety, the response to the language learning situation will be to avoid contact with the TL (or in the case of the formal environment, with classroom participants and activities). If the learner feels facilitative anxiety, he/she will try to improve and increase contact with the TL.

In this model, Bailey also allows for cases in which the learner is still competitive, but has a successful self-image. In such cases, anxiety drops out of the equation and the learner enters a self-fulfilling prophecy, whereby the positive self-image leads to success which leads to a more positive self-image. It is thus possible for facilitative anxiety to lead to success and an improvement in the individual's self-image. However, for debilitative anxiety Bailey only envisages a lack of success and/or the abandonment of any effort to learn (in a formal context this means dropping out of a course). Bailey's model is represented in Table 3.1.

Bailey meticulously goes through the 11 diary studies showing how the different learners involved manifested different paths in her model. She first discusses her own diary, which charted her experiences attending a French grammar and reading course meant to help her pass a translation test which was a requirement on her PhD programme. Bailey notes how over the ten-week course she exhibited competitive behaviour and both debilitating and facilitating anxiety. From the first day of class, she constantly sized up her classmates, seeing how she compared to them, while at the same time wondering if she was pleasing the teacher. The following excerpt, written during the first two weeks of the course, illustrates how:

Table 3.1 The role of anxiety in language learning (based on Bailey, 1983: 97)

Competitive → SL learner	successful → positive experiences → learning enhanced self-image
Competitive → SL learner	unsuccessful → anxiety → facilitating → effort → learning enhanced self-image → debilitating → avoidance → abandonment

> I hope Marie [the teacher] will eventually like me and think that I am a good language-learner, even though I am probably the second lowest in the class right now (next to the man who must pass the ETS test). The girl who has just been in France seems to think that she's too good for the rest of us, but she didn't do all that well today. I want to have the exercises worked out perfectly before the next class. Today, I was just scared enough to be stimulated to prepare the next time. If I were any scareder I'd be a nervous wreck. I feel different from many of the students in the class because they have been together for a quarter with the other teacher. They also don't seem very interested in learning French. Today Marie was explaining something and some of the students looked really bored. (Bailey, 1983: 74–5 [Bailey, 1978: 41])

Bailey goes on to explain how she came to feel so anxious that she deliberately missed her fourth class. This represented for Bailey a temporary abandonment of her studies, the worst possible result for debilitating anxiety in a formal context. Nevertheless, over the next several weeks, Bailey managed to channel her competitiveness into more facilitating anxiety and by the end of the course she was relatively successful.

In several of the other cases described by Bailey the same twin concerns emerge: how the diarist compares him/herself to classmates and the wish to please the teacher. However, in one case cited, Marjorie Walsleben's (1976) account of her experience of learning Farsi as a foreign language, there is open conflict between the diarist and the teacher. Like Bailey, at the beginning of the course Walsleben felt anxious when comparing herself to students she perceived to be at a more advanced level. However, Walsleben's anxious feelings came to be more related to her teacher than to her classmates, with whom she did not feel as competitive as Bailey had. The point of conflict with the teacher was the practice of administering frequent vocabulary tests to students unprepared to take them and who viewed them as a waste of time. Walsleben tells the story how one day matters came to a head:

> After the break [the teacher] announced that he would give the vocabulary test, 'If that's OK.' Shirley stated again her difficulty in

studying uncontextualized words for a vocabulary test, and [the teacher] explained that he nonetheless felt that it was a justifiable way of building up our vocabularies. When he repeated that he was going to give the test and looked at me when he said, 'If that's okay,' I responded tersely, 'You're the professor, but in my opinion it's a poor use of time.' That was the proverbial last straw. For the next hour and a half the whole class was embroiled in a very emotional exchange of opinions dealing with what the class was and was not, what it could and should be, who would let whom do what. (Bailey, 1983: 87 [Walsleben, 1976: 34–5])

As Bailey puts it, in this case it seems that the diarist is not competing with her classmates; rather, she 'is struggling with the instructor for control of her language learning experience' (Bailey, 1983: 87). A week after the blow-up with the teacher, Walsleben dropped out of the class.

Examining Bailey's review of the 11 diary studies some 25 years later, I see that while she was moving in the direction of identity as framed in Chapter 2, she was still bound to the socio-affective variables tradition of Lambert and others. Thus, while her research relied on accounts of language learning as opposed to questionnaires and measures of language learning, her analytical framework was solely about competitiveness and anxiety. With the benefit of hindsight and access to broader and more expansive analytical frameworks, a researcher today would likely see competitiveness and anxiety as by-products of a more global phenomenon, and that is the ongoing process of self-positioning that diarists engage in. From this perspective, Bailey, Walsleben and the other diarists were engaged in an ongoing process of discursively constructing an identity in the context of their participation in a language course. I will have more to say about the discursive construction of identity in this kind of foreign language classroom context in Chapter 5. For now, however, I would like to move to another study, also published in 1983, which to my mind could be interpreted as a precursor to current identity and SLL research in naturalist settings, that is settings in which the learner is immersed in the second language with little or no formal classroom-based instruction. I refer here to Richard Schmidt's (1983) oft-cited study of Wes.

The professional migrant experience and fossilization

Richard Schmidt (1983) tells us the story of Wes, a Japanese photographer living and working in Hawaii. In a study carried out from 1978 to 1981, Schmidt charts the development of Wes's communicative competence. He draws on Canale and Swain's (1980) well-known four-part model which breaks the construct down into four components: grammatical, sociolinguistic, strategic and discourse. In Schmidt's view, Wes showed a fair degree of competence as regards the latter three components: he was able to produce language deemed socio-pragmatically appropriate enough in different contexts; he was able to negotiate his way through communication problems; and he was actually a good conversationalist, able to provide adequate descriptions as well as deliver and sustain well-constructed narratives. However, as regards his grammatical development, Wes did not make very much progress. For example, over the entire period he was monitored by Schmidt he continued to produce utterances which denoted a shaky command of English grammar. The following examples are Wes's use of the verb 'be':

> I'm cry (meaning 'I almost cried' or 'I would cry')
> I'm always listen (repetitive habitual)
> Tomorrow I'm finish (future)
> Before I'm finish (past)
>
> (Schmidt, 1983: 148)

Such utterances do not seem surprising when one considers Wes's metalinguistic awareness. In the following excerpt, Schmidt asks Wes about the difference between progressive and non-progressive verb forms:

> RS: So what's the difference between "paint" and "painting"?
> Wes: Well, if I go to exhibition, I saw "paint," but "I'm start painting" means I do it, not finish.

RS: Yeah, OK < sort of, so what's the difference between "think" and "thinking"?
Wes: "I'm think" means now. "I'm thinking" means later.

(Schmidt, 1983: 147)

Schmidt draws a comparison between Wes and Alberto in Schumann's study, arguing that Wes, like Alberto, manifested very little morphological development during this period of time and that he managed to carry out his day-to-day affairs using a repertoire of formulaic utterances. However, Schmidt suggests that unlike Alberto, Wes's social and psychological profile was nearly ideal for language learning to take place. He did not see himself as inferior to the TL community at any level and he was not positioned as inferior by this community. And although he did spend time with Japanese speakers at the beginning of his stay, he progressively found himself immersed in English-speaking circles, due to his increasingly successful professional activity. Schmidt never asked Wes to complete attitude and motivation questionnaires; however, he observes that Wes always manifested a positive attitude towards his host country and that integrative motivation seemed to dominate.

As has been the case in the other studies cited, I see identity lurking in the background of Wes's story, but never coming forward. This being the case, one has to read between the lines in Schmidt's article to catch a few glimpses of how Wes's language development was related to his sense of self. Wes may be seen as the English speaker he needed to be for his particular social context. For example, the lack of development in grammatical competence, but the ability to tell stories, reminds me of Teutsch-Dwyer's (2001) study of Karol, a Polish man living in California, about which I will have more to say in Chapter 4. Like Wes, Karol's grammatical development fossilized, although he was still able to tell stories. Teutsch-Dwyer ties Karol's lack of grammatical development to his dependence on his American girlfriend and her two friends who effectively did not push him to do better as a conversationalist. Wes, it seems, was in a similar kind of dependent situation, as Schmidt explains:

A final communication strategy which I believe Wes has quite consistently relied upon, no doubt valuable in the short term but

probably detrimental in the long run, is to expect native speakers
to learn his interlanguage, both to understand him and to speak in
a way that is comprehensible to him, and to consider it the native
speaker's problem as much as his own if this does not happen.
(Schmidt, 1983: 167)

As Teutsch-Dwyer notes, a big part of Karol's self-image as a
heterosexual man was being accepted as a good storyteller. He
came to be this in the eyes of his female friends, albeit with an
underdeveloped grammatical competence. One can only speculate
about Wes's self-image as regards his social life, as Schmidt does not
open up this particular line of inquiry. However, it is quite likely that
the many friends and associates he is reported to have had provided
him with a kind of support bubble. This support bubble in turn led to
a situation in which the 'funny English', which Wes claimed that he
spoke, became part and parcel of who he was. The following story
was told by Wes spontaneously:

W = Wes   S = Schmidt

1. W: listen / today so funny story
2. S: yeah / what happened?
3. W: you know everyday I'm go to McDonald for lunch
4. S: yeah
5. W: and today I saw so beautiful woman / so beautiful clothes /
    make-up / everything / but / so crazy!
6. S: how? / what do you mean?
7. W: talking to herself / then she's listen to some person /
    everybody watch / but no one there / then / somebody / local
    woman I think say 'are' / but beautiful woman she doesn't want
    talk to local woman / she's so snobbish! / so funny!
8. S: Jesus

(Schmidt, 1983: 159; NB transcription conventions adapted)

For Schmidt, this story is well-formed according to Labov and
Fanshel's (1977) framework. This framework classifies good stories
as ones in which there is an attention-getter, a general framing of the
story and what it is about, mention of the time and place and who is
involved, the introduction of a complicating action, a resolution of the

complicating action and an evaluation. In addition, Schmidt concludes that: 'The story is not only well formed but cleverly formed and funny' (Schmidt, 1983: 159). Wes is thus cast not only as a good storyteller, but an entertaining one. The profiling of Wes as funny and witty continues as Schmidt moves to his conversation skills. The following conversation was recorded in a restaurant:

W = Wes   S = waitress   M = friend   G = friend

1. M: I would like eggs benedict <to waitress> / that's the speciality <to Wes>
2. S: how about you?
3. W: here eggs benedict is good?
4. M: yeah
5. G: it's the speciality
6. W: yeah? / OK / I have it <waitress leaves>
7. M: you never ate before?
8. W: no, I ate before / but not this hotel
9. M: it's very good over here
10. W: but only just English muffin / turkey / ham and egg / right?
11. G: right
12. W: so how different? / how special?
13. M: because it's very good here / maybe it's the hollandaise / I don't know
14. G: maybe it's just the atmosphere
15. W: yeah / I think so / egg benedict is eggs benedict / just your imagination is different / so / this restaurant is belong to hotel?
16. G: no / not exactly

(Schmidt, 1983: 159–60; NB transcription conventions adapted)

According to Schmidt, '[t]he good-natured, teasing type of humour of this page (unfortunately and inevitably less obvious from a transcript than from the recording, which preserves tone of voice) is typical of Wes's conversations' (Schmidt, 1983: 160). Wes is further framed as a good listener who is good at picking up and re-introducing comments made by others and who never shows signs of not understanding what is going on. Schmidt even cites comments made by Wes's Japanese friends who reported that in Japanese he was 'considered a very good conversationalist, thoughtful, witty, and refreshingly direct' (Schmidt, 1983: 160). The overall image of Wes as an English speaker, therefore, is one impervious to the strictures of formal grammar, with an extraordinarily pleasant and entertaining personality.

As regards Wes's migrant status, he is at the opposite end of the socioeconomic scale from Alberto. Indeed, he would appear to be an early precursor of what migrant theorists in recent years have called 'middling transmigrants', described by Conradson and Latham (2005) as follows:

> They are often, but not always, well educated. They may come from wealthy families, but more often than not, they appear to be simply middle class. In terms of the societies they come from, and those they are travelling to, they are very much in the middle. (Conradson and Latham, 2005: 229)

Middling migrations are often centred on one particular activity that is carried out in the host country. This activity might be leisure, as in the case of retirees from Northern European countries who migrate to resort communities located on the Mediterranean coast. However, it might also be educational or academic in nature, as in the case of adolescents and adults on gap years or students enrolled on graduate programmes in countries such as the UK or France. Or, it can be professional, as in the case of Wes, who was trying to forge a successful career as a photographer in Hawaii. Middling transmigrants are also individuals with near or total control over their movements, who go somewhere to live with one particular or general purpose in mind. In addition, they do not subject themselves to poor living conditions, awaiting a better future for their children, as labour migrants often do; rather, they make the most of their stay in the host country.

Seeing Wes as a middling transmigrant seems more appropriate than seeing him simply as a deficient ESL learner, as Schmidt does. To be sure, Wes's arrested grammatical development might have had something to do with some kind of in-built syllabus (Corder, 1981) or the Critical Period Hypothesis (Singleton and Ryan, 2004) or any number of other dimensions related to fossilization (Han, 2004). However, comfortable with who he was, confident in his professional abilities and the citizen of one of the wealthiest countries in the world, Wes really had very little incentive to improve his English as a means of acculturation to the host community he dealt with. Indeed, his English worked quite well for the different subject positions he adopted and the communities of practice in which he had attained membership. From this point of view, trying to situate him in Schumann's Acculturation Model does not produce entirely satisfactory conclusions. Trying to pigeonhole him as a deficient speaker achieves even less.

In fairness to Schmidt, his research was not – and indeed could not be – about identity as described in Chapter 2. Nor, obviously, could Schmidt have been expected to incorporate constructs from current research on migration, such as 'middling transmigrant'. Situating himself in the mainstream of SLL research 25 years ago, Schmidt focused on the fossilized grammar of one particular language learner and whether or not Schumann's Acculturation Model might offer an explanation for this fossilization. Nevertheless, as I have suggested here, there is quite a lot of identity work emergent in Wes's speech samples, even if it is not brought to the fore and developed in detail.

The professional sojourner experience: Learning Portuguese in Brazil

At about the time that he was completing his data collection with Wes, Richard Schmidt spent five months in Rio de Janeiro, Brazil, teaching in an applied linguistics department at a major university. During this period, Schmidt set out to learn Portuguese to the best of his ability, and alert to a research opportunity, he kept a diary of his language learning experiences from the outset of his stay. In addition, from the seventh week onwards, he made recordings of his spoken Portuguese with his colleague Sylvia Nagem Frota.

Schmidt and Frota (1986) is a lengthy and detailed account of Schmidt's language learning experiences in different contexts: in classrooms, socializing at the beach and in restaurants and clubs and in the workplace. From the beginning, Schmidt made efforts to learn

Portuguese naturalistically by seeking contact with native speakers and it was not until the fourth week of his stay that he began attending classes, adding a formal learning environment to his experiences. The latter experience proved to be useful in that it allowed Schmidt to make connections between what he was hearing and even saying in his social contacts and the language as a formal system. In the workplace, however, Schmidt never really used Portuguese and this proved to be the least useful context for learning Portuguese. As Schmidt and Frota explain:

> R's [Schmidt's] use of Portuguese throughout his stay in Brazil was exclusively for social, not professional purposes. He lectured in applied linguistics at a university in Rio de Janeiro and gave workshops at various institutions for language teachers, but always in English. He felt that he could not have carried out these functions in Portuguese, even at the end of his stay[.] (Schmidt and Frota, 1986: 248)

Schmidt and Frota's account is concerned primarily with Schmidt's linguistic development over the five months and above all, with how and when he noticed new language features in the speech of his numerous interlocutors. However, examining Schmidt's reproduced diary entries within more current identity frameworks allows one to see that while it is interesting to chart his linguistic progress, it is also interesting to explore to what ends he progressed linguistically.

In the diary accounts pertaining to the first three weeks of his stay in Rio, when he was trying to learn naturalistically with no formal instruction, Schmidt writes about his efforts to assert for himself a subject position as a competent Portuguese speaker. During this period, he tried to pay close attention to what was said to him and tried to imitate his interlocutors. He also used the television and radio as easy ways to get input. However, in this early period he was already frustrated at not being able to be himself in Portuguese:

> I hate the feeling of being unable to talk to people around me. I'm used to chatting with people all day long, and I didn't like this silence. (Schmidt and Frota, 1986: 242)

Once he began his classes in week 4, Schmidt took on a new subject position in his diary entries, that of applied linguist/language teacher. As was observed in Bailey (1983), and as will once again be the case in Chapter 5, it is almost axiomatic that language teachers or former language teachers assert a very pronounced teacher identity as soon as they step into the classroom as language learners. After his first day of class, Schmidt was happy: he liked the conversation practice he had had and above all, he valued being able to think about and discuss some of the language he was encountering outside the classroom in a formal classroom environment. In addition, after classes he went out with some friends and made connections between what he was exposed to naturalistically. Schmidt describes the situation as follows:

> I'm sure I'll be asked all these questions thousands of times before I leave here. So, I went out last night and talked to four people. It worked, and I'm invited to a party tomorrow night. Of course, I quickly ran out of things to say and quickly stopped understanding what people said to me, but that just makes me eager to get back to class. (Schmidt and Frota, 1986: 243)

Anticipating his first recording in Portuguese with Frota, Schmidt noted how he was ashamed of his bad Portuguese:

> . . . with native speakers of Portuguese who are English teachers . . . I am ashamed to show my ignorance of their language when they speak mine so well. With monolinguals, it's different: we are equally ignorant of each other's language and feel no embarrassment at all. (Schmidt and Frota, 1986: 245)

Schmidt found that he was able to make good progress in class despite the teacher. However, when he was allowed to skip a level, he found himself in a class that was too difficult for him. Rather than go back to a lower level, Schmidt decided to quit. Thus, after just five weeks of instruction, he was back in a completely naturalistic context. In this context, Schmidt soon became aware that the native speakers he encountered always spoke very slowly and simply for him, a strategy that bothered him immensely. He observed that foreigners who settled in Brazil seemed to learn Portuguese rather quickly and in doing so, they did not fall into the ex-pat trap he had fallen into of being dependent on English speakers.

As weeks went by, Schmidt's social life became increasingly active and this meant that he came into contact with a more varied and richer input. He found a restaurant where he would go regularly and see the same people. Schmidt describes the situation as follows:

> Between 11 and 1 about 20 regulars show up for dinner. Everyone knows everyone, and there's lots of moving about and putting tables together. Later, smaller groups split off, either to party in someone's apartment nearby or to go dancing. I've seen a lot of sunrises, and I think I've found a place where I can really fit in. They have welcomed me, and there's a critical mass of very intelligent people which I find very stimulating. The people I've met so far have been mostly writers (journalists, novelists) or theater people (actors, producers, directors). (Schmidt and Frota, 1986: 247)

For the last six weeks of his stay, Schmidt spent time with these friends and his Portuguese improved to a point that he could at least communicate and engage in basic social interactions. Nevertheless, even by the end of his stay, he did not feel as though he was a whole human being in Portuguese, although making the progress he had made was rewarding:

> The language problem is severe. I frequently get so exhausted trying to keep up at least with the main topic of each conversation that I just drift off for a while. In spite of that, I've felt positively euphoric since I started to hang out there. (Schmidt and Frota, 1986: 247)

Schmidt and Frota present Schmidt's experiences in Brazil with a view to charting his linguistic development. The end result of their efforts was the 'discovery' of the concept of 'noticing', that is, the phenomenon whereby language learners register that particular language features occur or are used in particular ways where previously their occurrence and use would have gone undetected. Schmidt's increasing capacity to notice during his stay in Brazil is, no doubt, an important finding for SLL researchers of a cognitive bent. However, it does not say much about

Schmidt's emergent Portuguese language identity. Nevertheless, as I have attempted to show in this section, reading between the lines of the diary entries reproduced in Schmidt and Frota allows us some insight into how Schmidt's engagement with particular communities of practice, such as his Portuguese classes and his circle of friends at the restaurant, afforded him opportunities to develop second-language-mediated subject positions.

Conclusion

In this chapter, I have discussed research from the 1960s to the early 1980s in which identity has seemingly been lurking in the wings without ever coming out as a full-blown object of interest. One impression emerging from my admittedly selective survey is that in three decades of research on bilingualism and language learning, identity was generally framed as a fixed and measurable phenomenon, clearly relatable to successful or unsuccessful language learning experiences. In an article surveying the history of SLL research focused on affective and social factors, Pavlenko (2002) sees the kind of research carried out by researchers such as Guiora, Bailey, Schumann and Schmidt as part of a general 'Socio-psychological Approach' to language learning. For Pavlenko, the great flaw in this work is that it is, in effect, a structuralist approach to phenomena requiring a more poststructuralist framework (or a modern approach to phenomena requiring a postmodern framework). In an attempt to show how a generally poststructuralist/postmodern approach is preferable to the Socio-psychological Approach, Pavlenko outlines what she considers to be the basic assumptions of the latter along with what she sees as the problems with each of these assumptions. In Table 3.2, I have adapted her views on the main assumptions of the Socio-psychological approach to language learning and what the problem is with each of these assumptions. The solution to the problems raised by Pavlenko is very clearly the poststructuralism-inspired approach to identity described in Chapter 2.

Table 3.2 The problem with Socio-psychological approaches to language learning (based on Pavlenko, 2002: 279–81)

The assumptions	The problems
The norm is for human beings to be members of discrete monolingual cultures.	So-called monolingual communities are not as monolingual as they are often portrayed. In addition, the majority of people in the world live in and among two or more languages.
In language contact situations, it is a question of abandoning one language for another.	Individuals around the world tend to inhabit multiple sociolinguistic communities.
Acculturation, that is, adapting to the ways of the target language community, is the goal of L2 learners.	Learners of languages, both in naturalistic and foreign language settings, vary greatly as regards acculturation as a key goal.
Cultures remain stable through time.	Cultures are in a constant state of flux and ongoing change as they both assimilate the incoming while accommodating the existent.
Constructs such as 'motivation', 'in-group membership', 'attitudes', 'acculturation', 'beliefs' and so on, are in and of themselves explanatory of sociolinguistic phenomena such as accent and code switching.	They tend to name observed phenomena but they don't explain them. Indeed, the constructs themselves are in need of explanation. To say that one learns due to 'acculturation' is to raise the question of what causes 'acculturation'.
The above-cited constructs are deemed to move in one direction, as causes leading to effects.	There is two-way traffic between structure and agency as individual characteristics feed into structures and in turn are shaped by these structures.
There is a clear separation between social factors, such as the physical context of learning, and individual factors, such as ethnicity.	The social and the social psychological interrelate so that ethnicity is not the same everywhere the individual goes.

(Continued)

Table 3.2 (Continued)

The assumptions	The problems
Questionnaires are the best way to access and measure key constructs such as motivation.	Questionnaires cannot tell us much about a construct like gender or ethnicity as responses often can only claim to have the status of 'person A circled this particular number on this occasion'.
English-dominant contexts are representative of all language-contact situations.	These contexts are not the norm in the world.
Ultimately, language learning is an individual phenomenon.	Language learning is a socially situated activity.

The studies discussed in this chapter cover a good range of SLL contexts: adult migrants in the US (Schumann and Schmidt), FL study in the US (Bailey), fixed term study abroad (Schmidt and Frota, 1986) and adult SLL in Canada (Lambert, Guiora). In the next three chapters, I will discuss research carried out in the past 15 years in the former three contexts. Unlike the research discussed in this chapter, the research discussed in Chapters 4 to 6 has been carried out with a more explicit orientation towards identity, as discussed in Chapter 2. Whereas my aim in this chapter has been to seek ways of inserting this approach to identity into research which was designed and carried out for other purposes, in Chapters 4 to 6 my intention will be to explore exactly what identity issues emerge in each of the contexts discussed, offering critiques of this work along the way.

Note

1 H. Douglas Brown (1980) offers the following definitions of these two types of motivation, which in recent years have come to be questioned (Dörnyei, 2001, 2005):

Instrumental motivation refers to motivation to acquire a language as means for attaining instrumental goals: furthering a career, reading technical material, translation, and so forth. An *integrative* motive is employed when a learner wishes to integrate himself within the culture of the second language group, to identify himself with and become a part of that society. (Brown, 1980: 114; italics in the original)

4

Identity in adult migrant contexts

Introduction

In this chapter, I discuss research that has examined in detail the emergence of second language identities in adult migrant contexts. By adult migrant contexts, I mean cases in which adults (understood to be 18 years of age or older) have moved across geographical borders and immersed themselves in new cultural and linguistic environments. In some cases, the migrant is immersed, sink or swim, in the new cultural and linguistic environment and must get on with all aspects of the new life without the help of language classes. In other cases, language classes form a significant part of the migrant's story of adaptation and even assimilation. In either case, I will argue that it is the adult migrant case which carries the greatest potential of all the language learning setting for the 'critical experiences' (Block, 2002a), as described in Chapter 2. In short, it is in the adult migrant experience that identity and one's sense of self are most put on the line, not least because most or all previous support systems in terms of history, culture and language have been removed and must rapidly be replaced by new ones. It is in the maelstrom resulting from this relative vacuum that individuals are forced to reconstruct and redefine themselves, both for their own sense of ontological security (Giddens, 1991) and the positions ascribed to them by others in their new surroundings. Nevertheless, these processes of reconstruction and repositioning do not take place in predictable manners and it is certainly not the case that the naturalistic context guarantees sustained contact with longer-term inhabitants of the second language context.

I begin my discussion by examining in detail a study which is, in a sense, a bridge between the research examined in Chapter 3, in which identity was not an explicit issue, and research described in this chapter, where identity is one of the main – if not the main – focus. I refer here to Broeder, Bremer, Roberts, Vasseur and Simonot (1996) analysis of data collected as part of the European Science Foundation (ESF) Project in Second Language Acquisition, carried out in the early to mid-1980s. This study was primarily concerned with misunderstandings arising in migrants' contacts with gatekeepers in five different European countries. However, there is also some attention to identity work, which I see as historically significant. In effect, Broeder *et al* is an important piece of research linking sociolinguistic issues with an interest in life stories, which has become a common way of exploring identity issues in SLL research. Nevertheless, as I will make clear, the study did not really go far enough in this direction and it is only with the work of researchers such as Tara Goldstein (1996) and Bonny Norton (2000) that there have been book-length, in-depth accounts of how migrants make their way in a new cultural and linguistic environment, and above all, how they engage with the languages in their new environment. My discussion of Goldstein's study of Portuguese women in a factory in Toronto and Bonny Norton's study of five immigrant women in Toronto, is complemented by a smaller scale study by Teutsch-Dwyer (2001), published as a book chapter. Having examined in detail this body of research – a selective sample to be sure – I move finally to some of my own recent research on Spanish-speaking Latinos. An examination of my own research allows me to engage in a general critique of the research discussed previously.

Adult migrants and gate-keeping encounters in Western European countries

Although it was published in 1996, Broeder, Bremer, Roberts, Vasseur and Simonot (1996) *Achieving Understanding: Discourse in Intercultural Encounters* is based on data collected from 1982 to

1986, as part of the European Science Foundation Project in Second Language Acquisition. The project, easily the most extensive and ambitious of its kind in the 1980s, set out to study the acquisition of five languages – English, German, Dutch, French and Swedish – in five countries – the UK, Germany, the Netherlands, France and Sweden – by speakers of six languages – Punjabi, Italian, Turkish, Arabic, Spanish and Finnish. While Perdue (1993a, 1993b) is a general report on the project which focuses primarily on the linguistic development of the over 30 participants, Broeder *et al* (1996) take a decidedly more sociolinguistic perspective. The authors focus on the acquisition of four different languages – English, French, German and Dutch – in the UK, France, Germany and the Netherlands by immigrants who were L1 speakers of Italian, Spanish and Arabic. However, more importantly, they focus on what they call the 'negotiation of understanding' in service and other public encounters in which one interlocutor is an immigrant second language learner and the other is a local service provider who communicates with his/her interlocutor exclusively in the local language.

Broeder *et al* therefore represents a break from the studies discussed in Chapter 3 on several counts. First, it involves 30 individual cases and therefore is far more extensive than the other studies. Second, it is based on data collected over a longer period of time than any of the other studies. Third, it involves more languages, and in particular, it gets away from a certain English language bias, which is manifest in much SLL research. Fourth, perhaps because it is socio-linguistic in focus, the starting point is not based on assumptions about how languages are learned or what affective factors might be important in the language learning process; rather, it is primarily concerned with the detailed characteristics of conversations and above all, the dynamics of misunderstandings and the pre- and post-utterance actions taken by immigrants to repair them or avoid them, respectively. Fifth, and more importantly, Broeder *et al* challenge several assumptions held by SLL researchers about naturalistic SLL contexts.

The first assumption challenged is that naturalist contexts provide learners with more opportunities to be exposed to TL input than other contexts (e.g. foreign language contexts). Part and parcel of this assumption is the idea – prevalent in many contexts around the world – that the best way to learn a language is to 'be there', that is to be physically located in a country or place where the TL is the predominant linguistic mediator of day-to-day activity. In Broeder *et al*, this assumption was generally born out in gate-keeping encounters, such as visits to the doctor and contacts with government agencies; however, it did not hold up in informal social encounters, such as conversations with family and friends. Indeed, many of the 18 informants in the study used anything but the TL in their encounters with friends and relatives. Thus, Santo, an Italian migrant living in London claimed that he hardly ever used English among co-workers, friends and relatives, and Berta, a Chilean immigrant in Paris, claimed that she had no French-speaking friends.

The second assumption challenged in Broeder *et al* is that in second language encounters, negotiation of meaning takes place, whereby all interlocutors involved in a conversation work towards mutual understanding. Consistent with earlier publications such as Sarangi and Slembrouck (1992), the authors found that the responsibility for achieving mutual understanding and maintaining the flow of conversation fell in most cases on the shoulders of the migrants, and that these migrants were neither prepared nor ready to take on this responsibility in most cases. Thus, in cases where migrants were not able to initiate and monitor the negotiation of understanding, conversations tended to have inconclusive and often frustrating outcomes for all parties involved. In the following example, Berta, a Chilean woman who had been living in Paris with her family for just a few months, struggles as she asks a carpenter how much it would cost to have some shelves cut. The exchange appears first in French, followed by the translation into English.

B = Berta   C = Carpenter
*NB Spanish portions are in **bold** with translations immediately afterwards in brackets: {xxx}.*

1. *C: ouais on peut vous découper les planches avec – vous venez avec les mesures on vous découp euh les planches*
2. *B: bon c'est de (.) un mètre*
3. *C: (.) un mètre sur quelle euh?*
4. *B: ah y **yo no sé** {je ne sais pas} (.) je crois qué c'est (.) vingt comme ça*

5. C: *ouais on peut vous les découper (.) que les planches simplement*
6. B: *ouais combien coûte le?*
7. C: *ça depend en quoi vous le prenez en soit du contreplaqué ou du latté*
8. B: *no c'est (.) pour mettre le – sur le mur*
9. C: *sur?*
10. B: *sur le mur*
11. C: *avec des equerries?*
12. B: *ouais*
13. C: *oui?*
14. B: *ouais? (.)* **y** *{et}quoi?*
15. C: *excusez-moi*

1. C: yes we can cut up the boards for you with – you come with the measurements we cut up the boards for you.
2. B: well it's (.) one meter
3. C: (.) one meter by what eh?
4. B: ah I **yo no sé** {I don't know} (.) I think it's (.) about twenty
5. C: yes we can cut them up for you (.) only the boards
6. B: yes and how much the?
7. C: it depends what type of wood you want either plywood or slat
8. B: no it's (.) to put the - on the wall
9. C: on?
10. B: on the wall
11. C: with braces?
12. B: yes
13. C: yes?
14. B: yes? (.) **y** {and}what?
15. C: excuse me

(Broeder *et al*, 1996: 91; NB transcription conventions adapted)

Midway through this exchange, Berta loses the thread of the conversation and by the end she understands very little of what is going on. The technical terms introduced in turns 7 and 11 – *contreplaqué* (plywood), *latté* (slat) and *equerries* (braces) – no doubt throw her off course, making it impossible for her to find out how much she would have to pay to have the shelves cut. The carpenter makes no effort to adapt his language so that Berta can understand him and therefore appears to put all of the responsibility for creating understanding on her shoulders, not his. The end result is that 'Berta . . . leaves the shop with a sense of failure' (Broeder et al 1996: 91), adding to her sense of frustration and consolidating her ascribed position of unworthy interlocutor.

The third assumption that Broeder et al challenge is that learners learn the second language through conversational interaction. The authors found that in many interactions, the migrant's language competence was, in effect, being assessed and judged rather than serving as a resource to be drawn on. Their interlocutors seemed to be operating according to dominant discourses about migrants, which positioned them as inadequate interlocutors. In a sense, the migrants were put in an impossible situation: they needed language skills in order to communicate more effectively and improve their life prospects, but they could not get the communicative practice necessary to better these skills.

A fourth and final assumption about the naturalistic context, often implicit rather than explicit in much work, is that there is somehow a level playing field of opportunities and a right to speak and be spoken to. However, as Broeder et al note in some of their examples, an inattention to power differentials in service encounters is not advisable.

In the following excerpt, Abdelmalek, a Moroccan man who had been living in Paris for several months, is trying to buy a train ticket to Casablanca. However in the execution of such a simple act, he indexes his own relative powerlessness by the way that he understands questions and how he responds to these questions.

1. *A: je partir à Casablanca, maroc*
2. *N: par quoi vous voulez partir?*
3. *A: [se] beaucoup problems law-bas papa malady je partir tout de suite*
4. *N: je comprends pas law. qu'est-ce que vous voulez où vous voulez aller?*

1. A: I am leaving for Casablanca Morocco
2. N: how do you wish to go?

3. A: a lot of problems there father is ill I'm leaving right away
4. N: I don't understand that, what do you want where do you want to go?

(Broeder *et al* 1996: 12–13;
NB transcription conventions adapted)

In this exchange, Abdelmalek understands the question *'par quoi vous voulez partir?'* (how do you wish to go?) as *'pourquoi vous voulez partir?'* (why do you wish to go?). In other words, he understands it to be about <u>why</u> he wants to travel to Casablanca rather than <u>by what means</u> he wants to travel. Broeder *et al* use this exchange as an example of misunderstanding at the linguistic level. However, they also note how Abdelmalek's on-the-spot understanding is not just linguistic and may be related to the fact that in other public encounters, his official French interlocutors exercised the right to ask him such personal and even inappropriate questions. His manifest compliance in answering such questions wrongfoots the ticket seller who at first does not understand and then later adopts a stance of: why are you telling me this? The upshot is that migrants may come to inhabit spaces of relative inferiority, as regards power, where such positionings are neither necessary nor appropriate. The result is that they are, in effect, excluded from the mainstream as incompetent interlocutors by the gatekeepers with whom they come in contact.

In her survey of research on 'adult immigrant language learners', Norton (2000) views Broeder *et al* as a landmark study, above all because of how the authors debunk the first three assumptions outlined above. However, Norton also points to two shortcomings. First, she argues that Broeder *et al* lacks the kind of detailed life story information contained in her own work (more on Norton's study below) and in particular that the study does not focus on language practices related to communities of practice. Thus, the reader is privy to service encounters but sees almost nothing of participants' other day-to-day activities and how these activities are language mediated. Perhaps because the life story element is considerably downplayed, Broeder *et al* is also deemed not to have gone far enough as regards social analysis. For Norton, the study does not sufficiently address power issues, in particular the assumption that 'those who speak regard those who listen as worthy to listen, and that those who listen regard those who speak as worthy to speak' (Norton, 2000: 8). She laments that there is insufficient focus on how migrants develop identities as what Bourdieu (1977) calls 'legitimate speakers', that is how they come to be accepted and fully functioning members of different communities of practice.

Reading Broeder et al (1996) some ten years after its publication, I get roughly the same impression as Norton, namely, that there are more identity issues here than initially meet the eye. Thus, in Berta's conversation, Broeder et al do not analyse specifically how the carpenter might have positioned Berta – as a woman, as a Spanish speaker or simply as a foreigner. They do note that that such behaviour might cause immigrants like Berta to 'retreat permanently and avoid contact with the majority ethnic group', effectively narrowing the number of social circles and communities of practice in which a French language identity might develop. However, this kind of socially-informed analysis is not pursued in very much detail. As regards being judged and assessed rather than engaged with in conversations, the net effect for migrants might be simply to give up on possible contacts with speakers of the target language and to seek refuge, speaking to friends and family in the L1. Again, Broeder et al do not directly relate this state of affairs to identity; however, surely there are issues related to judgements about race, ethnicity and gender on the part of gatekeepers and other speakers of the target languages. Finally, one lesson to be learned from Abdelmalek's misunderstanding is not only that migrants themselves may inappropriately take up subject positions of relative inferiority and powerlessness vis-à-vis their interlocutors, as Broeder et al note, but also that this self-positioning leads to their being positioned and treated by gatekeepers as different.

In fairness to Broeder et al (1996), the authors were dealing with a database collected several years earlier which, crucially, was meant to answer questions about language development and interaction, not identity. In addition, it is worth noting that, particularly at the end of the book, the authors actually do show that they are interested in the connections to be made between language practices engaged in by participants and the social (institutional) power structures which impinge on these practices. In their closing chapter, there is a discussion of how participants in the study were disadvantaged by virtue of being positioned as unskilled or under-skilled, when often they were skilled or over-skilled, and as incompetent communicators, when they were perfectly good communicators in their first languages. Beyond these other-generated ascriptions, Broeder *et al* also acknowledge that there are discursive subject positions consciously adopted by migrants, and they note that it would be wrong to frame migrants as passive victims of institutionally driven, classist, anti-migrant and racist discourses. Indeed, the conversation excerpts reproduced in the book show migrants fighting back in different ways. Thus, there are examples of migrants using their linguistic resources to maintain conversations when breakdowns occurred, migrants trying to maintain their sense of dignity and face when and where these had been challenged and or put under threat, and migrants openly engaging with or even defying their interlocutors if this was the only way to get things done.

Nevertheless, Broeder *et al* is, above all else, a thorough account of immigrant language use, in the context of a focus on understanding (*à la* Gumperz, 1982). As such, it is not primarily about the life stories of immigrants and the ongoing development of different subject positions in their new social environments. In order to find such life stories in the context of language socialization studies, one must look elsewhere, specifically to research being carried out at the end of the 1980s and the beginning of the 1990s.

Portuguese on the factory floor in Toronto

Published in the same year as Broeder *et al,* Goldstein's (1996) *Two Languages at Work: Bilingual Life on the Production Floor* is first and foremost a challenge to the commonly held idea that immigrants need as thorough and complete a command of the host language as possible in order to be fully functioning employees. While this assumption may be valid in the case of what Reich (1991; see Chapter 2 of this book) calls 'in-person servers' (e.g. sales staff at department stores, secretaries, hairdressers, bus drivers and teachers) and 'symbolic analysts' (i.e. the superclass of highly educated and skilled individuals in high-level professions), it is not valid in the case of 'routine producers', whose work is not carried out in the presence of those who will ultimately consume its products. In addition, in situations where routine producers of a particular ethnolinguistic background are clustered together, it is likely that a command of the language of that ethnolinguistic group is far more valuable than a command of the host language. This is the case both for the practicality and efficiency of work carried out, as well as for the maintenance of a good working atmosphere based on phatic, affectively oriented communication among workers.

In her research, Goldstein focused on 27 Portuguese immigrant women working in the production department of a family-run toy and textile company called 'Stone Specialities' in Toronto from January 1988 to March 1990. Goldstein was interested in assumptions being made at the time by some educational authorities in Ontario about the English language needs of immigrants. An English language instructor herself, she found that there was a dominant discourse among educational authorities in Ontario that the inability to speak English well was a 'deficiency', not only in workplace settings but also in family and other social settings. However, when Goldstein explored the language needs of her informants, using observation, interviews and recorded workplace conversations, she found that many assumptions made by authorities were totally unfounded. In effect, English was not essential to the lives of these Portuguese women, and as regards the work context specifically they had formed a Portuguese-mediated network of relationships which encompassed matters related to work as well as social matters both inside and outside the workplace. For Goldstein's informants, Portuguese had 'social value as a symbol of distinctness and as a symbol of a speaker's identification with others in the Portuguese manufacturing "family"/community' (Goldstein, 1996: 144). English, by contrast, was 'used by people outside the Portuguese manufacturing "family"/community and . . . [was] associated with talk, paper work and work roles . . . not part of the line work and the assembly of different products' (Goldstein, 1996: 144–5).

In this context, a language-based dichotomy had emerged, whereby Portuguese was the language of power at the very local level of these women's lives while English was the language of power at higher levels in the company as well as most of the world outside of the factory. Getting a job was more than likely a process carried out primarily in

Portuguese rather than English, as 24 of Goldstein's 27 informants were reported to have found their jobs through their Portuguese family and friends. In addition, Portuguese was the dominant language on the assembly lines, which meant that one's job efficiency could be affected by a lack of knowledge of Portuguese. Indeed, Goldstein describes how Spanish- and Italian-speaking co-workers had felt the need to learn elementary Portuguese in order to survive at work. Their survival at work, however, might not have been exclusively about the basics of assembly; they might also have observed how the use of Portuguese at work fulfilled the phatic side of workplace communication (Holmes, 2000), as all social life was mediated by Portuguese and not English. Indeed, using English among Portuguese-speaking colleagues was considered a rather bad or rude thing to do. The speaker might choose to use English because she wished to say something bad about another person, who might not understand English very well. Alternatively, the speaker might choose to use English in order to show off the possession of cultural capital not possessed by others.

Before she began her study, just one out of 26 women she interviewed had attended English classes offered by the local government to immigrants. When asked why they had not attended classes, informants provided a variety of reasons, which clustered around four general arguments. First, there were mentions of male family members who did not like the fact that their daughters or wives were attending classes with other men. Goldstein sees this male control over these women's decisions and movements as part of a more pervasive gendered hierarchy in the Portuguese community. In effect, these women had to toe the line between acceptable public activity – work almost exclusively with well-known Portuguese female colleagues – and unacceptable public activity – educational development with unknown non-Portuguese men and women.

Second, there was the matter of not feeling safe going out at night. One informant, Luísa, responded as follows when asked about whether or not she had considered attending English classes when she first arrived in Toronto:

I was scared to walk on the streets at night. Because I came in August and in September the school starts. And I was scared because I hear so many strange things. (Goldstein, 1996: 210)

Whether this fear was originally based on documented cases of Portuguese women being harassed at night on the streets of Toronto, or it was just a rumour, is not particularly important. What is important is that in their conversations with Goldstein, informants invoked this view as a reason not to study at night. However, the strength of this argument was questioned by Goldstein and when she asked Luísa about why she had not attended classes offered in the daytime, she was told: 'I had to help my friends because we had to start a new life' (Goldstein, 1996: 210). In this case, a new argument is brought in, one that is about home and family-related responsibilities that could never be relegated to a secondary position by the desire to study English. Thus, childcare and bringing home money were priorities and must always come first.

A fourth and final reason for not studying was not so much invoked directly by informants as it was a part of their personal biographies. Goldstein notes how many of the women working at Stone's Special-ities had come to Toronto from the Azores Islands where they had only had about four years of formal education. According to Goldstein, acquiring a good level of proficiency in English was effectively beyond the means of most of her informants. In this sense, attending English class might be seen as a waste of time because these women would never attain a respectable level of English. However, I see an additional way in which just four years of formal study might shape decisions about attending English class, namely that formal education was simply a foreign activity for these women.

The women in Goldstein's study apparently made very conscious decisions not to attend the English classes on offer to them prior to taking their jobs at Stone Specialities and these decisions were linked primarily to the need for the security which the Portuguese community provided. Studying English would have meant upsetting their valued community or 'family' life. However, their choice in the matter was very much shaped not only by the Portuguese community environment, but also by Canadian society in general, which ascribed to them the subject position of under-skilled working immigrants. For Goldstein, these women were caught between these contradictory forces, which prevented them from acquiring better English language skills. Better English language skills would have given them greater cultural capital, which in turn would have allowed them access to greater social, political and economic capital, and ultimately, more independence and prosperity.

Running through the comments that the women made to Goldstein was a lack of ambition with regard to work. For most of the women, the prospect of improving their lot by moving to another company was ruled out, as was, in many cases, accepting an offer of promotion from the assembly lines to a supervisory post. Goldstein relates this lack of ambition to gendered subject positions occupied by her informants:

> It can be argued that the views these women hold of work are tied to the gendered dynamics of their families. For example, women who are expected to raise a family, maintain a home, and contribute to the families' income may not value a better paying job off the line if such a job entails additional responsibility. Similarly, women who work both inside and outside the home – and whose income is supplemented by the income of other members of the family – may value the close proximity of the workplace to their home over the extra money they can make at a factory that requires them to travel long distances. (Goldstein, 1996: 187)

Goldstein's study is mainly about Portuguese immigrant feminine subject positions and how the key focal point in the lives of these women is the family: childcare, financial obligations to the family and acceptance of masculine hegemony, both inside and outside the home. Mixed in are classed subject positions emergent from the minimal formal education of the women (often only four years in the Azores, as noted above) and their at-best moderate professional skills, which left them with few prospects for jobs outside of Stone Specialities. And finally, there is a patriarchal Portuguese culture which relegates women to subordinate positions in all aspects of their lives, which has seemingly been transferred intact from villages in the Azores to urban Toronto. Goldstein does a good job of melding together these different strands to explain why the women, in many cases, seemed to be taking decisions which went against their long-term work-related interests. Ultimately, their professional ambition came second to their personal life ambitions of being part of the Portuguese community.

Goldstein represents an advance over Broeder *et al* in that it contains considerably more background information about the informants who are discussed. It also brings to the fore, far more explicitly, specific subject positions around language, gender, culture and class, showing how these different positions come to be inextricably linked. In short, one cannot understand any of these women without seeing how their gender and class identities shape and are shaped by particular patterns of language use that draw on particular repertoires, and how all of this is linked with their membership in the broader Portuguese cultural group. However, despite the originality and depth of Goldstein's study, there are some noteworthy shortcomings.

First, Goldstein came into the lives of most of her informants several years and even decades after their arrivals in Toronto. As a result, she is completely reliant on recollections of the past of her informants. This is not so much of a problem if one considers the importance, not of factual history itself, but how individuals choose to explain history in the present. However, there is still a sense of staticity in Goldstein's contacts: there is more historical re-telling than here-and-now language socialization in progress. An additional problem is how the data were collected, using an English-Portuguese interpreter because Goldstein did not understand or speak any Portuguese. To her credit, Goldstein admits that this might be problem. She also acknowledges that most readers of ethnographies expect the ethnographers to speak the language of their informants so as to engage actively with them as equals and co-producers of phenomena in a multitude of contexts. However, Goldstein is really not able to address these points satisfactorily for the simple reason that there is, in effect, nothing she can do about them after the fact. She states that working with the interpreter was a positive experience because she provided Goldstein with vital background information about the history and sociology of the Azores. However, to my mind, the inability to speak Portuguese in the case of this study was surely a big limitation on Goldstein's ability to get inside the assembly line culture of Stone Specialities and above all, to 'be with' her informants.

The life stories of female immigrants in Toronto

At about the time that Goldstein was completing data collection for her study in Stone Specialities, in another part of Toronto, Bonny

Norton was beginning data collection for her study of five female immigrants. *Identity and Language Learning* (Norton, 2000) is a detailed account of her longitudinal study of five immigrant women in Canada which examines the interrelationship between identity, power and access to English in classroom and naturalistic settings. The main thesis put forward by Norton is captured in the following quotation:

> While the women can have exposure to English through television, radio and newspapers, the opportunity to practice speaking English outside the classroom is dependent largely on their access to Anglophone social networks. Access to such networks was difficult to achieve for these immigrant women. (Norton, 2000: 135)

Norton shows the relative degrees to which the women achieved access to English-speaking networks in the five individual case studies she develops. These case studies were based on a database consisting of two questionnaires, two interviews, numerous diary entries and diary discussion meetings and essays written by the informants on three occasions. All data were collected between October 1990 and December 1991. The women participating in the study were from Poland (two informants), Vietnam, Peru and Czechoslovakia. They varied along several variables, such as age (early 20s to mid-40s), marital status (single and married), family situation (with children or not) and educational level (high school to MA). Only one of the women knew any English before arriving in Canada, although the other four had varying degrees of proficiency in two or more languages each. This basic information about the five women is presented in Table 4.1. I will now examine in detail two of the cases – a younger informant, Eva, and the oldest informant, Felicia – in order to see the kinds of identity issues arising in Norton's work.

Eva left Poland when she was 20, living for two years in Italy, where she became proficient in Italian. She had left Poland seeking a better life economically, and she chose Canada because of its relatively open immigration policy. She shared an apartment with a Polish man and got a job at an Italian store frequented by an Italian-Canadian clientele. Here she was able to use her Italian, but as soon she could, she changed jobs, moving to a restaurant where she was the only non-Canadian employee. Eva was happy to be in Canada,

Table 4.1 Basic information about Norton's five informants

Name	Country of origin	Age in 1990	Marital status (Children)	Education	Languages spoken	English level
Mai	Vietnam	22	Single (0)	High school	Cantonese, Vietnamese	Beginner
Eva	Poland	23	Single (0)	High school	Polish, Italian	Beginner
Katarina	Poland	35	Married (1)	MA Biology	Polish, German, Russian	Beginner
Martina	Czechoslovakia	38	Married (3)	BA Surveying	Czech, Slovak, Russian, German	Beginner
Felicia	Peru	45	Married (2)	BA Education	Spanish	'some'

seeing it as a country of opportunity, and she was very optimistic about her prospects, once she learned to speak English well enough. However, as she settled into life in Canada, she came to see that the path to full acceptance as an equal in her new home was impeded by her Polish immigrant status.

The only place where Eva was regularly exposed to English was at work, in a restaurant called 'Munchies'. At first, Eva reported experiences in which she was marginalized and even exploited by her fellow workers, who made sure that she did the worst chores, such as cleaning up. Observing that she tended to do the jobs which required no speaking, such as cooking and cleaning, the restaurant manager simply assumed that she could not speak English well enough to do the easier jobs requiring direct contact with customers, such as taking food orders. Not surprisingly, Eva was not happy with this situation, telling Norton: 'I don't want like somebody takes me for a stupid person who just came and doesn't know nothing and cleans the floor . . .' (Norton, 2000: 63).

However, matters changed when she began to socialize with her fellow workers away from the restaurant and they, in turn, began to see her as more than just a silent immigrant worker. For example, on one occasion her European background became the focus of conversation, and this allowed her to position herself vis-à-vis her monolingual Anglophone Canadian colleagues in a different light: as someone who had lived an interesting life, who knew about Europe and who spoke Italian. She spoke of this conversation with Norton as follows:

Eva: They ask me a few more questions and then we were talking about languages. They asked me, because my manager she has got married with an Italian – and I help her with a few words in Italian . . .

Bonny Norton: Were people impressed that you could also speak Italian?

Eva: mmmm. They already knew before. Maybe they were because they asked me if I can speak another languages and I told then I can understand Russian and I said that I understand Czech and I learnt for example German and I know almost well Italian. They were surprised I think. (Norton, 2000: 69–70)

Feeling more legitimate as a co-worker and human being, Eva began to lose her self-consciousness about speaking English and eventually engaged in far more interactions in English, both on and off the job. Eventually, she told Norton that she felt more a part of things at work, and that, in effect, she had carved out an identity as a fully functioning co-worker who was a worthy interlocutor:

> Firstly, I have more practice. I feel more comfortable there when I speak. And I'm not scared anymore to say something. Because before I wasn't sure if I say something the right way or they like understand me or not – because sometime I say something but they don't understand me. (Norton, 2000: 71)

Eva's relative success on the job did not erase the fact that Polish continued to be her home language. Nor did it mean that she never had problems with Anglophones because of her accent. However, it did mean that she had achieved membership in her workplace-based community of practice, an English-mediated subject position.

Eva's experiences, not surprisingly, contrast markedly with those of Felicia, the oldest informant in the study. Felicia was a 45-year-old Peruvian woman who moved to Canada with her husband and three children when the political and social turbulence of 1980s Peru was making life uncomfortable for the family. University-educated and upper middle class, Felicia was accustomed to a very high standard of living and the move to Canada meant a serious curtailing of her opulent lifestyle. In her contacts with Norton, Felicia presented her husband as a highly qualified, English-speaking international business specialist, who despite being in Canada on a professional visa, had trouble getting a job similar to the one he had had in Peru. One of Felicia's central themes in her contacts with Norton was her frustration and bitterness at not being able to live her life as she had in Peru. Her conclusion was that Canadians look down on immigrants, something that she repaid by professing no interest whatsoever in ever identifying with her host country. For Felicia, Canada was a good place for 'people who lived in countries under communism . . . or people who never had anything in their countries' (Norton, 2000: 56), but it was a bad place for 'professional people or wealthy people [who] lose a lot coming to Canada' (Norton, 2000: 56). Felicia clearly put herself in the latter category and she chafed at the treatment she claimed that she and her family had received, as the following interview excerpt shows:

> We downed our standard of living in Canada. We used to have a relaxed life in our country. My husband had a very good job. Canada doesn't give my husband the opportunity to work. I never will understand why the government gave him the professional visa. (Norton, 2000: 102)

In her contacts with Norton, Felicia very self-consciously positioned herself as a wealthy Peruvian, who just happened to be living in Canada, but never as an 'immigrant'. She was only comfortable speaking English to people she knew well and she avoided speaking English with 'new people' and Peruvians who spoke English well. Most of the people in the former category (i.e. the people she knew well) were colleagues and acquaintances at a recreational centre where Felicia worked as a babysitter. She seemed to have negotiated membership in a social circle of middle class women, playing the role of someone who owned property in Peru and was looking to buy a house in the neighbourhood. However, in her contacts with these acquaintances, she still felt inadequate and feared being classified as an uninteresting foreign person. She explained:

> Sometimes the ladies ask me something about my country or my family, but I think that I'm not an interesting person because my English is limited and I have to think before talking. (Norton, 2000: 106)

Far worse, however, were her contacts with strangers, such as the mothers of the children she babysat in the centre. In these contacts, Felicia was more circumspect and spoke very little. This was because she feared that the mothers, not knowing her background, would take her for an 'immigrant'. This impression was borne out when Felicia took another childcare job, this time in an after-school programme, dealing with older children. On her own, she had to speak English a great deal both with the children and their parents. However, this context exposed her to being positioned as a needy immigrant woman, with poor English language skills – not as the wealthy Peruvian property owner, married to a successful businessman. Felicia described what she considered to be a negative experience at this new place of work as follows:

> Yesterday I went with Maria [Felicia's daughter], she spoke to me in Spanish many times, there were different children that the day before, two of them were very active and the kind of children that don't like to obey. I had to call them the attention many times and I felt that my English was limited. One of the older children asked me, you have an accent, don't you? I answered yes, I do. He asked me if my language was French, and I answered not, but it is close to French. When his mother came to pick him up, I asked him his name, and he answered 'I don't know to tell my name in Spanish', and I answered him, 'you don't have to tell me your name in Spanish, you have to tell it in English.' Yesterday, I didn't feel very well there. (Norton, 2000: 106)

Feeling humiliated by this experience, and perhaps others of a similar nature, Felicia quit this job just a few days after starting it.

In general, Felicia intentionally limited her contacts with English speakers and this self-imposed isolation led her to feel less confident about her English, and quite likely limited her progress in learning it. She was effectively in a vicious circle whereby practice with strangers, which would have helped her to develop greater confidence and competence in English, put her sense of self at risk. At the same time, her limited competence meant that strangers would always position her as an immigrant, and probably a poor one. This was an ascribed subject position she avoided at all costs.

In the cases of Eva and Felicia, there is a contrast between a younger woman, determined to succeed in Canada as her English improves, and an older woman, more tied to her past as a wealthy, educated Spanish speaker for whom the move to Canada has meant a substantial 'declassing' and a loss of social and economic capital. The cases of the other women in the study fall somewhere in between these two cases, whilst throwing up unique issues of their own. For example, Mai, a young Vietnamese woman, was like Eva in that she was young and determined to succeed in Canada. However, unlike Eva, she had to navigate through a more difficult job situation and a complex set of family relationships. Her work situation as a seamstress worsened when economic hard times led to lay-offs at the factory, which in turn led to a less agreeable social environment at work. As regards her family, Mai eventually got married, a move that allowed her to get away from the oppressive patriarchy imposed by her domineering brother, a successful businessman in Toronto.

The other two older women, Katarina and Marina, were like Felicia in that they migrated to Canada with their husbands and children. Like Felicia, Katarina was unhappy at how she and her husband, both university-educated professionals, had been declassed in the process of moving to Canada. However, her declassing is linked more to their professional activity, whereas Felicia's seemed to be more related to wealth and a luxurious lifestyle. Although she often complained, much as Felicia did, at being treated as an immigrant, Katarina seemed to work harder than Felicia to overcome her declassing, attending computer and English courses.

In marked contrast to Katarina and Felicia, Martina did not have a professionally trained English-speaking husband who, at least in theory, would have been able to get decent employment in Canada. Her husband was a plumber by trade and spoke no more English than she did, effectively none. With three children ranging in age from 11 to 17, Martina found that she had to learn fast and get on with getting things done in English, as she became the primary caregiver and fixer in her family. Martina was a trained surveyor in Czechoslovakia, and in common with Katarina, she had to settle for jobs well below her capabilities. However, she seemed more disposed to putting her pride on hold as she was determined to prosper in Canada and was resigned to accepting jobs far below her capabilities on the way to greater prosperity.

Taken together, the five case studies provide the reader with a clear picture of how language and other subject positions develop over time and how identity is a complex site of struggle. Interestingly, the strongest ties among Norton's informants seem to be family, work and friends as opposed to community, which certainly was an overarching identity marker in Goldstein's study. This difference is no doubt due to the fact that Norton's research did not focus on one particular ethnolinguistic community, but on five individuals. However, it is also likely due to the fact that Norton's informants were decidedly more upwardly mobile, or in any case, already relatively well situated in their countries of origin prior to emigration.

Nevertheless, in her move to consider key issues of identity and the social conditions of migrants, Norton leaves behind the kind of microanalysis of interactions that Broeder *et al* engaged in or the linking of documented language use with her informants' senses of self, which Goldstein did. Thus, unlike Broeder *et al* and Goldstein, Norton provides no examples of recorded conversations in which her informants participated. Her cases are, therefore, constructed narratives of language learning and use. They are powerful and compelling narratives to be sure. But they lack the extra perspective that examples of interactions would have provided. The next study to be discussed in this chapter, Teutsch-Dwyer, serves as somewhat of a remedy to the shortcomings of Norton's study. It provides the life story of a language learner *and* it links the development of subject positions to language learning.

The language-based masculinities of a Polish immigrant in California

Interested in how a new cultural and language environment might lead to the development of new masculine subject positions and how the development of these new masculine subject positions might impact on second language development, Marya Teutsch-Dwyer (2001) carried out a detailed study of Karol, a 38-year-old Polish man living and working in the US. Teutsch-Dwyer made bi-monthly recordings of Karol's naturally occurring speech and took observation-based field notes. She also carried out interviews with Karol, as well as his American girlfriend and co-workers. These databases allowed her to chart the development of Karol's English language story-telling ability and his general development as a valid interlocutor in English. Teutsch-Dwyer focused on devices such as the positioning of time markers in stories, the use of time-marking adverbials and the use of inflected verbs. She observed that over a 14-month period of time, Karol showed very little progress in the use of such devices and that he was even using fewer time-marking adverbials at the end of the period. The following excerpt from a conversation with Karol, recorded in the latter part of the study, shows the grammatical limitations of his speech:

> John this John have mother is born here and grandmother and grandfather born in Poland and he very good speak Polish. He read Polish book. Lota know of Polish history, geography. (Teutsch-Dwyer, in Pavlenko *et al*, 2001: 192; punctuation added)

Teutsch-Dwyer suggests that Karol was actually living in a fairly comfortable environment when he arrived in California. For his first month, he lived with his sister, her English-speaking American husband, the couple's young daughter and a Spanish-English bilingual nanny. At first, his brother-in-law showed an interest in talking to him, asking him about politics in Poland and other matters of common interest. In these exchanges, Karol's sister had to act as a translator, but as Teutsch-Dwyer notes, Karol at least felt validated as a male interlocutor. He was, in effect, worthy to speak to and listen to, even if anything that he said had to be passed through his sister. However, after a month, the brother-in-law apparently tired of Karol's company and asked him to leave the household. Karol moved into a hotel where he became friends with four other Polish men.

In conversations with Teutsch-Dwyer, Karol was disparaging about his brother-in-law. For Karol, the latter's hobby was money and business, and as Karol had no money and was not interested in business, he was not an interesting interlocutor. However, the brother-in-law's rejection of Karol was not just about topics of conversation or even that speaking with him must have been a torturous process; rather, it had more to do with conflicting masculinities. On the one hand, Karol's brother-in-law saw adherence to a work ethic, ambition, financial solvency and responsibility to family as markers of masculinity. In contrast, Karol thought that being a good conversationalist (and story teller) and adopting a more bohemian lifestyle were far more important and attractive as markers of masculinity. Teutsch-Dwyer sums up the situation as follows:

> Karol realized that his brother-in-law's standards of what constituted an appropriate male conversational partner was far

from what he could offer at the time. Karol was not a man of means, nor did he have friends with money. He was not about to enter business deals, and above all, he had insufficient English language skills. For face-saving reasons, however, he repeatedly criticised this over a materialistic approach to life. (Teutsch-Dwyer, 2001: 188)

Karol's other contacts with American males was in the factory where he worked. Karol was happy with the relationship he had with his male boss, who would take the time to explain to Karol what he wanted him to do and who seemed to appreciate his work. However, matters took a turn for the worst when he found out that the boss had slighted him by telling a co-worker in the factory that Karol's English was too poor for him to get a promotion within the company. After finding that he could not really participate as an equal partner in conversations with his American brother-in-law and his male boss, Karol found that it was only with three female co-workers that he was able to participate fully as a respected interlocutor. He would meet with these women during break times, regaling them with his 'funny' and 'incredible' stories about his previous life in Poland and his experiences in the US. Crucially, these three women actively listened to what he had to say and they made an effort to understand him. As Teutsch-Dwyer notes, this kind of interaction was new to Karol and was a big boost to his ego and morale:

> This new linguistic reality stood in sharp contrast to his social position vis-à-vis his brother-in-law and his boss, where his position of power was minimized and his English tolerated to the bare maximum. In the new situation, he regained the 'power to speak' . . . His maleness among the female circle of friends was restored, and he felt his position was elevated to the position of an equal in conversations. (Teutsch-Dwyer, 2001: 190).

However, his elevation to equal status in conversations was not based on his English getting substantially better. Rather, it was because the three women – especially the one who became his girlfriend – simplified their vocabulary, spoke slowly and even came to anticipate his speech to the extent that he was under no pressure to produce more elaborate or accurate language. As Teutsch-Dwyer explains:

> Karol reported that after a while he did not have to struggle to use 'very correct English' among his circle of female friends because he knew they could by now understand what he intended to say – that is, they got used to his language and his communicative strategies. (Teutsch-Dwyer, 2001: 190)

In Karol's contacts with his girlfriend, this kind of linguist obsequiousness transferred to other realms his life as she began to take care of his personal business, for example, taking and making phone calls on his behalf to banks and doctors. The end result was a degree of learned helplessness on Karol's part, as he was doted upon by his girlfriend in so many aspects of his life. As regards his language development, Teutsch-Dwyer concludes that Karol's 'substantial lack of the grammaticalization process during his language acquisition over a period of fourteen months is closely related to his perceptions of positive acceptance by the social female circles he was a member of and by the sheltered conditions he experienced in his private life' (Teutsch-Dwyer, 2001: 192).

Thus, Karol's modest English grammar development cannot really be explained by the limitations of gate keeping encounters, as in the case of Broeder *et al*'s informants. Nor is there any question of limited contact with English speakers in favour of almost exclusive contact with members of the same ethnolinguistic group, as was the case for the women in Goldstein's study. In short, in no way was there, in Karol's life, a lack of exposure to the target language, a lack of opportunity to interact with English speakers or a lack of opportunity to speak. However, like Norton's women, Karol did experience serious gendered and social class readjustments in the process of adapting to life in California. Teutsch-Dwyer focuses in particular on the interrelationship between gender identity and communities of practice, and above all, Karol's struggle for an acceptable male identity in his interactions with others. He failed in his attempts to develop relationships with his brother-in-law and his boss, but he managed to become a valued member of a social group of women for whom he became 'a very popular guy'. However, becoming a popular guy came at a price, as it led to the adoption of a masculine subject position that worked against his longer-term goals of bettering his English.

As I note elsewhere (Block, 2003), Teutsch-Dwyer's study is somewhat unique in SLL research in that it links identity issues to language development issues in a clear and effective way. Above, I stated that it remedies, to some extent, the shortcomings of the Norton study because it relies not just on what Karol said about his life and experiences, but also recordings of Karol in action, using English among friends, co-workers and family. Nevertheless, the study has only been discussed in one publication (Teutsch-Dwyer 2001), and in that publication, the reader does not see instances of extended interactions between Karol and members of his social and work-related networks. I now turn to a study which attempts to link an adult migrant's ongoing uses of the target language with his accounts of his life as a migrant, all with a view of seeing how language development and use intertwine with identity issues.

Spanish-speaking Latinos in London

In Block (2006a), I report on a small-scale study of a growing ethnolinguistic group in London, Spanish-speaking Latinos (hereafter SSLs). The study was based on contacts with a small sample of six informants. Here I focus on one informant, a Colombian migrant named Carlos, with whom I conducted four interviews over a period of nine months. In these interviews, Carlos and I discussed the unfolding story of his life in London and, importantly, conversations at work and at home that he had recorded with the permission of his interlocutors. Before moving to these recordings and how they relate to the different subject positions adopted by Carlos in his day-to-day life, I will first provide some background information.

Carlos was born and raised in a working-class family in a small city in the southwestern part of Colombia. He studied philosophy at university and by the late 1980s, he was a philosophy lecturer at a university in Colombia and was married with two children. He was also at this time heavily involved with left-wing political movements in Colombia, an activity that landed him in prison on more than one occasion. In 1991 his marriage ended and during a trip to London, he met Kelly, a British national, whom he soon after married. The couple moved to Colombia, where their son, Eduardo, was born in 1992. From 1992 to 2001, Carlos, Kelly and Eduardo formed a middle-class family unit in Colombia: Carlos was a university lecturer and Kelly was a Spanish/English translator. However, in autumn 2001, the family decided to move to London because Kelly wanted to be close to her family and both she and Carlos were concerned that Eduardo would never learn English, given that the couple spoke only Spanish at home.

As regards his own English language skills, Carlos's profile is perhaps not typical of many university-educated Colombians. Throughout his formal education, he had studied French as a matter of protest against what he perceived as the imposition of English by the US. In addition, he and Kelly never spoke in English with each other during the time they lived in Colombia. The lack of contact with English during his lifetime meant that upon his arrival in London in 2001, he spoke hardly any English and this meant, in turn, that he could not find any employment beyond low-level manual service jobs. He was thus effectively declassed when he arrived in London, falling from professional middle class to unskilled low-level service provider overnight. At the time of my contact with him, Carlos was working as a porter in a university building in central London. The job involved duties such as delivering mail, dispensing information at the reception desk and acting as a liaison between his line manager and a crew of Spanish-speaking workers whose company was hired to do tasks in the building such as cleaning and moving.

Although I never asked Carlos to take a battery of English language proficiency exams, I heard enough of his English to be able to describe it, in general terms, as stabilized at a level that allowed him to get done what he needed to get done. His on-the-job conversations – both social and more work related – were handled with relative ease. Typical of the latter is the following short exchange taking place at the reception desk (NB: W = unknown woman; C = Carlos):

W: would it be possible for you to tell someone that there's no
     paper in the loo?/
C: yes, sure [madame =
W: [thank you =

C: = I'm sorry about that=
W: = thank you/
C: OK, yeah/

Away from work, Carlos showed himself to be particularly adept when dealing with professionals, such as doctors and lawyers, as his part of a phone conversation with a barrister suggests:

> Good morning sir (.) can I speak to Mr Fulham please/ (.) oh right good morning sir/ (.) I'm Mr Carlos Sanchez/ (.)/ Carlos Sanchez / (1)/ yes (.) you was on my flat yesterday/ (.) in our place yesterday/ (.)/ you was yesterday in my place in <provides his address>/ (.)/ no/ (.)/ ah (.) yes/ (.)/ I received the notice/ (1)/ erm/ (.)/ (xxx)) yeah OK <laughing>/ (.)/ yeah erm/ (.)/ yes/ (6)/ sorry Mr Coram/ (.)/ yeah/ (.)/ yeah/ (.)/ yes sir/ (.)/ yeah/ (.)/ yes sir/ (3)/ but I yes I yes yesterday we were in erm erm hearing because I / (.)/ in the court/ (.)/ yes sir erm/ (.)/ yes sir erm we were in an appeal we made erm (.) with the erm (.) home office/ (.)/ yes and we spent all the day there because/ (.)/ yes we started at 10 o'clock and we spent all the day there/ (1.)/ yeah/ (12)/ yes that's fine/ (10)/ yes please/ (4)/ yeah/ (8)/ yes sir/ (12)/ yes/ (4)/ yes/ (4)/ OK could you let me know when exactly? because in that in that/ (1)/ no/ (3)/ yeah/ (5)/ yeah

Examining Carlos's side of the conversation – all that we have here – one sees the odd grammatical anomaly (e.g. 'you was on my flat') and lexical anomaly (e.g. 'notice' for 'news'); however, on the whole, Carlos comes across as a perfectly coherent and competent interlocutor. When I first listened to the recording, I was struck by the confidence that Carlos conveyed during the call, how he seemed very calm and assured throughout the exchange. When I suggested that unlike relatively less educated migrants, he did not seem intimidated by contacts with professionals, he explained:

> . . . la experiencia mia anterior, digamos académica . . . te da confianza para ir al médico, por ejemplo, para hacer un poco las cosas en tu vida normal. Pero es un poco sentirse como afianzado en esa situación intelectual que te permite como

ganar la confianza. Y he pensado también o he visto que la gente que no tiene, digamos, ese sustento . . . es más débil, es más vunerable . . . (Carlos, 4/12/03)

. . . my previous experience, let's say academic . . . gives you confidence to go to the doctor, for example, to kind of do things in your normal life. But it's a little like feeling strengthened by that intellectual situation that allows you to gain confidence. And I have thought about this and I have seen how the people who don't have, let's say, this support . . . are weaker, more vulnerable. (Carlos, 4/12/03)

However, none of his contacts in English had the effect of making him want to improve his English beyond the level he had attained. His declassing had not spurred him to increase his contact with English, and there was no emergent instrumental motivation moving him to study the language more intensively and with any degree of urgency. Nor, perhaps more importantly, did he feel any sense of personal investment in English, as described by Norton in her study.

This lack of interest in developing his English language skills was perhaps due to how he experienced the majority of his contacts in English. These contacts tended to take place at work and they were either brief service encounters with the general public, as in the loo paper example above, or conversations with his English-speaking colleagues. Regarding the former, Carlos was able to acquit himself fairly well, especially because such contacts tended to be short, generally involving only a few turns. By contrast, his contacts with colleagues were more extensive, albeit no more rewarding for Carlos. Indeed, in interviews with me he maintained that apart from a passion for football, he did not really have anything in common with his colleagues.

The following exchange is part of a conversation recorded in the reception area at work in early 2004. The participants are Dan (D), Carlos (C) and Bob (B). Bob is Carlos's line manager and Dan is a recently retired ex-employee who stops in to visit his old workmates when he has travelled to London from his home in a town north of the city.

1. D: I feel a bit rough like I've got a bad cold and ((xxx)) and uh
    (1) I can't shake it off I've had it for over a week so I thought
    I'd come up to town a bit <phones ringing in background> oh,
    gosh thought I'd come down/
2. C: yeah?=
3. D: =and we had a poor performance/ 'cause see he can't get down
    very often so he booked the tickets about four weeks ago=
4. C: =and it was easy game for Chelsea/
5. D: I know ((xxx))(1) and really I felt so rough I didn't feel like
    going but I thought don't want to let im down/
6. C: yeah=
7. D: =cause what I've been taking and carrying this cold and
    then they played like that awful!=
8. B: =poor=
9. D: =yeah, very poor[
10. B: [no
11. C: [he was very poor performance for
                       Chelsea=
12. D: =but a lot of the play=
13. B: =[yeah
14. C: [yeah
15. D: %we're not scoring the goals we're not scoring the goals I
    can't make it out not scoring many goals%
16. B: ((xxx))
17. D: yeah but last Wednesday I mean ((xxx)) I got the fucking
    shivers and I that day all of a sudden I couldn't stop shivering
    even though it wasn't that cold really=
18. C: =yeah/
19. D: I just had the fucking shivers later then I went to see the
    doctor and me own doctor's been ill funnily enough so I see
    another doctor (2) and he examined me and said 'no, don't
    seem too bad' so he says 'no use in giving you any antibiotics'
    HE WASN'T EVEN GONNA GIVE ME ANY MEDICINE
20. C: <laughing>
21. D: I said well what about you know cause I've been taking
    Lemsips and all [that
22. C: [that's that's the worse really=

23. D: =and like last night I took a fucking Lemsip before <In the background, Bob asks if he can help someone who has come to the reception counter> about ten o'clock in bed (2) and uh about two in the morning I've got this fucking cough. Oh I couldn't shake it off (2) Oh, I just feel terrible.

Examining Carlos's contributions to this exchange, I see several things worthy of mention. First, in turn 2, he provides an appropriate interjection that splits Dan's opening statement about his cold and travelling to London to see a Chelsea football match. In turn 3, Dan begins with an assessment of the match – 'we had a poor performance' – and then shifts to the problems that he and his friend have to go through to get from their homes, located somewhere north of London, to Stamford Bridge to see Chelsea matches. Carlos interrupts the latter half of Dan's intervention to add his own assessment of the match in question: 'it was easy game for Chelsea'. However, Dan carries on talking about travelling to London as opposed to the match and Carlos provides a back channelling, 'yeah', in turn 6, to keep the conversation going. In turns 7–10, Dan and Bob make comments about the match and this seems to spur Carlos to come back in turn 11 with a repetition of Dan's statement about Chelsea's poor performance, first uttered in turn 3. Carlos and Bob then collaborate with Dan who lays out Chelsea's problem, dramatically whispering 'we're not scoring the goals'. However in turn 17, Dan returns to the topic of his cold. Carlos follows him, laughing when Dan loudly condemns his doctor's reluctance to prescribe him medicine. He even interjects his views on having to take Lempsip (a cold medicine in Britain) instead of prescribed medicine: 'that's the worse really'.

Carlos thus appears to do a good job of acting as an active co-participant in this conversation. He cedes protagonism to Dan, but his interventions all seem appropriate, as regards content and function. What he says is grammatical, although he omits the article in turns 4 and 11, refers to the match as 'he' in turn 11 and uses 'worse' instead of 'worst' in turn 22. The latter anomaly could be a case of repeating what he has heard ('worse' is not uncommon usage in this context) or it could be question of pronunciation, not producing the word final phoneme /t/.

However, when asked about this conversation, Carlos did not seem convinced that he had been such an active and appropriate interlocutor.

Estoy escuchando y ya hay una parte de la conversación, que yo te digo, la pierdo porqué la otra persona con quien habla . . . tiene el problema, es tartamudo, y luego su dicción, la forma de pronunciar, es muy cortante, y pierdo ya el ánimo, el interés, en la conversación. Entonces los dejo ya entre ellos allí. Yo estoy allí pero . . . (encogiéndose de hombros) (Carlos, 6/2/04)

I'm listening and there is a part of the conversation, that I tell you, I lose it because the other person he is talking to . . . he has this problem, he stutters, and then his diction, how he pronounces, its very sharp, and I lose spirit, interest, in the conversation. So, I just leave them there, to talk between themselves. I'm there but . . . (shrugging) (Carlos, 6/2/04)

Of course, the conversation itself is not really about information exchange, or even work for that matter. Sociolinguists such as Janet Holmes (2000) have noted how a good proportion of workplace conversation is not about work-related topics, strictly speaking. A large part of doing one's job, of being part of a group at work, is engaging in informal conversations around topics ranging from football to one's personal life. In the English-mediated, White, working-class and male dominant atmosphere in which he worked, Carlos found that he had little in common with his fellow workers. He was Colombian, mixed race in British census terms, a university lecturer by profession and not completely familiar with the kind of masculine subject positions adopted by his colleagues. Indeed, as I noted above, there was only football, and even when football was the focus of conversation, he could not always keep up with his colleagues.

However, Carlos had other conversation interests beyond football and in his interviews, he cited a catalogue of frustrated attempts to talk about workers' rights and matters related to the world of politics, which generally fell on unwilling ears. In the following exchange, again with his line manager Bob (B), there is an attempt by Carlos (C) to take a conversation about life in ten years' time to a discussion of the life of Spanish-speaking Latino labour migrants in London:

1. C: in ten years I will be living in Colombia again/
2. B: <expressing surprise> would you like to live in Colombia again?/
3. C: yes B/ (.) yes I like living there/
4. B: you [know
5. C: [and I miss a lot to my country/ and I I miss everything I was doing before=
6. B: =yeah but the only thing is/ it's very poor environment isn't it?
7. C: no:o it depends B/ because erm (.5) people are in some difficulties/ but we were living in a very good situation (.) very good level/ (.) yeah (.) well it's not erm it's not erm it's not a normal way for all the population=
8. B: =no no [no
9. C: [no it's [not
10. B: [lots of [people
11. C: [but you can live with commodities there with/ (.2) obviously you're never=
12. B: =you can't [compare
13. C: [with the first world/ nah nah nah=
14. B: =it won't it doesn't compare with living in Europe (.) does it?
15. C: no/ it no/ (.) you can't compare except if you are one of the erm erm rich ones in the country/ (.) (.) you are the one of the biggest man in the country or you are one of the big [politicians
16. B: [well those/ (.) well I mean/ (.) I suppose it's like when you were a lecturer there/ it was you were the sort of/ I suppose above average income weren't you? for people there=
17. C: =yes (.) I was making good money and my income was very [good
18. B: [in relation to=
19. C: =and also Kelly/ (.) she was working and (.2) we had very good level and standard of living/ but it's not the common/
20. B: no/

21. C: no/
22. B: a lot of the people like the guys who come and work ((xxx))/ (.) most of them come from poor areas don't they?
23. C: yeah ((xxx)) most of them they come from very very poor areas erm/ (.5) they have not many erm level education/
24. B: no/
25. C: but from there they come to pay for everything for their families that's=
26. B: =so all their [money
27. C: ⠀⠀⠀⠀⠀⠀⠀⠀⠀[they use to do/ (.) they send the money for buying houses for food for . . .

<B changes the subject at this point, mentioning that a friend has moved to Thailand, where he will be able to buy a home very cheaply.>

In this exchange, Carlos and Bob seem to be speaking at cross-purposes. First, Bob tells Carlos that he is fortunate to be in Britain because Colombia is a 'very poor environment' (turn 6). Carlos then explains to Bob that he actually did not have such a bad life in Colombia, that he and Kelly 'had a good situation', although he does acknowledge here that their situation 'is not a normal way for all the population' (turn 7). The fact that Carlos has to explain to Bob that he and Kelly had enjoyed a good standard of living in Colombia is odd because, as Bob reveals in turn 16, he already knew that Carlos had been a university lecturer in Colombia. In turns 17 and 19, Carlos once again asserts that he and Kelly had lived well in Colombia but that their situation was 'not the common'. In turn 22, Bob shifts the focus from the relative poverty of Colombia, vis-à-vis Europe, to the poverty of Colombians working in London. Picking up on this reference to labour migrants, Carlos attempts to draw Bob into a conversation about the poor living conditions of labour migrants and remittance payments. However, his mention of how remittance payments might be 'for buying houses' back home prompts Bob to introduce the new topic of his friend's home purchase in Thailand. He thus frustrates a move by Carlos to take the conversation to a topic that would allow him to feel more fulfilled as an interlocutor and as someone knowledgeable of the workings of capitalism in the world today. In so doing, he indexes his distance from Carlos, a work colleague but not someone with whom he shares any interests.

Not all of Carlos's workplace recordings involved his immediate White English colleagues. Another type of workplace conversation took place when Carlos met other members of the support staff of the university, in particular those working for the catering service at the university. In the conversation that follows, Carlos is talking to two such employees, Ricardo (R) and Jozef (J). At the time of the study, Ricardo was a Brazilian university student spending a year in London. Carlos and Ricardo spoke fairly frequently and together they had developed a code that drew on a combination of Spanish and English, with the odd Portuguese word thrown in. However, this conversation is mostly in English, no doubt because Jozef (J), a Polish national who spoke no Spanish or Portuguese, was present.

N.B. This conversation took place in the kitchen area amid the constant background noise of machinery. Spanish portions are in **bold** with translations immediately afterwards in brackets: {xxx}

1. C: do you know Lonnie the cleaner?
2. R: ah yes=
3. C: =the black guy /(.5) always his happy happy face/
4. R: nahh/ (.) with you/
5. C: yes/
6. R: **me he peleado algunas veces con el y con el otro**
   {I've fallen out with him a few times and with the other one}/
7. C: why? **por qué peleaste?** {why did you fall out?}
8. R: **quería que que quería que yo li <sic> pase las aulas con la basura conmigo (.5) y que uhh pusharse (?) conmigo y ponía lo lo la basura dientro <sic> de esta mierda y** {he wanted he wanted wanted me to go through the classrooms with the rubbish with me and that uhh 'push it' with me and he was putting the the the rubbish inside this piece of shit}
9. R: I said, no, no <Carlos laughs> I'm sorry/ (.) it's not my work/
10. J: he always complains/
11. C: yes?
12. J: yes/

13. C: but with him I have good relations/
14. J: but actually he always complains <imitating Lonnie> oh, don't put boxes in there ohh <Ricardo and Jozef laugh>/
15. C: well, he was the same with me but I didn't pay attention at that/ I said take it easy <Ricardo laughs>/ yes/ (.) life's short/ (.) yeah don't worry about that/
16. J: [yeah, yeah
17. R: [yeah, yeah <Jozef and Ricardo think Carlos is talking to them about their current work>
18. C: NO/ (.) that I told him to Lonnie (.) just relax be calm/
19. J: he said are you fucking kidding? <laughing>/
20. C: yes/ (1) they use to employ that people because they are very good workers (.) you know and very cheap you know/ (.) four pounds per hour/
21. R: [how
22. C: [four pounds=
23. J: [four
24. C: [four pounds/
25. J: ((xxx))/
26. C: he starts it at six o'clock and he finish eight/ fourteen hours a day/
27. J: Jesus Christ man/
28. C: Monday to Saturday/
29. R: fucking hell/
30. C: erm?
31. R: much work/
32. C: and [that way
33. R: [how much per hour?
34. C: four pounds/
35. R: huh?
36. C: FOUR POUNDS/
37. J: ((xxx))/
38. C: yes/ (1) he was living here in this country for maybe three years/ and in that way he bought the house (.) big house in Kenya (1)/
39. R: he bought the house?
40. C: yes it's hard/ (.) it's hard
41. R: ((xxx)) <loud noise of meal tray trolleys moving around>/

42. C: huh?
43. R: he's quite intelligent/
44. J: four pounds/ ((xxx))/ making only two pounds/ ((xxx))/
45. C: at the end of the day they (.) the rate is three seventy five after tax/
46. J: after tax/
47. C: yeah (.) more or less/ (1) and it's peanuts/

Carlos begins the conversation by asking Ricardo and Jozef if they know Lonnie, a cleaner from Kenya. Both Ricardo and Jozef acknowledge that they do, but they make clear that they do not like him, the former describing a run-in with Lonnie (turns 6 and 9) and the latter imitating him (turn 14). For his part, Carlos attempts to be more balanced, saying that he is on good terms with Lonnie, although he admits that he had also noticed that Lonnie could be difficult. In turn 20, Carlos manages to move the conversation to a topic of interest to him, the low wages of support staff at the university. Over several turns, he tells Ricardo and Jozef about how Lonnie has managed to buy a house in Kenya, despite earning just four pounds an hour, by working fourteen hours a day, six days a week. Lonnie's success story surprises Ricardo and Jozef. Indeed, in turn 43, Ricardo seems to have changed his opinion of Lonnie, saying that 'he's quite intelligent'. When I asked him to comment on this exchange, Carlos produced the following analysis:

Somos cuatro personas de diferentes 'backgrounds', que se dice en inglés, y con diferentes intereses. En el contexto del 'Brasileiro', es muy joven y va muy tranquilo por el mundo. Todavía no tiene afanes, no tiene compromisos. Entonces . . . lo que le llegue va bien. El polaco es igualmente joven pero está pensando en ese momento en casarse y . . . tiene otra visión. Entonces en esa situación ellos ven en inferioridad al amigo de Kenya porqué el gana menos y su trabajo es mucho más difícil. Y tratan . . . de tomar ventaja . . . de esa situación, entonces le transfieren como su trabajo a el y claro . . . se ha dado cuenta y por supuesto viene el choque entre ellos. Pero pasa eso, por el tipo de migración, el tipo de intereses . . . que siempre hay una tendencia a menospreciar un poco la gente de otra . . . especialmente si el color de tu piel no es como el de ellos. (Carlos, 3/9/04)

We are four people from different 'backgrounds', as they say in English, and different interests. In the case of the Brazilian, he is very young and takes his life easy. He doesn't have any worries yet, he doesn't have any obligations. So . . . he takes whatever life throws up. The Pole is just as young, but he is thinking about getting married at this time and . . . he has a different view. So in that situation they see our friend from Kenya as inferior because he makes less money and his job is a lot harder. And they try to take advantage of that situation, so they kind of transfer their work to him. And obviously . . . he has realized this and of course they are on a collision course. But this happens because of the type of migration, the type of interests . . . that there is always a tendency to underestimate people a little . . . especially if the colour of your skin is different from theirs. (Carlos, 3/9/04)

One interesting aspect of this conversation is the way that Carlos acts as a tutor for his younger colleagues. By telling them the story of how Lonnie overcame exploitatively low wages and overall hardship, he moves Ricardo and Jozef from outright contempt for Lonnie to respect and admiration for him. As Carlos explains above, he sees Ricardo as young and carefree and Jozef, though perhaps not carefree, as young as well. In addition, he suggests that racism might be behind the treatment bestowed on Lonnie by the two young men. In this sense, Ricardo's attempts to shift his work to Lonnie and Jozef's attempt to make fun of him are manifestations of disrespect for someone deemed to be inferior. It is worth noting that Ricardo and Jozef are both phenotypically European in appearance, while Lonnie is Black. As Carlos puts it, 'there is always a tendency to underestimate people a little . . . especially if the colour of your skin is different from theirs'.

Given his lack of engagement with and interest in English, Carlos might have been expected to live his life as part of the growing SSL community in London. However, when asked about such a community and his relationship with it, he was rather categorical in maintaining his independence:

Es curioso, David, porqué trabajo en contacto con Colombianos basicamente, y latinos en general. Pero por fuera, y estando ya en casa, no queremos el contacto con más latinos, supuestamente porqué queríamos desarrolar más mi inglés o porqué el niño también hablara más inglés. Pero creo que [el contacto con SSLs] no está funcionando al final del dia [porqué] son personas que tienen objetivos muy precisos. Por ejemplo, ellos necesitan trabajar un número de horas por dia, que no les permite hacer una vida social muy amplia tampoco. Y luego, ya el tipo de actividades sociales a que ellos acuden, a mi no me interesan, por ejemplo, que es ir a beber y ir a bailar y ir a comer una comida que he comido durante todos los años de mi vida . . . no puedo compartir este tipo de cosas porqué no, o sea no me llegan . . . (Carlos, 12/9/03)

It's funny, David, because I work in contact with Colombians basically, and Latinos in general. But away from work, and being at home, we don't want contact with more Latinos, supposedly because we wanted to develop more my English or so that our son also could speak English. But I think that [the contact with SSLs] doesn't really work at the end of the day [because] they are people with specific objectives. For example, they need to work a certain number of hours a day, which does not allow time to have a very broad social life either. And then I'm not interested in the type of social activities that they go to, for example, going out drinking, going out dancing and going out to eat a type of food that I have eaten every year of my life. I can't share this type of things just because they just aren't enough . . . (Carlos, 12/9/03)

In effect, it was Carlos's cultural and, to some extent, his social capital that made him feel very different from the majority of SSLs with whom he came in contact at work. Most of these SSLs, to whom Carlos referred in the third person, were living a marginal life in London in social, economic and political terms. As I have noted elsewhere (Block, 2006a), Carlos's political consciousness pushed him towards contact with these people when he attempted to help them solve some of their day-to-day problems. For example, Carlos and Kelly would often help SSLs who needed to communicate with their employers or government agencies but could not do so because they lacked the requisite knowledge of English and the overall know-how to carry out such transactions. Such contacts with more marginalized SSLs notwithstanding, Carlos found that his background as a philosophy lecturer in Colombia and his cosmopolitan lifestyle pushed him away from the majority of SSLs and towards better-educated, middle-class Spanish speakers. He described his social life as follows:

> . . . por casa vienen unos amigos españoles que tienen profesiones, que están desarrollando otro tipo de actividades, diferente a los latinos y claro es un nivel un poquito más interesante. También vienen a casa unos amigos argentinos que trabajan en esto de psicologia y algunos son profesores. Entonces es un poquito diferente. . . . (Carlos, 12/9/03)

> Some Spanish friends come round who have professions, who are engaging in another type of activities, different from the Latinos and obviously it's a slightly more interesting level. Some Argentinian friends also come round who work in psychology and some of them are teachers. So it's a little different. . . . (Carlos, 12/9/03)

Carlos is thus an individual who is comfortable carrying out his life as much as possible in Spanish. In this sense, he adopts a form of cultural and linguistic maintenance. However, this maintenance contrasts markedly with that displayed by the Portuguese women in Goldstein's study because it is more cosmopolitan in nature, its reference point more a transnational community of university-educated Spanish speakers than a sense of pan-SSL. In other words, it is transnationalism more related to social class and language than to nationality and culture. In this sense, Carlos is also very different from Schumann's (1978) Alberto, a socially and economically marginalized labour migrant; Schmidt's (1983) Wes, a professional middling transmigrant; and the labour migrants and political refugees discussed in Broeder et al (1996). Indeed, Carlos presents us with a new type of migrant language learner, as a member of something akin to Perlmutter's (1991) horizontal communities of shared interests and experiences, in his case, the shared interests and experiences of cosmopolitan educated Spanish speakers.

Importantly, Carlos's affiliation to these speakers of Spanish has had an impact on his English language development in that it has allowed him to reserve important parts of his day-to-day life – his family and his social life – for Spanish, not English. Because his English language use is confined primarily to the workplace, and because his workplace communication is in no way fulfilling (or following Norton, 2000, investment-inspiring), Carlos remains stabilized as a more or less competent speaker of English for the kinds of things he needs to do in English on the job. Interestingly, he does not display any inclination towards using colloquial English in his interactions with male colleagues, where such language might be appropriate. Thus, while Ricardo and Jozef show an affiliation to colloquial English through their use of expressions such as 'are you fucking kidding?' (Jozef, line 19), 'Jesus Christ man' (Jozef, line 27) and 'fucking hell' (Ricardo, line 29), Carlos speaks an English bereft of such embellishment.[1] Of course, this may be due to the topic he chooses to develop in the conversation and the didactic subject position he adopts. Or, it may be a more general choice related to a desire to speak a more academic variety of English, much as he does in Spanish, as opposed to a 'street' variety. In any case, whatever the reason for his avoidance of colloquial English in his speech, it marks Carlos off from his colleagues, be they White English or foreign born, who do use colloquial English. He can thus engage in activities with members of different communities of practice at work, but he always does so as a relative outsider as regards the topics he attempts to introduce in conversations and the variety of English that he employs when talking about them.

In my study of Carlos, I have attempted to combine interview accounts of language related experiences with actual recordings of some of these experiences, collected over a 12-month period of time. While I have not been able to chart his development from his early days in London, I have managed to gain insights into why his English language development has fossilized to a large extent (though, by no means, completely). As I stated above, Carlos's English is the English he needs to do things in English, above all work-related activities and day-to-day service encounters. Beyond work and service encounters, he has no incentive or sense of investment in English that is sufficiently strong to move him forward to any significant degree. In addition, Carlos's personal history and his current sociohistorical context, as described in his interviews, allow me to understand

Carlos not as marginalized and downtrodden labour migrant, but as declassed professional transmigrant who survives via membership in a community of practice organized around social activity with educated Spanish speakers.

Conclusion

In this chapter, I have discussed in some detail five studies that have dealt with the issue of identity in adult migrant SLL contexts. Broeder *et al* (1996) was written just when applied linguists were beginning to turn their eyes to identity as a useful construct in SLL research. Therefore, of the five studies, it is the one which least draws on the poststructuralist-inspired model of identity outlined in Chapter 2. Goldstein (1996), Norton (2000), Teutsch-Dwyer (2001) and Block (2006a), however, were all conceived within such an identity framework. In my discussion of these five studies, I have suggested that Broeder *et al*'s greatest strength was its reliance on recorded encounters between informants and gatekeepers. Goldstein, Teutsch-Dwyer and Block also benefit from such recorded data. While it does not have recorded conversations involving informants, Norton (2000) is perhaps the most complete study among those discussed as regards the depth of the five life stories that form its backbone. Ultimately, however, what is needed are more studies that follow migrant adults for long periods of time, drawing not only on their accounts of their experiences but also on recordings of their experiences.

Having examined in detail these five studies, I think it is clear that the adult migrant experience is one in which critical experiences, leading to the emergence of new subject positions, are likely to occur. In effect, the sustained immersion in a new cultural and linguistic milieu seemingly cannot but impact on the individual's sense of self. Thus in Norton (2000), all five women experienced a break with their pasts mediated entirely by their first languages. In effect, English had come to mediate their lives in Canada to varying degrees, sometimes making inroads into home and family life, and at other times remaining outside these more personal spheres of activity and being. More importantly, these new English-mediated subject positions were inseparable from changes in the social class subject positions available to and adopted by the five women. For example, a professional migrant like Katarina found that she and her husband, both university educated, had to re-orient their careers in Canada accepting, in the short term, significant declassing. Meanwhile, Felicia found her high standing in society, linked entirely to her husband's professional status, has withered away in the move to Canada.

The five women were also immersed in new gendered subject positions shaped by the migrant experience. For example, Martina found that because her husband was not proficient in English, she had to take primary responsibility for heading her family, a subject position she had not occupied in Czechoslovakia. Meanwhile, Mai struggled to become an independent woman, exchanging a domineering brother for a husband, in the hope that marriage would allow her greater scope for self-realization, both professionally and as a person.

Even when the first language and culture were strongly maintained by migrants, both at home and in more public spheres such as the workplace, as in the case of Goldstein's Portuguese factory workers, the new work environment and macro-level phenomena in Canadian society reshaped the apparent cohesion of the Portuguese community in Toronto. In short, doing being Portuguese in Toronto was qualitatively different from doing being Portuguese in the Azores, no matter how much the Portuguese language and Portuguese customs were maintained. In the case of Carlos, there is a more individualistic twist on this lesson. Although he maintained Spanish as both a home language and a clear marker of his own identity, he did not do so as he would have done in Colombia. His maintenance of Colombian cultural customs was rather limited, above all because he did not actively seek out other Colombians in London to socialize with. He thus lived as part of a porous and emergent community of educated Spanish speakers living and working in London.

To varying degrees, the adult migrants in the five studies discussed here were all immigrants, likely to stay in the countries in Europe and North America where they had settled. To be sure, there are differences as regards the extent to which individuals embraced this status. Felicia explicitly denied her status as an immigrant in Canada, saying that she 'never felt an immigrant in Canada, just as foreigner person who lives here by accident' (Norton, 2000: 101). Meanwhile, Carlos positioned himself as a cosmopolitan living a floating existence in London, somewhere between middling transmigrant and expatriate: he came to London accustomed to a middle-class existence in terms of economic capital, cultural capital and social capital and he has always made it clear that he could and would return to Colombia one day. However, for the 30 migrants in Broeder *et al* (1996), Eva, Katarina, Mai and Martina in Norton (2000), the 27 Portuguese women in Goldstein (1996) and Karol in Teutsch-Dwyer (2001), there seemed little doubt that permanent settlement in the host countries was the most likely scenario. And, as stated above, it is this sustained, if not permanent, settlement that makes possible the critical experiences so essential to the emergence of new subject positions.

Note

1   I am grateful to Jan Blommaert for this observation.

5

Identity in foreign language contexts

Introduction

In this chapter, I focus on how identity is an issue in Foreign Language (FL) contexts. The FL context is the context of millions of primary school, secondary school, university and further education students around the world who rely on their time in classrooms to learn a language that is not the typical language of communication outside the classroom. Conditions in these different FL contexts vary considerably as regards teacher/student ratios, the age of students, teacher preparation, intensity (hours per week), accommodation, technological backup, availability of teaching materials, the relative importance of learning the FL and, above all, the language studied. However, they all have in common the predominance of the classroom as a site of exposure to the TL.

In the sections that follow, I discuss in detail studies taking place in different FL contexts in different parts of the world. I begin by examining Anthony Liddicoat and Chantalle Crozet's (2001) study of the teaching of interlanguage pragmatics to French FL learners in Australia. I then discuss a key construct arising from this study, 'intercultural language learning'. This done, I move to consider Claire Kramsch's work on 'textual identities', and research drawing on this construct in the form of Julie Belz's (2002) study of German FL learners in the US. I then examine James Lantolf and Patricia Genung's (2003) study of a Mandarin FL learner in the US, before revisiting research of my own (Block, 1995, 2000) on an EFL learner in Spain.

In all four of these studies, identity is an issue, although the specific focus on it varies somewhat. Thus, while Liddicoat and Crozet (2001) is about interlanguage pragmatics, identity is, in my view, an issue arising. Meanwhile, Belz (2002) and Lantolf and Genung (2003) explicitly invoke identity as a key construct, the former examining textual identities and the latter the variable adoption of applied linguist, teacher and student subject positions. As regards my research, originally about students' perceptions of their classroom language learning experiences, I have revisited my original database and framed excerpts from interviews with one informant as enactments of subject positions *vis-à-vis* the teacher and classmates.

Having examined in detail these four classroom-based FL studies, I conclude that the FL context provides few opportunities for the emergence of significant new subject positions mediated by the TL. However, I then move to discussions of two variations on the more traditional FL context that show some promise in this direction. First, I examine Cheiron McMahill's study of a feminist EFL class in Japan. This study shows how an engagement with English as an international language (and not as the patrimony of native speakers), coupled with an explicit and intensive engagement with feminine subject positions, can have a significant impact on an FL learner's sense of self. Second, I look at FL contexts where Internet-mediated communication with users of the TL is an important component. Specifically, I examine the case study of an American university student learning French at an American university, who develops a friendship with her French key pal.

Interlanguage pragmatics
and the identity of the FL learner

The first FL study I examine in this chapter is based on research focusing on interlanguage pragmatics. Elsewhere (Block, 2003), I claim that this area of research is promising because it allows a focus not only on the finer aspects of language as grammatical system, but also on sociocultural context and identity issues. In the context of SLL research, pragmatics has been defined by Kenneth Rose and Gabriele Kasper as 'the way speakers and writers accomplish goals as social actors who do not just need to get things done but must attend to their interpersonal relationships with other participants at the same time' (Rose and Kasper 2001: 2). Defining pragmatics in this way, Kasper and Rose position themselves as part of a tradition in applied linguistics that goes back to the earlier work of Geoffrey Leech (1983) and Jenny Thomas (1983), and connects with more recent research (see collections such as Bardovi-Harlig, 1999; Bouton, 1996, 1999; Rose and Kasper, 2001; Kasper and Rose, 2002). In this more recent research, a distinction developed by Leech and Thomas between pragmalinguistics and sociopragmatics is taken as axiomatic. The former term refers to the linguistic resources needed in order to carry out speech acts and the latter refers to the social knowledge one needs to understand both how things are done in a particular sociocultural context and how to do them. In the collections cited above, there are a good number of studies carried out in FL contexts. In general, these studies share the view that language learners need to learn not only TL linguistic knowledge (i.e. morphology, syntax, phonology and lexis), but also knowledge about TL sociocultural practices, as well as the TL-mediated public personae they wish to project. In my view, the latter dimension is the point at which interlanguage pragmatics research enters the realm of second language identity, making it relevant to my discussion in this chapter.

How pragmalinguistics, sociopragmatics and identity work come together is well illustrated in a study carried out by Anthony Liddicoat and Chantalle Crozet (2001). Working with Australian learners of French as a FL, these authors follow up an earlier study by Béal (1992), who examined the acquisition of the apparently simple functions of asking and answering questions about weekend activities. In the Australian context, such an exchange might go as follows between two work colleagues, a woman (W) and a man (M):

1. W: Did you have a pleasant weekend?
2. M: I did. What about you?
3. W: I did too.
4. M: What did *you* do?

5. W: We went to a birthday dinner on Saturday and a barbecue on Sunday.
6. M: Food, food, food . . .
7. W: Yes, we ate our way through most of the weekend.

(Liddicoat and Crozet, 2001: 128)

Liddicoat and Crozet refer to this exchange as 'formulaic questions . . . followed by formulaic answer' (Liddicoat and Crozet, 2001: 128), noting that some exchanges are even shorter, ending after the equivalent of turn three above. In a French language context, by contrast, the question and answer exchange about weekend activity seems to be quite different. Liddicoat and Crozet note how such exchanges generally involve more than just a short response, as the following example, involving a woman (W) and a man (M) illustrates:

1. *Woman: Le weekend a été bon?*
2. *Man: Très bon, très bon. [under his breath] très bon . . . On a fait du train.*
3. *W: Du train?*
4. *M: Du petit train à vapeur, qui se ballade [dans les Dandenongs*
5. *W: [Ah, dans les Dande-gongs, oui c'est sympa ça.*
6. *M: Une bonne partie de . . . le retour on s'est retrouvé entre deux wagons, sur le marche-pied [short laugh].*
7. *W: Tellement y avait du monde?*
8. *M: Tellement y avait du monde.*

. . .

1. Woman: Was your weekend nice?
2. Man: Very nice, very nice ((under his breath)): very nice . . . We took a ride on a train.
3. W: A train?
4. M: That little steam train, the one that snakes [through the Dandenongs
5. W: [Ah, in the Dandegongs! Yes! It's a lot of fun, that!
6. M: For quite a bit of the . . . on the way back, we ended up in between two carriages, on the stepladder! ((short laugh)).

7. W: Because it was so crowded?
8. M: Because it was so crowded.

. . .

(Béal, 1992: 32–34; cited in Liddicoat and Crozet, 2001: 129;
NB transcription conventions adapted)

Over the next nine lines, the man finishes his story and then asks
the woman:

Et vous ça (a) été bien?
What about you. Was it good?

(Béal, 1992: 32–4; cited in Liddicoat and Crozet, 2001: 129;
NB transcription conventions adapted)

The woman answers this question over the next ten lines.

As presented by Liddicoat and Crozet, these two prototypical
exchanges are obviously very different. The Australian exchange
seems to be more of a conversational routine requiring very little effort
on the part of the participants. Little or no information is exchanged
and there does not seem to be any degree of personal revelation
or investment. In other words, person B does not incorporate any
personal information in the response. Nevertheless, such an exchange
must still be seen as part of the ongoing process of maintaining
relations, formulaic as it may be. By contrast, the French exchange
would certainly appear to require more effort than the Australian
version. This animated exchange shows quite a lot of information being
exchanged and there is also a fair amount of personal revelation as
well. Thus, while the function of the two exchanges is similar – more
phatic than informational – their surface features are very different.

Doing the Monday morning exchange in French could, of course,
be studied by Liddicoat and Crozet's Australian students as an
opportunity to develop further their morphosyntactic and discourse
competence as well as their communication strategies. However,
as the authors point out, while greetings across languages might
generally be formulaic and even ritualistic, they are not so in the
same way and language learners need to engage in some form of
sociocultural analysis in order to work out what differences exist and

how to make sense of them. In pragmatic terms, FL learners need to work cross culturally, examining not only the pragmalinguistics of the situation, but also the sociopragmatics.

Liddicoat and Crozet investigated whether or not a group of Australian students of French would benefit from awareness-raising activities about the French and Australian ways of doing the post-weekend exchange. They were interested to see if teaching methodology might overcome the reticence of Australian learners to take on French sociopragmatic norms, as presented in Béal's study. The students first examined examples of French speakers and Australian English speakers performing this exchange and then discussed in detail with classmates and the teacher the differences they observed.

Liddicoat and Crozet argue that learners who engaged in the sociocultural analysis of greetings in both French and English manifested changes in how they dealt with the Monday morning greeting: 'How was your weekend?' In general, these learners adopted a more French, topic-based orientation than had previously been the case. They also seemed to develop an 'understanding that learning to speak a FL is not a matter of simply adopting foreign norms of behaviour, but about finding an acceptable accommodation between one's first culture and the target culture' (Liddicoat and Crozet, 2001: 137–8). However, one has to wonder if it is wise to set up such stark contrasts between the 'first culture and the target culture' and specifically how individuals in both France and Australia do the Monday morning conversation. Surely, not all French people would take the time to engage in elaborate conversations. And even for those who do have a tendency to do this, would they necessarily do so with all of their work colleagues? And if the answer to the preceding questions is 'no', then what are the micro-contextual and other factors that shape whether or not the Monday morning conversation is long or short? Also, what does doing a shorter, less elaborate conversation index? The same questions surely must apply to Australians, as regards their purported propensity to engage in very short Monday morning conversations. Nowhere in their paper do Liddicoat and Crozet make such gross generalizations; nevertheless in trying to engage with cultural differences between France and Australia, they seem to have inadvertently presented a rather essen-tialist and over-simplified view of sociolinguistic norms in France and Australia.

Another concern I have about this research is related to whether or not the pedagogical activity described by Liddicoat and Crozet led to any French-mediated identity work. On the one hand, I learn that the learners gain a better understanding of how to do the Monday morning conversation, albeit according to a rather oversimplified model of TL conversation norms. In this case, they have gained cross-cultural knowledge in the form of an awareness not only of how French people do the 'How was your weekend?' conversation, but also how Australians do it (they may or may not have ever analysed this particular part of their L1 repertoire). However, the use of this more creative, awareness raising pedagogy does not put these learners in a situation in which a critical experience is likely to occur. In other words, engagement in such activity does not constitute a 'period [. . .] of time during which prolonged contact with an TL and a new and different cultural setting causes irreversible destabilization of the individual's sense of self' (Block, 2002a: 4).

In this case, the impediment to a classroom based experience having a greater impact on learners' senses of self is, to a great extent, down to the nature of the activities investigated by Liddicoat and Crozet. These activities of compare and contrast ultimately seem to be more about *cross-cultural learning* than *intercultural learning*, where the former refers to learning about cultural differences while the latter is about learning through the cultural differences emergent during interactions with members of the target culture and users of the TL. I now examine how intercultural learning intersects with SLL and ultimately second language identity work.

Intercultural language learning

There is a fairly extensive literature on intercultural language learning and the development of intercultural speakers in FL contexts (e.g. Kramsch, 1993; Byram, 1995, 1997; Byram and Fleming, 1998; Byram and Grundy, 2002; Byram, Nichols and Stevens, 2003). An intercultural speaker is defined by Byram as

someone who can operate their linguistic competence and their sociolinguistic awareness of the relationship between language and the context in which it is used, in order to manage interaction across cultural boundaries, to anticipate misunderstandings caused by difference in values, meanings and beliefs, and thirdly, to cope with the affective as well as cognitive demands of engagement with otherness. (Byram, 1995: 25)

Intercultural competence, that is, what intercultural speakers are said to have, is defined as

the ability to behave appropriately in intercultural situations, the affective and cognitive capacity to establish and maintain intercultural relationships and the ability to stabilise one's self identity while mediating between cultures. (Jensen, Jaeger and Lorentsen, 1995: 41)

Intercultural competence is said to rely on two pre-conditions: the ability to relativize one's own culture, consisting of beliefs, value systems and behaviours (*savoir être*) and an acquired knowledge about cultures other than one's own. Three skills which arise from these two pre-conditions may be glossed as follows:

● *savoir comprendre* – knowing how to read culture via various media;

● *savoir apprendre* – knowing how to learn from contacts with new behaviours, belief systems, values and so on;

● *savoir faire* – knowing how to interact in an interculturally appropriate manner.

In recent years some authors have preferred to define the person possessing these *savoirs* not so much as an 'intercultural speaker' but as an 'intercultural mediator', because the latter term gives 'more emphasis to the individual's potential for social action rather than to the competencies acquired as a consequence of teaching' (Alred and Byram, 2002: 341).

In their discussion of intercultural mediators, Alred and Byram (2002) draw on the earlier work of Berger and Luckman (1966), specifically, their models of socialization. Berger and Luckman argued that there were two types of socialization. Primary socialization is the result of interaction and engagement in practices shaped and mediated by the first and most immediate significant others in one's life. In lay terms, this is the socialization of childhood, during which the individual is purported to learn the fundamentals of being a member of a particular cultural matrix or matrices. Secondary socialization comes later in life and represents the individual's induction into institutions such as education, work and leisure. In effect, it is about how an individual builds up communities of practice with other human beings.

To this, Byram (1990) adds a third type of socialization, what is termed tertiary socialization. Tertiary socialization is about induction into the norms of behaviour, beliefs and values of a second culture, either early in life or later in life. For Alred and Byram, this type of socialization includes social class movement, religious conversation and growing up in a multicultural environment. However, more importantly it includes the FL learning experience, which ideally is about breaking with beliefs, concepts and schemata acquired during primary and secondary socialization.

The work of Byram and others on interculturality has received a great deal of attention in recent years, particularly among European language educators for whom it provides a theoretical justification for innovative pedagogical practices such as project work (e.g. Ribé and Vidal, 1993; Ribé, 1997; Roberts, Byram, Barro, Jordan and Street, 2001; Byram, Nichols and Stephens, 2003). However, on a theoretical level, it does suffer from a few shortcomings. First, despite its rejection of cross cultural approaches, which generally involve translating the TL culture in terms of the language learners' home cultures, it still essentializes cultures as metaphorical spaces, divided by 'borders', that individuals can occupy. In doing so, it also does not take on board the emerging diversity and complexity of societies around the world due to social changes wrought by advanced information technology or the influx of migrants, or both. Thus, to talk about 'difference[s] in values, meanings and beliefs', in countries like France, Britain, Germany or the US, begs the question of whose 'values, meanings and beliefs'? In addition, interculturality carries with it certain assumptions about conversation breakdowns taking place when interlocutors come from different sociocultural and linguistic backgrounds. For interculturalists, these breakdowns are seen as 'misunderstandings' resulting from a lack of intercultural competence on the part of the non-local interlocutor. However, as authors such as Blommaert (2005) suggest, breakdowns can be related to any number of phenomena such as a refusal to conform, a desire to disagree or a different perspective on the function of an exchange (see Carlos's conversations in Chapter 4 for examples of all three of these phenomena).

Notwithstanding these rather serious theoretical problems, the work of Byram and others on interculturality has at least opened up discussions of the nature and extent of emergent TL-mediated subject positions in FL contexts. In such discussions, some authors, such as Claire Kramsch, have managed to develop what I think are more sophisticated conceptual frameworks

Textual identity, language play and the identity of the FL learner

In recent years, Kramsch has developed the idea that through writing in the TL, there is the prospect, or at least the possibility, of the language learner developing a sense of self in the TL. She calls this sense of self a 'textual identity' (Kramsch and Lam, 1999; Kramsch, 1998, 2000, 2003). Kramsch's starting point is a broadly semiotic approach to language learning and use, one that sees communication not only as linguistic in nature, but as being about making and using signs. Following Peirce ([1902] 1955), Kramsch sees signs as entities standing for something else, which can be of three distinct types. Signs can be 'indexical', that is they point toward something (e.g. smoke or flames index fire). They can be 'iconic' when they bear a topical similarity to their referent (e.g. a photograph of fire is an icon of fire). Finally, they can be 'symbolic', representing something because there are conventions that say so (e.g. the letter combination in English 'fire' is a symbol for fire).

The relevance of Peirce's three-part breakdown of signs to language and language learning is summed up as follows by Kramsch:

Any linguistic sign can be seen as combination of index, icon, and symbol. For example, the utterances produced by language learners can be viewed in three ways: (a) as indexing a certain reality, (b) as being icons or metaphors for the reality they refer to, (c) as enacting the arbitrary conventions of the code and its socially conventionalized uses . . . (Kramsch, 2000: 136)

Kramsch recognizes that it is difficult for FL learners to make their own signs in the TL, given that they are not in the sociocultural context which in principle affords the creation of such signs. However, she argues the FL learners can draw on the TL input provided to them in the FL context and become sign creators. In so doing their language productions thus can be viewed: '(a) indexing a certain reality, (b) as being icons or metaphors for the reality they refer to, [and] (c) as enacting the arbitrary conventions of the code and its socially conventionalized uses' (Kramsch, 2000: 136). The question is how these language productions might lead to the development of textual identities, which in turn would have a significant impact on the language learner's sense of self.

An attempt to answer this question can be found in the work of Julie Belz (2002) who explores the hypothesis that 'multilingual language play (i.e. language play that involves hybridizations or combinations of L1 and TL) may function as a textual indication of changes in learner self-conceptualizations' (Belz, 2002: 15). She examines written samples produced by 31 advanced level German students at an American university. These students were fulfilling the task of writing a 300–500 word essay in which they were encouraged to work multilingually, that is to use German, English and whatever languages they thought they needed to get their ideas across (Belz states that in the end a total of 16 languages were used). As a follow-up, Belz interviewed some of the students.

Belz analyses the data from two perspectives: the 'hybridized metaphorical play with language names', that is how the learners invented names for their multilingual forms of expressions, and 'hybridized syntactic play', that is how within their texts learners mixed the syntax of the languages they drew on as resources of communication. In the former case, the learners created what Belz calls 'textual icons', such as 'Engleutsch', which she argues 'signify changes in these learners' self-conceptualizations' in that 'they are signs of their textual identities constructed in and through language'

(Belz, 2002: 32). In the latter case, they manifested multicompetence, in simple terms 'the knowledge of more than one language in the same mind' (V. Cook, 1996: 65), using German syntax in their English and English syntax in their German.

Belz examines not only how language play can aid linguistic development (Lantolf, 1997; G. Cook, 1997, 2000; Broner and Tarone, 2001), but also how it can be linked to the multicompetence emerging as learners encounter new linguistic forms and functions. In her study, I think Belz does a good job of operationalizing the concept of language play in the context an FL classroom setting. However, what can be said about the emergence of TL-mediated subject positions? The following excerpt from a composition entitled 'meine Sprache' ('my language') was written by a student Belz calls Lin, who had studied German for five semesters:

> *Deutsch und English are so good zusammen. Die Beide fließen zusammen so wonderschön**lich** [bold in the original], und man kann weird words make up and with word order play . . . Ich mag California. Hier kann man das Fahrrad fahren, schilaufen gehen oder to the beach gehen all in one state. Und knowing Deutsch makes alles even besser! Was würde ich ohne Deutsch tun? Ich weiß nicht. I wouldn't be able to speak meine Sprache. I couldn't express myself echt, ganz genau . . . (LINTXT lines 127–35, 151–86)*

> German and English are so good together. Both of them flow together so wonderfully-**like** [bold in the original], and you can weird words make up and with word order play . . . I like California. Here you can ride bikes, ski, and go to the beach all in one state. And knowing German makes everything even better! What I do without German? I wouldn't be able to speak my language. I couldn't express myself for real, precisely . . .

> (Belz, 2002: 27)

In this case and others, learners make claims about feeling different and even special in using their new language. From this point of view, these students can be said to have developed a new subject position and a new discourse of self-expression, which did not exist before.

In addition, they can be said to belong to an emergent community of practice of students of German, who have the capacity, via their agency, to constantly redefine what this community is about and what their membership in it actually means. Belz sums up matters as follows:

> I submit that these textual icons signify changes in these learners' self-conceptualizations (i.e., they are signs of their textual identities constructed in and through language). In particular, they mark their growing multicompetence, a new state of mind brought about by the learning of another language. [The learners] conceptualize themselves as multicompetent language users with respect to all languages they know as opposed to deficient L2 communicators with respect to only their L2(s). (Belz, 2002: 32)

However, have the students in Belz's research achieved a profound level of interculturality and more importantly, have they moved towards new third place subject positions in the TL? In one sense, they have, for the simple reason that they have created new languages that are neither L1 nor TL, but something beyond the component linguistic repertoires drawn on. However, as I suggest above with reference to Liddicoat and Crozet (2001), this raised awareness of language, and even self-awareness as language user and creator, does not take students to feelings of ambivalence that come with critical experiences. Indeed, there is nothing in the students' experiences of creating their own languages or in their talk about these experiences that would suggest that significant identity work is taking place. For example, a student named Carl seems to revel in the experience of creating his own language, 'Carlsprache' or 'Carlolanguage':

> *Ich liebe Wörter. Ich liebe Wortspiele. Ich heisse Carl, Charles, Carlo, карп Kaaaaaaaaaarl: l'homme que no puede wählen welche Язьk él quiere parler. . . . Even though I think in many languages, it's like it all comes together in one language called 'Carlsprache' or 'Carlolanguage'. Ich verstehe mich . . .*

> I love words. I love words games. My name is Carl, Charles [English], Carlo [Italian], карп [Russian], Kaaaaaaaaaarl [German]: the amn who cannot choose which language he wants to speak . . . Even

though I think in many languages, it's like it all comes together in one language called 'Carlsprache' [German] or 'Carlo [Italian] language [French].' I understand myself. (Belz, 2002: 26)

However, it is not altogether clear to me that beyond linguistic playfulness much else is happening. Meanwhile, another student, Danny, seems to focus on the experience as one that raised his awareness of syntax rather than one that destabilized his sense of self:

I liked the playful parts [of the multilingual essays] where people were obviously experimenting: I mean Lin . . . because it really takes a certain amount of force to push words into alternative grammar, at least for me it's really hard. You have to think about it . . . Lin really made me think about separable prefixes. (Belz, 2002: 32)

Thus while language play has become a promising framework as regards alternative ways to view learner generated language (Lantolf, 1997; Cook, 1997, 2000; Broner and Tarone, 2001), I am not convinced that the kind of language play discussed as significant in these publications constitutes serious and profound TL-mediated identity work (NB not all of the previously cited authors would make such a claim). I now move to a study in which a language learner does experience ambivalence and conflict as regards her sense of self, even if such feelings are not mediated by the TL.

FL language learning diaries revisited

In an article that echoes Bailey's work 20 years earlier (Bailey, 1983; see Chapter 3), Lantolf and Genung (2002) monitor the experiences of one of the authors, Patricia Genung (hereafter PG), learning Chinese as FL at an American university. Like Bailey, PG had enrolled in an FL course as a requirement for her PhD. In her case, however, she had to study a 'non European' language. PG had studied up to varying degrees of proficiency in several languages including German, reported as her best FL. The authors thus describe her as a 'successful language learner'. One biographical note that the authors emphasize relates to PG's occupation: at the time of the study she was a Colonel in the US army. Lantolf and Genung state their belief that PG's 'history as a high ranking officer in the US military was a central factor in her willingness to challenge, albeit unsuccessfully, the community structure and rules of interaction imposed by the instructional staff' (Lantolf and Genung, 2003: 179).

PG attended her classes with 15 other students, a heterogeneous group with different backgrounds and different motives for studying Mandarin. However, she was normally in class with seven other students, as the group of 16 students was split into two cohorts. There were four instructors on the course: three Chinese women – two from mainland China and one from Taiwan – and one L1 English speaker, who was also director of the programme. The students divided their time between the native speaker teachers and the L1 English speaker. Although the goals of the course were in part communicative, the general style and organization of time mitigated against, for example, conversation activities. Drilling seemed to be the primary methodology.

As it turns out, this methodology question came to be the source of PG's problems with her Mandarin course. Lantolf and Genung note that 'the Chinese language program seems to have insulated itself from the dominant belief system about language teaching and learning that served to organize the department at large' (Lantolf and Genung, 2003: 184) and the dominant teaching methodology consisted of explicit grammar explanations and pattern drilling. As lessons went by, PG reported in her diaries how she had begun to feel a certain tension between her expectations and what was going on in lessons. However, her initial reaction to this tension was to try to do as well as she could. She did complain to the head of the department (the L1 English speaker), but he told her that Chinese had to be taught in the way that it was being taught.

What emerged as the class went on was a situation in which teachers stuck to a carefully controlled programme of grammatical presentation and drilling while the students in the class began to feel more and more frustrated. To make matters worse, the teachers resorted to teaching strategies that could only damage the affective atmosphere in the classroom. Lantolf and Genung report that teachers would try to humiliate students by publicly reprimanding them when it was thought that they had not done homework or prepared sufficiently for classes. And there were cases of intimidation as when students were interrupted and told that their responses were 'not good!' The authors note that: 'From PG's perspective, the dominant tone of the community that emerged in this classroom was one of hostility' (Lantolf and Genung, 2003: 187). In addition, PG's classmates said that such treatment by teachers made them feel 'verbally abused' and 'beat up' (Lantolf and Genung, 2003: 187).

PG endured this situation feeling progressively frustrated that she was not learning to form sentences, in short that she was not progressing in the way that she had expected and wanted. Slowly, her motives shifted from what Lantolf and Genung term 'social learning motives', including the desire to communicate with others, and 'self-related motives', including a drive towards self-fulfilment, to 'cognitive motives', in particular the learning of facts and achieving a high grade. In a sense, she shifted from what Breen (1987) terms an 'achievement orientation', that is she oriented to her language learning activity primarily with the aim of self-fulfilment, to a 'survival orientation', that is, her chief aim was to endure the course and get by the best she could (and get an acceptably good grade). In doing so, she adjusted her self-image as a 'successful language learner' from 'success = learning' to 'success = getting a good enough grade'. Lantolf and Genung sum up the situation as follows:

> From PG's perspective, the unyielding authoritative posture adopted by the instructors and program director short-circuited her attempts to participate in authentic language activity . . . Her attempts to challenge the authoritative discourse failed and she opted to give her 'allegiance' to their authority. (Lantolf and Genung, 2003: 192)

However, the subject position of language learner was not the only one being played for in this case. In Lantolf and Genung's account, there are clear links with the diary studies discussed in Bailey (1983), as well as Richard Schmidt's experiences in Brazil, documented by Schmidt and Frota (1986). In all these cases, the diarists are applied linguists with language teaching experience and they all take on, to varying degrees, the professional identity of a teacher informed by applied linguistics. This self-positioning is manifested in the way that the diarists find their teachers to be incompetent or in any case lacking in some way. PG went even further than the diarists in Bailey and Schmidt and Frota, however, when she went to the director of the programme and questioned the teaching methodology, alas to no avail.

A third subject position emerging in this study is related to Lantolf and Genung's statement above about PG's military background. PG must have found herself in a rather difficult position, coming from a profession in which authority is respected, but probably not accustomed to having her principles trampled on. She therefore confronted her teachers as authority figures to be respected while feeling deep down that they violated everything she understood about what constitutes good teaching and professional behaviour, as well as respectful treatment of others. Her ambivalent feelings were assuaged when she eventually came to acquiesce, accept her lot, and get on with her life on the Mandarin course. Lantolf and Genung conclude that 'her attempts to challenge the authoritative discourse failed and she opted to give her "allegiance" to their authority' (Lantolf and Genung, 2003: 192).

The interpersonal language learner

Some 12 years ago, I carried out research in which my chief aim was to document and analyse what language learners found salient about their EFL classes and how they evaluated their teachers and the lessons they were attending (Block, 1995). The context was a large language school in Barcelona. Six students were interviewed, face-to-face, on a weekly basis during one ten-week term. All interviews were carried out in either Catalan or Spanish, depending on the individual's preference. One of the cases I examined in this study was that of Silvia. In Block (2000), I present Silvia's case as an example of how students possess a great deal of 'meta-pedagogical awareness' that is, the knowledge about what constitutes good and effective language teaching practice and the ability to produce fine grained descriptions, analyses and evaluations of teaching practice that have been experienced.[1] However, here I would like to consider two strands running through Silvia's ongoing accounts of her lessons, which relate to particular subject positions she adopted in the process of producing these accounts.

Silvia was from a wealthy family in Barcelona. At the time of the study, she was living with her husband and three daughters in one of the wealthiest and most exclusive neighbourhoods in the city. Silvia had studied law at university, but soon after finishing her studies, she got married and for most of the ten years preceding this study, her life revolved around raising her three daughters. Still, she occasionally worked, helping her husband, also a lawyer, at his law firm.

During this study, Silvia was doing a Cambridge First Certificate (FCE) exam preparation course that met on Monday and Wednesday mornings from 10 to 12, and lasted eleven weeks. After an initial pre-course interview, in which we discussed Silvia's language learning background, the two of us met for interviews on nine occasions during the course, usually on Wednesday just after class. Silvia chose to speak to me in Spanish during these interviews.

In the pre-course interview, Silvia revealed herself as someone who valued a good atmosphere in a class, in particular the interpersonal relations between teacher and students and between student and student. Thus, when discussing her past experiences, she frequently made mention of her relationships with teachers, from the enjoyment she experienced talking to a private French teacher about literature to going out to dinner with a 'nice' teacher and classmates with whom she had done her first course in the same school some 15 years earlier. As regards fellow students, she said it was important for everyone to participate and feel comfortable in the classroom.

Silvia and her teacher

Perhaps the most salient concern to emerge during Silvia's ongoing accounts of her lessons was her intense one-on-one relationship with her teacher. What most mediated this relationship were compositions and the teacher's way of correcting them. The comment below, made when the course was about two thirds over, is typical of what Silvia had to say about this topic (NB In this interview excerpt, and in all subsequent ones presented, the portions in bold were produced in English in the original).

> . . . *el otro dia porqué me dio tanta rabia que me tachara en las* **compositions**, *que le dije que se pasaba conmigo. Y me dice 'sí,* **I recognize I am very hard with you and . . .** *pero* **you should** *esto y lo otro . . .' Sí,, el otro dia me molestó mucho, la verdad . . . había tachado y luego en clase, ironiza un poco a veces sobre los errores y a mi no me gusta . . . la verdad, no me gusta. . . . Tengo mucho amor propio, de acuerdo, y entonces no me gusta que nadie me corrija, quizás. Porqué ya me corrijo yo bastante a mi misma porqué quizás sea muy exigente, entonces . . . Claro, reconozco que está en su derecho, lo tiene que hacer, ¿no? Pero no lo acepto tan fácilmente. Es como cada vez que vienes y te dan un palo en la cabeza, ¿sabes? Después de haber hecho un esfuerzo . . . Yo escribo con muchas ganas y con mucha ilusión y con ganas de hacerlo mejor, ¿no?*

> . . . the other day because it made me so angry that she crossed out things in my **compositions** that I told her that she overdid it with me. And she says 'yes, **I recognize I am very hard with you and . . .** but **you should** [do] this and that . . .' Yes, the other day it really bothered me, really . . . she had crossed out things and then in class, she ridicules the errors a little at times and I don't like it . . . I really don't like it . . . I have a lot of self esteem, all right, and so I don't like people to correct me, perhaps. Because I already correct myself enough because I am perhaps very demanding, so . . . Of course, I admit that she's within her rights, she has to do it, doesn't she? But I don't accept it so easily. It's like every time you come and they knock you in the head with a stick, you know? After making an effort . . . I write with a lot of hope and desire and I always want to improve, right? (Silvia – 26/5/93)

In this excerpt, Silvia manifests a great deal of ambivalence as regards her relationship with her teacher as corrector of her English. She says that the teacher admitted being deliberately hard on her, but at the same time, she admits that she cannot accept being corrected. She accuses the teacher of ridiculing students who have made errors, but then cedes ground momentarily to a question of institutional normativity: 'she's within her rights'. She finishes by likening the teacher's treatment of written error to hitting students over the head with a stick. This metaphor is reminiscent of PG's classmates in Lantolf and Genung (2003; see above), who said that they felt 'verbally abused' and 'beat up' (Lantolf and Genung, 2003: 187) by their Mandarin teachers.

The conversation then returned to the question of intention, with Silvia suggesting that the teacher was not looking after her best interests, but only trying to maintain authority and control over her:

> S: *No sé si realmente lo hace por mi bien . . . o porqué . . . no sé.*
> D: *Yo no creo que lo haga por tu mal.*
> S: *No, pero no sé en el fondo si es para que yo mejore o para que no me pase de lista, ¿me entiendes? Tampoco le debe gustar que me pase de lista y entonces me casca . . .*

> S: I don't know if she really does it for my own good . . . or because . . . I don't know . . .
> D: I don't think she does it to hurt you.
> S: No, but I don't know if deep down it's to keep me from improving or to keep me from being too clever by half, you understand? She must not like me being too clever by half, either, and for this reason she punishes me {NB literally, beats me up] . . . (Silvia – 26/5/93)

The suggestion that the teacher wants to keep Silvia in her place ties in with a general construction of the teacher as having some kind of power over her through her superior knowledge of English. In addition, as she had done in the reference to being hit on the head with a stick, Silvia continues to employ physical metaphors to describe her relationship with the teacher, saying that 'she punishes me'. In the following excerpt she concludes by qualifying her relationship as 'special', suggesting once again that the teacher takes advantage of her vulnerability.

> *No lo sé . . . pero. . . hay una relación así especial. Yo noto que . . . y además ella lo nota, cuando yo estoy cabreada porqué se me nota en la cara. No lo puedo esconder. Y cuando estoy decepcionada también.*

I don't know but there's a sort of special relationship. I notice it . . . and she does, too, when I get pissed off, because you can see it in my face. I can't hide it. And when I'm disappointed, too. (Silvia – 26/5/93)

In an interview taking place one week later, Silvia went one step further in her accusations, suggesting that English teachers as a collective think they are better than their students.

> S: *Lo único es que a veces . . . pienso que los profesores por el hecho de hablar inglés y que tu no lo hables, están un poco por encima tuyo. Y esto da un poco de rabia, la verdad, porqué, no sé, pero da un poco esta sensación y le he comentado con alguna otra persona y me han dicho que sí. O sea que no es cosa mía que no voy a tener ningún complejo de inferioridad. Es que es un poco la . . .*
> D: *¿Qué? ¿Que yo tengo algo que tu no tienes?*
> S: *Que yo no tengo y que a mi me está costando mucho tenerlo y por eso* **look** . . .
> D: **look down on**
> S: *Eso es.*
> D: *Nunca lo había pensado. . . . ¿Pero no crees que esto también está intermezclado un poco con la relación de poder que puede haber entre profesor y alumno?*
> S: *Sí, claro, siempre hay una relación de poder entre el profesor y alumno y a mi a veces me ha molestado. . .*

S: The only thing is that sometimes . . . I think that teachers, because they speak English and you don't, they are above you. And this infuriates me, actually, because I don't know, but you get this feeling a little and I've mentioned it to other people and they've told me I'm right. I mean it's not just my thing, I'm not going to have any kind of inferiority complex. It's just it's a little . . .

D: What? That I have something you don't have?

S: That I don't have and it's costing me a lot to have it and for this reason **look** . . .

D: **look down on**

S: that's right

> D: I've never thought about that. . . . But don't you think that it's also mixed up with the power relation that there might be between teacher and student?
> S: Yes, of course, there is always a power relation between the teacher and the student and at times, it has bothered me . . . (Silvia – 2/6/93)

Silvia concluded this exchange by saying:

> *Y dices: ¿Pero qué te has creido? Si tu solo eres un profesor'.*
> *Claro, es que es verdad. Sabrás mucho inglés pero yo sé muchas*
> *otras cosas.*

> And you say: 'Well who do you think you are? You're just a teacher.' It's true. You might know a lot of English but I know a lot of other things. (Silvia – 2/6/93)

Here, Silvia makes reference to what seems to be question of social class. A well-educated woman from a wealthy family, with a law degree and a home in one of Barcelona's most exclusive residential areas – in short, someone with an excess of economic, cultural and social capital – certainly does not have to take certain things from someone who is 'just a teacher'. She seems to resent the fact that the classroom situation puts her in a less powerful position, albeit for only four hours a week. However, by the time of our last interview, held just after the last day of class, everything had come full circle and Silvia talked of reconciliation with her teacher:

> S: . . . *al final también le he dicho lo que quería decirle y me he*
> *quedado tranquila porqué se lo he dicho.*
> D: *¿Qué le has dicho?*
> J: *No, un dia le dije que me tenía que escribir algo en las*
> ***compositions*** *y no tacharlo todo y poner solo un visto y . . . y*
> *le dije* **'you should have written something here to cheer me**
> **up' and the last composition I got a sentence: 'Good work'**
> **or something like this which I appreciate a lot**. . . . *y hoy*
> *también hemos estado hablando con ella. Me preguntaba que*
> *qué iba hacer el año que viene . . .*

S: . . . in the end, I also told her what I wanted to tell her and I
am at peace with the world because I told her.

D: What did you tell her?

S: No, one day I told her that she should write something on my
compositions and not scratch out everything and only write
a check . . . and I said **'you should have written something
here to cheer me up' and the last composition I got a
sentence, 'Good work' or something like this which I
appreciate a lot** . . . and today we were also talking to her.
She was asking me what I was going to do next year . . .
(Silvia – 16/6/93)

She then surprised me with a revealing statement about her
relationship with teachers, which seemed less than congruent with
her remarks about teachers being 'just teachers':

> *a mi me gusta hablar con los profes. No sé por qué pero me gusta
> mucho . . . Y además hemos ido al bar y hemos tomado una copa
> de cava . . . Pero claro, como no habíamos ido nunca al bar con
> ella, pues no llegas a conocerla mucho. Entonces le hemos estado
> preguntando a ella de donde era y como es que había venido a
> parar aquí y todo. No sé, situas la gente cuando sabes más su
> historia porqué si no . . .*

> I like talking to teachers. I don't know why, but I like it a lot . . .
> And besides, we went to the bar and had a glass of cava . . . But
> of course since we had never gone to the bar with her, you never
> get to know her very well. So we were asking her where she was
> from and how she had ended up here and everything. I don't know,
> you situate people more when you know a little about their past
> because if not . . . (S – 16/6/93)

In these comments about her teacher, Silvia once again manifests an
ambivalent attitude. On the one hand, she appreciated the structure
and clarity that the teacher provided; on the other hand, she resented
the control that the teacher exercised over her in the classroom.
Behind Silvia's ambivalent feelings towards her teacher there was also
perhaps a degree of envy at a lost opportunity to break with tradition.
Listening to Silvia's 'off-the-record' comments made outside our

interviews about her course, I had the impression that she perhaps would have liked to have done what so many expatriate teachers have done: pack her bags and go to live in another country. Instead of doing this while she could, however, she got married and settled down to raise a family. Given this situation, her language classes, and above all her contact with teachers, were to some extent an escape from a life she found far too routine and confining.

Like the participants in other FL diary studies, such as Walsleben (in Bailey, 1983; see Chapter 3 of this book) and PG (in Lantolf and Genung, 2003), Silvia was critical of teaching practice and how the teacher made her feel. Nevertheless, her criticisms came from a student subject position as opposed to a teacher/applied linguist subject position, and Silvia could only seek to resolve her conflict with her teacher from this student subject position. She did this by talking to her teacher, which both changed her teacher's behaviour and satisfied her desire to be close to her teacher, which, as she makes clear in the last excerpt cited above, was something that she valued. Her teacher conflict as well her ways of dealing with it, therefore, are very different from Walsleben's and PG's situations. The latter were not able to establish positive rapports with their teachers and the end result was that Walsleben dropped out of her Farsi course, while PG, in effect, downgraded herself from successful learner and achieving student to unsuccessful learner and surviving student.

Silvia's need to be respected is inextricably linked and intertwined with a second struggle going on with her teacher, that is, her quest for a textual identity in English. As was explained above, a TL textual identity is about an individual becoming a 'text creator' in the TL, of gaining a voice in the TL. In her comments, Silvia constructs her journey from feeling victimized by her teacher, who is said to have ridiculed student errors and made her feel as though she was being physically abused, to feeling that her writing was appreciated. Thus, just as the she was able to have a person-to-person (rather than student-to-teacher) conversation with her teacher at the end of the course, she was also able to gain the teacher's recognition as a competent writer and therefore a validated written text creator in English.

Silvia's ongoing accounts of her lessons touch on issues similar to those found in Lantolf and Genung (2003) and Belz (2002), as she was involved in an ongoing struggle to gain the respect of her teacher, both as a person and as a user of English. However, the teacher-student dyad captures but one dimension of the FL classroom experience and often relationships with fellow students can be far more important.

Silvia and the problem student

The group attending classes with Silvia was small – some ten students – and the students ranged from a young male university student to women, like Silvia, in their mid-thirties. In an early interview, Silvia mentioned in passing that there was a classmate, Rosa, whom she avoided:

> *Pero ésta es un poco pelma . . . no, a veces te pega algún corte o piensa de otra manera y te dice que tu eres loca por pensar así . . . y ya me parece que es el tercer curso que voy con ella y estoy un poco harta y prefiero evitarla. Si ella opina distinto, pues yo opino de otra manera y se acabó.*

> But this one is a little bit of a pain in the neck . . . no, sometimes she puts you down or she thinks differently and she says that you're crazy to think how you think . . . and I think it's already the third course I have done with her and I'm a little sick of her and I prefer to avoid her. If she thinks differently, I think another way and that's it. (Silvia – 28/4/93)

Silvia was conscious that she tried to sit in a location where she was 'protected' from Rosa. However, such a strategy did not always work, as she explained in a later interview:

> *. . . el otro dia me intenté sentar al lado de una que es nueva y bueno luego vino esta persona y se me sentó al lado. Pero cuando hicimos grupos de dos, me puse al lado de [the new student] y por suerte cuadró bien . . . o sea me puse al lado de la que yo quería y no se notó . . . si tengo suerte procuraré evitarla porqué . . . para mi es un poco rollo . . .*

> . . . the other day I tried to sit next to someone new and then this person came and she sat next to me. But when we got into

groups of two, I sat next to [the new student] and luckily it worked out . . . I mean I sat next to the student I wanted to and it wasn't noticeable . . . if I'm lucky, I'll be sure to avoid her because . . . for me she's kind of a drag . . . (Silvia – 5/5/93)

When asked exactly why she felt such animadversion for Rosa, Silvia related the following incident, with a view to highlighting her difficult personality:

> S: *Estaban hablando sobre un tema de estos y tenía que ser un dialogo y entonces . . . bueno, claro yo también soy un poco puñetera porque . . . bueno, entonces estaba un chico del grupo del año pasado que empieza a hablar. Y entonces este chico cuando se lanza habla mucho, mucho, mucho y no para. Entonces yo le dije a ella, 'le puedes interrumpir si tienes alguna idea'.*
> D: *Pero, ¿lo dijiste en inglés?*
> S: *No, en inglés interviniendo le dije: 'oye le puedes interrumpir para que sea un dialogo' porque . . . y me dijo que como era su turno que a ella no le importaba y que por lo tanto que me callara. Y yo le dije 'bueno, Rosa, **I'm sorry'**.*

> S: They were talking about one of those subjects and it was supposed to be a dialogue and then . . . well, actually I'm a little picky because . . . so there was this guy in the group from last year who started to talk. And this guy when he gets going, he goes on and on and on and doesn't stop. So I said to her, 'You can interrupt him if you have something to say'.
> D: But you said it in English?
> S: No, in English intervening I said: 'listen, you can interrupt to make it a dialogue' . . . and she told me that since it was her turn, that she didn't mind and to shut up. And I said to her 'OK, Rosa, **I'm sorry**'. (Silvia – 5/5/93)

In this account, Silvia gets herself into trouble with Rosa when she takes on a teacher-like role, telling her how to carry out her dialogue with another student. However, beyond her previous admission that she is 'a little picky', she does not acknowledge that her behaviour might have been seen as inappropriate, the adoption of a subject position that she had no right to in the context of the classroom.

In the same interview, Silvia went on to provide her analysis of why she had such a conflictive relationship with Rosa:

Bueno, esta chica a mi me habían comentado que el curso que ella empezó aquí tuvo muchos problemas con la clase, que acabó peleada con media clase. Y yo al principio pensé, bueno, no es para tanto, que seria culpa de la gente y no de ella, pero ahora pienso que es culpa de ella. O sea, no me cabe duda en absoluto que si acabó mal con la clase es por ella, porqué es . . . Me parece que es una persona que se ha hecho a si misma y cuando las personas tienen las circunstancias adversas se vuelven más exigentes y más . . . Si tu tienes las cosas fáciles en la vida más o menos, eres más condescendiente. Pero si las has tenido un poco [difícil] . . . luego eres muy exigente, creo. Y yo creo que es lo que le pasa un poco a esta chica. . . . y luego que, bueno, tiene unas ideas muy fijas y no sé . . . a veces las cosas no son blancas o negras.

So, this girl, they had told me that in her first course here she had a lot of problems with the class, that she ended up falling out with half the class. And at first I thought, she's not that bad, that it must have been the other people's fault and not hers, but now I think it's her fault. I mean I have no doubt that if she fell out with everyone one it's down to her because she's . . . I think she is a self-made person and when people face adverse circumstances they become more demanding and more . . . If you have things easy in life, more or less, you are more condescending. But if you have them a little [difficult] . . . then you're very demanding, I think. And I think that's kind of the situation with this girl . . . and well, she has fixed ideas and I don't know . . . sometimes things are not black and white. (Silvia – 5/5/93)

Here Silvia plays both psychiatrist and sociologist, providing a fairly detailed analysis of her classmate's state of mind and social background. The theory seems to be that if a person has to fight to get to the top, then she becomes more aggressive; the contrary applies to people who have had it easy. Silvia once again displays a high degree of class-consciousness as she is from a wealthy background and in addition, she married into a wealthy family. Thus, if in the case of the teacher, she showed a degree of disdain for teachers, in the case of

Rosa, Silvia attributes her difficult personality to her membership in the class of the 'new rich'.

Silvia's fairly harsh criticisms of Rosa contrast markedly with her comments about other classmates. These ranged from students her age and older with whom she had studied in previous courses and younger students she had never met before. However, Silvia had good things to say about all of them. She even told me how she watched over one particular 18-year-old student, whom she considered unable to look after himself, collecting handouts for him when he was not present. Clearly, in this particular group, Rosa was the odd one out for Silvia. In addition, as was the case with the teacher, she seemed a little obsessed about her relationship with Rosa, as the following interview excerpt shows:

> . . . *todo el rato se está excusando porqué dice palabras en alemány . . . a veces pienso que quizás lo hace un poco a propósito, pero . . . y yo creo que esta chica a veces también lo hace porqué le gusta presumir de que ella estaba en Suiza, que tiene la nacionalidad suiza, y que no sé . . . que los suizos son tan perfectos, no sé . . . y que su hijo habla alemán y . . . cada uno tiene sus cosas pero yo no voy contando por ahí . . . normalmente si no me preguntan, no voy . . . alardeando por ahí.*

> . . . she is all the time excusing herself because she says words in German and sometimes I think she does it a little on purpose but . . . and I think that this girl also does it sometimes because she likes to show off that she was in Switzerland, that she's got Swiss nationality and I don't know . . . that the Swiss are so perfect, I don't know . . . and that her son speaks German . . . Everyone has their things but I don't go around telling everyone . . . normally if they don't ask me I don't go around boasting. (Silvia – 26/5/93)

This account was prompted by a question I had asked Silvia about language 'interference', a topic which had arisen when she told me that she was also attending French classes. Silvia began by talking about her own French-English interference, but then suddenly began to talk about Rosa again, as an example of language interference as pretence. Once again, she returns to her disapproval of how Rosa carries herself.

In essence, she presents a picture of Rosa as pretentious and lacking in grace, as she boasts about prestige elements in her life, in this case indexed by her Swiss nationality and her son's knowledge of German. However, as she had done with her teacher, Silvia ends the story of her relationship with Rosa on a high note. In an interview taking place after her last day of class, she explains how she had made up with her classmate:

> S: . . . *que me he reconciliado con todo el mundo después de todas mis . . . No hombre, tampoco ha sido nada conflictivo, ¿eh? pero bueno.*
> D: *¿te sientes mejor ahora que antes?*
> S: *Sí, además estaba preocupada por Rosa porqué hacía como cuatro o cinco diás que no ha venido y no sabia si le había pasado algo. Y ayer la vi y me contó cosas y bueno, no sé.*

> S: . . . I made up with everyone after all my . . . No, but it hasn't really been conflictive, has it? but anyway
> D: You feel better than before?
> S: Yes, and besides I was worried because she hadn't come to class for four or five days and I wondered if anything had happened to her. And I saw her yesterday and she told me things, I don't know. (Silvia – 16/6/93)

In this comment, Silvia seems keen to put all her differences behind her on the last day of class. As was the case in her relationship with her teacher, she seems to be saying that perhaps she was being unfair in her appraisal of Rosa. In addition, Silvia shows how in the context of classroom FL, the kind of identity work being done is much more about her classmates than putative communities of practice in the TL. In these two narratives, Silvia is positioning herself as a wealthy and educated person with a high degree of class-consciousness. She deals with those around her through this class-consciousness, which leads her to disparage those who are deemed to behave inappropriately, getting above their station. However, ultimately she seems to value harmony over all else and the happy endings to both stories seems to come as something of a relief to her.

Taking stock: Identity work in the FL context

Thus far in this chapter, I have discussed in detail studies taking place in four different FL contexts: one in Australia, two in the US and one in Spain. In Liddicoat and Crozet (2001) and Belz (2002), innovative teaching techniques are brought in by teachers to move students towards TL-mediated subject positions. In the former case, the authors chart how a teacher takes a cross-cultural approach to the pragmatics of Monday morning conversations with a group of Australian students of French. The teacher moves students towards a better understanding of purported cultural differences between French and Australian people and shows them how adopting new subject positions in French means abandoning the habitual and comfortable way of carrying out day-to-day quasi-ritualistic exchanges. The activities devised by the teacher seem successful as regards raising cultural awareness, but they seem to fall short as regards the development of French-mediated subject positions. In addition, the entire enterprise is based on a highly essentialized notion of sociolinguistic norms.

In Belz (2002), the teacher asks students to write in their own invented languages drawing on English (their L1), German (the language they were studying) and any other linguistic resources they had acquired previously, either formally or informally. The end result is something akin to third place linguistic repertoires, beyond the constituent parts of English, German and other languages. However, as I noted above, apart from stimulating language play and developing further multicompetence, the activities have not convincingly moved learners to profound new textual identities in German. I say this not least because there is no evidence that the new languages developed by the learners actually mediate new subject positioning in what might reasonably be called a community of practice.

In Lantolf and Genung (2003), very clear emergent subject positions are documented. In addition, they arise due to what look to be significant and therefore critical experiences for PG. However, these critical experiences are not mediated by Mandarin, the TL.

Rather, they are more about PG's ambivalent roles as: an unsuccessful language learner, lived from the perspective of someone who had always considered herself a successful language learner; a language student, lived from the perspective of an applied linguist with language teaching experience; and a disrespected interlocutor, lived from the perspective of a colonel in the US army.

Finally, in my research, Silvia works towards the development of an English textual identity via her writing activities, as witnessed by her ongoing exchanges with her teacher about these activities. Indeed, her accounts of how she struggled with her teacher over her voice in English seem far more convincing as evidence of an emergent textual identity than the accounts of Belz's students about their writing of essays in invented multilingual codes. Nevertheless, this struggle for a textual identity was inextricably linked to her larger, more general concern about how she was treated by her teacher. In Lantolf and Genung (2003), the authors show how PG also had an ongoing conflict with her teachers about their treatment of students. However, whereas in PG's case the relationship seemed to remain poor throughout the language course, in Silvia's case there was a happy ending with Silvia saying that she liked her teacher. In addition, Silvia also had an ongoing conflict with her classmate Rosa, although by the end of the course, this conflict too was resolved and Silvia had changed her mind about Rosa.

Examining Silvia's case, along with the cases documented in Liddicoat and Crozet (2001), Belz (2002) and Lantolf and Genung (2003), my conclusion is that the prospects for TL-mediated subject positions in the FL context are minimal to non-existent. This is not to say that there is no identity work going on; it is only to say that it is not linked directly to the TL being studied and has more to do with communities of practice emergent inside the classroom. However, despite my pessimism, I have found two variations on the FL context that at least do show potential for the construction of TL-mediated subject positions. The first is the development of an EFL course that stimulates student engagement with international communities of practice. The second, in the context of a French as an FL course, involves the provision of opportunities to communicate with regular users of French via the Internet.

Focusing on specific subject positions: Feminism and the EFL classroom in Japan

Cheiron McMahill (1997, 2001) charts the identity work done by a group of female Japanese EFL learners enrolled in 'grass-roots feminist English classes', defined as classes that are organized by the learners themselves, where English is taught via a 'feminist second language pedagogy' (McMahill, 1997: 612). In simple terms, such a pedagogy merges traditional linguistic roles of the language classroom (i.e. learning morphology, syntax, phonology, pragmatics and so on) with feminist concerns such as women's rights in Japan and the world. Example activities cited by McMahill include:

> . . . preparing to give presentations in English at, for example, the United Nations conference for women . . . working on a translation of a feminist book from English into Japanese while seeking help from native-speaking English feminists . . . simply taking part in a discussion of women's issues with women from other countries. (McMahill, 1997: 613)

The chief aim of such classes was to create an English-medium alternative 'female discourse community of resistance to sexism' in Japan and the world. In McMahill (2001), the author focuses on one particular session with one group that she co-facilitated over a period of two and half years, starting in 1996. The class was called 'Colors of English' and its stated aim was to empower Japanese women through the learning of English as means of communication with women around the world. Sessions were generally organized around topics, such as ethnic identities, discrimination in employment, problems with the learning of English, personal histories and so on. In the session discussed in McMahill (2001), the topic was mother/daughter relationships and the catalyst for discussion was a passage written by bell hooks (1996) in which the author talks of always being in conflict with her mother, who always puts her husband's needs before her children's needs. The passage concludes as follows:

> She is a religious woman. She has been told that a man should obey god, that a woman should obey man, that children should

obey their fathers and mothers, particularly their mothers. I will not obey. (hooks, 1996: 81; cited in McMahill, 2001: 317)

In the group discussion arising from the reading of the hooks text, the seven women present revealed their inner feelings about personal matters. For example, one woman, P5, told those present about a conflict with her mother, specifically how her mother had made her feel guilty about being over 30 and still not married. P5 explained how she felt about her mother's behaviour as follows:

[T]hen I couldn't stop crying and I couldn't leave the house and I – I just left home and I couldn't come I, back to home until 11 or 12 in the night (laugh), and yesterday in the night I was just – I couldn't stop crying still, and I – I don't know how to sleep. (McMahill, 2001: 325)

In an atmosphere of group collaboration, the seven women in the group emerged from the discussion of such conflicts with their mothers, their fathers, other women and societal norms and expectations, having adopted subject positions of greater clarity with regard to these different people in their lives. Thus, from initial recriminations of mothers, colluding in the oppression of their daughters and women in general, more hopeful subject positions emerged around an understanding that breaking away from patriarchal power structures requires a 'psychic price that every woman has to "pay"' (McMahill, 2001: 331). P7, a Korean woman born in Japan, who like P5 was single and lived with her mother, summed matters up as follows:

And so just hearing you, P5, I just want to say one thing, bell hooks – she can *see* the things you just suffered, because you can see, it's like a screen, the movie, once you see the structure, you are not *in* it, you are like the audience . . . see um – she – she talks about the pain a lot, because she is so smart she can see everything and she – she knows she's different from other kids, but and because of the pain that's a kind of *price* she has to *pay* for the freedom, so after the pain, she can get the freedom, so that's why her book is so – um – give you – why her book becomes important is that, it's *painful*, but that's the process you have to go through in order to get – to reach freedom, liberty . . . (McMahill, 2001: 331; italics in the original)

McMahill thus shows how through the 'Colors of English' classes, FL learners were moved into destabilizing, conflictive and often uncomfortable terrain, with the TL, English, as the medium. Through their participation in the class discussion of mother/daughter relationships, they seemed to move towards subject positions that did not exist before and which emerged in the immediate community of practice made up of session participants. Interestingly, the women had not moved toward these new subject positions through a comparison of Japanese and Anglophone cultures, à la Liddicoat and Crozet (2001). Nor, it seems, had there been any struggles with teachers over teaching style or general treatment of students, as was observed in Bailey (1983), Lantolf and Genung (2003) and the case of Silvia. There did seem to be a textual identity emergent in the talk of the students; however, it was neither ludic in nature, as it was in Belz (2002), nor a site of struggle between student and teacher, as it was for Silvia. It was instead about these women finding their voices as members of an international community of practice of feminists. Finally, there were no reported conflictive relationships among students as collaboration and support seemed to reign supreme.

Nevertheless, a caveat is in order before presenting McMahill's 'Colors of English' classes as a template for FL courses guaranteed to move students towards TL-mediated subject positions. I refer here to the fact that the students in McMahill's classes were classified as upper intermediate and many of them had spent substantial periods of time abroad in English speaking countries (P5 and P7, cited above, had both spent several years of their lives in the US). These women, therefore, were more comfortable with using English to communicate their feelings than would be the case for most EFL learners around the world. It seems doubtful that the shifts in subject positions documented by McMahill would occur as easily in FL classes in which students are far less proficient in the TL. From this perspective, the FL class organized around specific subject positions, such as membership in the international feminist community cited above, is likely the domain of a select few FL students among the millions in the world. These students already have considerable TL-mediated experience and they are part of a relatively wealthy international elite living in different countries around the world.

Internet-mediated FL learning and identity

Another variation on the FL class that offers the prospect of TL-mediated identity work is the addition of an internet-mediated communication component. Thorne (2003) examines three cases in which Internet-mediated communication led to the emergence of TL-mediated subject positions well beyond anything observed in the research discussed thus far in this chapter. Here I will discuss one such case, involving an American undergraduate student of French named Kirsten.

Kirsten was part of a cohort of students who in 2002 participated in an Internet-mediated exchange programme involving her university, Penn State, and the Ecole Nationale Supérieure de Télécommunications de Bretagne. Students from both universities were expected to be in contact via email and NetMeeting, a programme allowing synchronous communication, to exchange their views about a common bank of written texts and films. In addition, students were expected to exchange individual biographies and generally get on with chatting to one another, alternating French and English as they deemed appropriate.

In interviews with researchers, Kirsten explained how during her first week she had difficulty establishing contact with her key-pal, Oliver. This was probably due in part to an imbalance as regarded the number of participants in the programme: there were more than twice as many American students as there were French students signed up for exchanges. However, as Thorne suggests, another problem might well have been the actual Internet communication media being used: email and NetMeeting. It seems that once Kirsten and Oliver realized that they were both subscribers to American Online Instant Messenger (IM), another programme allowing synchronous communication, their communication increased dramatically. As Thorne puts it, 'IM was a pivotal and necessary condition for moving her relationship with Oliver to a more intimate plane' (Thorne, 2003: 4). In one intensive week, Kirsten and Oliver spent a great deal of time 'together', an estimated six hours 'chatting' on the first day and one hour a day thereafter.

During this intensive week of contact, much of the conversation was about language, with Kirsten and Oliver alternately acting as teachers/dictionaries in English and French, respectively. Thorne reports how through her sessions with Oliver, Kirsten was able to arrive at a better understanding of the pragmatics of *tu/vous* and the collocations of prepositions such as *au, en* and *dans*. For his part, Oliver learned from Kirsten the uses of the verb 'look', which he was apparently using in pragmatically inappropriate ways, and the distinction between 'book smart' and 'common sense'. In the following interview excerpt, Kirsten describes how she felt empowered by her ability to explain matters related to English to Oliver in French:

> And there was this whole portion of this conversation where he was like 'I'm really enjoying talking to you and I hope we can do it more often.' You know, 'I'll hear from you again soon.' I mean, it's kind of encouraging because it means he doesn't think my French is so bad that he (laughing) doesn't want to talk to me. (Thorne, 2003: 50).

Here, there is a glimpse at Kirsten's emergent subject position as valid interlocutor in French, in particular as English language expert for Oliver. Thus, from the rather functional subject position of teacher/dictionary she sees herself evolving to something far more interpersonal. Indeed, later in her interview, Kirsten describes how she and Oliver were developing a relationship adding up to more than just two exchange students exchanging comments about French and English:

> The click was that we were both so excited to hear from each other and we decided to listen to each other's ideas and whatever. And then to find out that we had so much in common . . . He's really sweet. We're gonna be good friends I think, if we aren't already. We're pretty good friends now. It all happened within a week, yeah. A week tomorrow. (Thorne, 2003: 53)

Still later, Kirsten jokes about how she and Oliver were getting close, suggesting a relationship beyond friendship. However, she presents this relationship as one-way: while Oliver has a crush on her, she has a boyfriend.

> He and I have become quite the (laughing) friends! I really do think he has a crush on me. It's really cute. The moment I mention my boyfriend he's like 'ohhh'. My roommates spent like 15 minutes saying (falsetto voice) 'you have a crush on him too!' but I'm like 'no, I don't', I just think it's really neat to be able to talk to someone in France, and in French! That's my goal. That's why I'm taking the class. (Thorne, 2003: 54)

In the course of this comment, Kirsten deftly moves from being touched by Oliver's putative crush on her ('it's really cute') back to her more functional, less emotionally charged position of exchange student who is only in the relationship to learn French. Nevertheless, her story, taken as a whole, raises several issues worthy of note as regards making the FL classroom a site for the emergence of TL-mediated subject positions. First, Kirsten seemed to be on the road to developing a textual identity in French as she became not only Oliver's English teacher/dictionary, but also someone able to talk to him about various aspects of her background or her day-to-day life. Second, in the development of her French-mediated textual identity, Kirsten could claim membership in an emergent Internet-mediated community of practice of French and English users involved in the exchange, and perhaps beyond the exchange. Third, it is significant that Kirsten and other students participating in the exchange programme found that they could only feel that they were actively constructing new subject positions in the TL when they used synchronous communication pro-grammes, such as American Online Instant Messenger, as opposed to asynchronous modes such as email. Grace, another student involved in the exchange programme, responded as follows when asked why email was not a communication option for her:

> I think it's also because we have, like we communicate with a lot of people now through AOL . . . That's so like that's how I talk to all my friends at different colleagues . . . We don't send emails back and forth to each other to like catch up. Like we just talk [using IM]. (Thorne, 2003: 56)

Thus, the addition of the Internet-mediated exchange programme to this classroom-based French FL context affords students opportunities to develop new subject positions in French that would not have existed otherwise. Nevertheless, a couple of caveats are in order.

First, the exchange programme described by Thorne was relatively short-term in design, lasting just three weeks, and we do not know what happened after these three weeks. For example, did Kirsten and Oliver remain in contact? Or did Kirsten move beyond the confines of her relationship with Oliver to participate in French-mediated Internet sites as an active contributor? Surely, continuity, in the form of prolonged and fairly intensive contact with Oliver or other French speakers, would open the prospect for more durable TL-mediated subject positions, as opposed to ephemeral and serendipitous ones.

A second caveat has to do with how feasible such a programme would be for many FL students around the world. The issue of inequality in Internet use is mentioned by Thorne (2003) and it is taken up in greater detail elsewhere by authors such as Warschauer (2003), who notes how Internet use is highest in the US and the wealthy countries of East Asia, Oceania and Western Europe. However, within nation state borders, there are great differences in Internet used across class and racial lines (Block, 2004) and beyond borders, its use declines commensurate with levels of national poverty. From this perspective, the likelihood of emergent TL-mediated subject positions being a part of the FL context seems relatively remote and the domain of a privileged minority on the world stage.

Conclusion

In this chapter, I have examined in detail a selection of studies carried out in FL contexts. These studies have varied as regards physical location, taking place in the US, Australia, Spain, Japan and (virtually and partially) in France. They have also involved the learning of different languages: French, German, Mandarin and English. The focus on identity has varied across the studies, from the more indirect (Liddicoat and Crozet focus on interlanguage pragmatics, which I see as related to identity) to the more direct (Belz, Lantolf and Genung,

McMahill, Thorne and my re-interpretation of Silvia's data, are all explicitly about TL-mediated identity work).

My examination of Liddicoat and Crozet, Belz, Lantolf and Genung and my own research has led me to the general conclusion that in the FL setting, there is usually far too much first language-mediated baggage and interference for profound changes to occur in the individual's conceptual system and his/her sense of self in the TL. This conclusion is perhaps not surprising if one considers that identity work is about drawing on semiotic resources available in the here and now, to participate in activities carried out in the here and now, and that for FL learners the most likely resources for this work are local multimodalities (which include local language repertoires) and not TL-related multimodalities. However, there are ways to transcend the multimodality of the local. As I noted when discussing McMahill, this transcendence might be achieved by disembedding the TL from a faraway native culture (e.g. US, British), and framing it as an international resource within reach of learners from Japan. Meanwhile, Thorne shows how Internet communication allows for the transcendence of great distances as learners in France and the US are able to spend time together whist remaining thousands of kilometres from each other, and to forge TL-mediated identities, albeit somewhat ephemeral ones.

The FL context, described here as relatively unfertile ground for TL-mediated identity work, contrasts markedly with naturalistic adult migrant settings discussed in Chapter 4, where there is the potential for partial or full immersion in the TL multimodality. It also differs significantly from the study abroad context discussed in the next chapter, where FL classroom instruction gives way to 'being there', which increases the potential for immersion in TL-mediated environments and the emergence of new TL-mediated subject positions.

Note

1   In Block (2000), Silvia is referred to as GJ.

6

Identity in study abroad contexts

Introduction

ISA program participants can study Spanish, French, or Italian at any proficiency level or can choose from programs taught entirely in English. Many ISA programs also offer the unique opportunity to enroll in courses with local students. As a result of the wide variety of ISA programs available, students are able to select the program that best suits their personal interests and individual academic goals. By becoming fully immersed in the culture, customs, and ideals of the host country, each participant gains skills, experiences, and memories that will last a lifetime. (International Studies Abroad website: www.studiesabroad.com/)

The study abroad context is viewed by many US foreign language professionals as the quintessential learning experience, where students have unlimited access to the kinds of activity that promote development of communicative competence. Confidence in the study abroad experience is such that one university recently abolished its home curriculum in foreign languages in favour of systematic sojourns abroad for students . . . However, systematic research has yet to demonstrate universal effectiveness of study abroad for language learning. Rather, findings of empirical studies point to the significance of individual differences in a variety of contexts and learning situations . . . or suggest that language development in study abroad may be less dramatic than anticipated . . . (Kinginger and Farrell Whitworth, 2005: 3)

Stripped of the comfortable mastery of their first language and culture and societal adroitness, learners in immersion environment, such as study abroad, often report feeling as if those around them may perceive them to be unintelligent, lacking personality or humor, or as having the intellectual development of a small child. (Pellegrino, 2005: 9)

In these three quotations, the contrast between the ideal and the reality of study abroad (SA) programmes in the US is patent. The first quotation is taken from a website with information about SA programmes available to US university students. It is manifestly positive as it extols the virtues of the SA experience. In the second quotation, Celeste Kinginger and Kathleen Farrell Whitworth note the general tendency for SA organizers in the US to frame SA programmes as invaluable opportunities for students to be immersed in a TL culture. This immersion raises the prospect of any number of possible encounters with regular users of the TL, which in turn are assumed to lead to improved TL communicative competence. However, as Kinginger and Farrell Whitworth note, research has shown that the gains in the communicative competence may not be as great as anticipated for any number of reasons, ranging from the individual personality traits of students to the idiosyncrasies of particular contexts. Meanwhile, Valerie Pellegrino's statement focuses on how the SA experience affects the participant's sense of self. In her research, SA programmes involve participants in a move from home, and a broad range of familiar settings mediated by English, to a new and strange environment in which they are, in essence, reduced.

Over the past 15 to 20 years, there has been an expansion in the number of SA programmes in operation in the US, Europe and other parts of the world. And with this expansion has come an increase in the amount of published research about these programmes. For example, in the European context, there have been numerous publications examining the organization, monitoring and evaluation of the ERASMUS (European Community Action Scheme for the Mobility of University Students). The ERASMUS programme, which was launched in 1987, was designed as part of a general initiative to bring European Union universities closer together, administratively, pedagogically and philosophically. It allowed students to complete and receive full credit for one year of degree programmes in a variety of disciplines in another EU country. In a string of publications (e.g. Maiworm, Steube and Teichler, 1991, 1993; Maiworm and Teichler, 1996; Teichler and Maiworm, 1997), researchers document the experiences of ERASMUS students, whose numbers grew from just over 3,000 in 1987–88 to some 80,000 by 1993–94 (Teichler and Maiworm, 1997: 37; Coleman, 1998: 170) and 123,907 by 2002–03 (UK SOCRATES/ERASMUS council, www.erasmus.ac.uk). However, all of these studies and publications focus primarily on questionnaire data converted to statistics and what is lost in the process is a sense of the how participants lived the ERASMUS experience. There is little mention of identity and where there is, it relates to questionnaire items linked to stereotyping of national characteristics or participants' estimations of how much they have learned about the cultures of host countries.

Another body of European literature has attempted to capture the SA experience by using not only questionnaires but also diaries, field notes and interviews (e.g. Byram and Alred, 1993; Parker and Rouxeville, 1995; Byram, 1997; Snow and Byram, 1997; Mübig-Trapp and Schnitzer, 1997; Byram and Fleming, 1998; Payne and Smith, 1998; ADMIT, 2000; Roberts, Byram, Barro, Jordan and Street, 2001). In these publications, many of which have been concerned with British university students on Year Abroad programmes, there are two discernable areas of focus. On the one hand, authors have focused on the development of communicative competence, that is, development in grammar, accent and pragmatic ability. On the other hand, the studies have focused on the creation of spaces within which students can develop their intercultural competence (see discussion in Chapter 5). Of particular interest in the latter category are publications in which Year Abroad participants become ethnographers (e.g. Roberts et al, 2001). This transformation means that participants do not just go to live abroad for a period of time; rather they do so as researchers, actively collecting data and putting together projects focusing on different aspects of host country culture. While these studies do show a shift in subject positions from relatively passive student to active researcher and 'intercultural mediator' (Alred and Byram, 2002), they do not focus specifically on identity issues, such as the development of TL-mediated subject positions. A notable exception to this tendency is Elizabeth Murphy-Lejeune's extensive study of young Europeans moving across borders as part of study and teaching programmes. I will return to this study later in this chapter.

By far the largest body of literature on SA has been produced by researchers working in North America and, in particular, the US. In this literature, there is a division as regards focus, similar to the one I noted above in European-based publications. On the one hand, following what Kinginger and Farrell Whitworth say about the language achievement expectations of SA programmes, there have been numerous studies focusing primarily on TL development – the communicative competence cited above, or more specifically, grammar, pronunciation, vocabulary, pragmatics or learning strategies. Thus, in Barbara Freed's (1995) groundbreaking collection, *Second Language Acquisition in a Study Abroad Context*, and more recently, a special issue of *Studies in Second Language Acquisition* devoted to study abroad contexts (edited by Collentine and Freed, 2004), the contributions are about the development of different aspects of communicative competence, such as TL grammar, lexis, phonology and pragmatics, TL skills (speaking and reading) and TL communication strategies. A still more recent collection of papers, edited by Margaret DuFon and Eton Churchill (2006), is slightly more balanced as regards focus, although the majority of contributions are more about the development of TL communicative competence than anything else.

Still, along with large number of studies documenting the development of TL communicative competence, there have also been a good number of publications focusing on identity issues in the SA context, relating much more to what Pellegrino has in mind in her quote above, that is the effects of SA on the individual's sense of self. Laubscher (1994) is an early attempt to explore the experiential side of SA, providing a broad brush of how SA participants from an American university became, on the whole, more culturally aware during semester and year-long stays in Europe, Africa, the Middle East and East Asia. While Laubscher provides interesting accounts of how participants' attitudes evolved during their stays abroad, he does not enter the realm of identity. Indeed, his analytical framework is much more consistent with the social psychological approaches critiqued by Pavlenko (2002) and discussed in Chapter 3.

In this chapter, I focus on SA studies that do deal directly with identity issues, attempting, as I have in the previous two chapters, to see how the context under examination affords emergent TL-mediated subject positions. I begin with a topic that has occupied a great deal of space in publications: the reported sexual harassment of female American students and how such harassment has affected their opportunities to develop TL-mediated subject positions. I discuss in detail the findings of three oft-cited publications (Polanyi, 1995; Twombly, 1995; Talburt and Stewart, 1999) that have explored this issue in depth. My aim is to gain an understanding of how the SA experience may, in the end, be primarily about frustration at the inability to develop TL-mediated subject positions, as women feel threatened by male TL speakers and in some cases come to avoid going out. From sexual harassment, I move to more nuanced views of gender issues in SA, discussing research by Meryl Siegel (1995, 1996), Pellegrino (2005) and Kinginger and Farrell Whitworth (2005), carried out in Japan, Russia and France, respectively. While sexual harassment and heterosexual practices are elements in this research, other gender-related subject positions are brought to the fore as well.

In the second half of the chapter, I discuss other subject positions arising in SA experiences. First, I examine SA host family environments in which participants play the part of students and host family members the part of teachers. I then move to the emergent subject position of national identity, documented by some researchers. These discussions lead me to an attempt to bring together gendered, student and national subject positions by focusing on one particular case study (Kinginger, 2004).

At this point, I shift gears somewhat, suggesting that the kinds of identity issues arising in the US-based studies might well be more about the cultural baggage that American university students carry with them than about SA as the potential site of TL-mediated subject positions. To make my point, I examine two general alternative perspectives on SA. The first perspective is provided by Elizabeth Murphy-Lejeune (2002), in her in-depth study of European young people on three different SA programmes. The second is provided by authors such as Renae Skarin (2001) and Ingrid Piller and Kimie

Takahashi (2006), who have suggestive data about how Japanese women experience SA programmes in English-speaking countries such as Australia, the US and Britain. I close the chapter with some comments about the connections between SA and second language identity construction.

Sexual harassment in Russia

As I noted above, from the mid–1990s onwards, some SA researchers moved beyond the then-dominant interest in how SA impacted on linguistic development as they began to take into account the intercultural and identity-related aspects of such experiences. Rather than being based exclusively on a pre- and post-test orientation, these studies incorporated diaries and interviews as ways of collecting data. One area of interest for these researchers was how male and female students reported very different experiences during their stays abroad. In particular, there was a focus on the ways that women were positioned in their contacts with local men and, above all, reports of sexual harassment by female students came to be salient. In the context of this book, sexual harassment is significant because of its negative impact on a context that might otherwise provide multiple opportunities for TL-mediated identity work.

In an early discussion of sexual harassment in SA programmes, Livia Polanyi (1995) makes a distinction between what she terms 'ritual flirtation' as 'part of the ordinary business of daily life' (Polanyi, 1995: 280) and sexual harassment, as experiences that 'are universally unpleasant and lead to self-doubt, social awkwardness and worry' (Polanyi, 1995: 280). For Polanyi, a market scene, in which female students are called 'beautiful' by a Ukrainian vendor, is an example of ritual flirtation: it is a relatively harmless, albeit gratuitous, sexual overture that is easily handled by the women involved. By contrast, the following experience, recounted by a student named Hilda in her diary, clearly qualifies as sexual harassment:

What happened was I had a meeting with a friend of mine who I had known three years ago, who I thought was a really big black-marketeer, and this meeting didn't go very well because he decided that I was his woman immediately and he started to be extremely demanding of me and telling me who I could see, when I could see them, what my life was going to be like and everything like that. And I was feeling extremely uncomfortable during this exchange and very disgusted, because I couldn't make myself clear to him. I kept trying to explain in a very nice way, without being nasty or very direct, but really explaining that I didn't – even though I thought he was an attractive person – that I didn't want to have that kind of relationship with him, and it was very difficult because he wouldn't listen to me. And I was rather fed up with the whole thing. (Polanyi, 1995: 281–2)

Here Hilda describes how a meeting with someone she thought was a 'friend' became very uncomfortable for her when she realized that he was interested not in friendship, but in a sexual relationship and control over her movements. In a similar vein, another student named Silvia wrote about how a meeting in a Russian Orthodox Church, with a Russian acquaintance named Shura, became uncomfortable when the latter began making strange sexual overtures, physically crowding her and likening her to the Madonna. Silvia explains the outcome of her encounter as follows:

So, it was rather interesting. It was just the two of us hanging round in front of these icons and me kind of trying to put space between us in an impossible situation because there were people crowding around us. It was slightly stressful. I mean, I did not want to insult him, he kept saying, 'Oh. Well, I know why you don't like me, it's because I'm Russian and you think that we're all the stalking bears and you don't like me.' And that's not true. He's a nice person, but I don't know him very well, and it was just a weird situation. (Polanyi, 1995: 282)

In both of these cases, Hilda and Silvia reported that they felt silenced by their initial inability to make their positions clear to their interlocutors. However, as their fluency in Russian improved, both women were able to extract themselves from uncomfortable situations. In a later journal entry, Hilda explains how she was able to talk about such situations with a female Russian friend, who in turn gave her advice about how to act around Russian men and what to say when she felt harassed.

Polanyi goes on to explain how the women in the SA programme did not perform as well as the men on post-programme exams. For Polanyi, this is because they did not learn the Russian required for exams, but the language they needed to survive as single women subjected to sexual harassment. Polanyi explains:

> In Russia, in the field they are learning not to be 'Russian language speakers' but to be 'women Russian language speakers.' Rather than discussing music, politics and debating the relative merits of a totally free market based economy, they are learning how to get out of humiliating social encounters, how to interpret the intentions of even polite-seeming educated young men, how to get themselves home in one piece after an evening spent in fending off unwanted advances. (Polanyi, 1995: 289)

My interest here is not in the exam results of male and female students on this particular SA programme. Rather, it is in how sexual harassment mediated the development of gendered subject positions in Russian. In a sense, Hilda and Silvia found that the only subject position available to them in their interactions with Russian men, was sexual partner. This meant that they were not able to replicate, in any way, their self-positioning in English as relatively well-educated young women, able to talk about a variety of topics. They could not, in other words, develop heterosexual relationships consistent with their self-images. By contrast, men on the programme apparently were able to develop heterosexual masculinities with Russian women that were more consistent with their self-images as men prior to the SA programme. Indeed, they described their encounters with Russian women as romantic and fun, as well as filled with conversations round a wide variety of topics. In the following diary entry, a male student named Dorian describes an evening out with three women, one of whom became something akin to his date, in glowing terms:

> My Russian felt good, and her ongoing barrage of smiles certainly helped . . . We joked and chatted . . . My Russian was smooth and

flexible . . . The evening went wonderfully. We discussed music, art, economics, and film, along with politics. (Polanyi, 1995: 281)

Still, one ray of light for the women in Polanyi's study was their contact – and in some cases, perhaps even friendship – with Russian women. Hilda's conversation with a female Russian friend about how to handle Russian men shows that there were subject positions to be developed with Russian women that would qualify as more normal and certainly less 'weird', to use Silvia's description of her encounter with Shura. However, the prospect of making friends with female TL speakers as a counterbalance to sexual harassment is not always in evidence in SA programmes, as Twombly (1995) suggests.

Sexual harassment in Costa Rica

Susan Twombly (1995) is an account of how sexual harassment, manifested in *piropos* – that is, amorous and/or sexually explicit comments made by men to women in the street – and other forms of assertive male heterosexual behaviour, became the defining features of some American women's experiences in Costa Rica. In her study involving ten female students on an SA programme in Costa Rica during the academic year 1993–1994, she concludes that: 'For many women interviewed, *piropos* served as constant and powerful reminders not only of their sex, but also their status as outsiders in a foreign culture' (Twombly, 1995: 5).

It should be noted that *piropos* were not a surprise to these students, who had learned about this social practice prior to arriving in Costa Rica. And, as Twombly notes, they recognized a difference between 'good' and 'bad' *piropos*. The former might be a comment about nice clothes or elegance, along the lines of *'hola, angel'* (Hi, angel) or *guapa* (beautiful). The latter, by contrast, would be explicitly sexual in an unsubtle manner, as in the case of *'vamos a hacer el amor'* (Let's make love) or, more likely, the use of more explicit sexual terminology.

What these female students were not ready for, however, was only being exposed to what seemed to be 'bad' *piropos* and being exposed to little else whenever they came into contact with unknown men in the streets. Indeed, most of the women reported feeling nervous whenever they had to pass a group of men in the street. As one woman explained:

> I just wish that I could walk down the street. I always think when I walk by a man, and I don't want to pass them on the street. And I don't want to walk by them in a restaurant to pay for a meal, for example. For a while I felt like I didn't have a right to walk down the street. There is no reason I should feel badly for walking down the street in the middle of the day. You have to either ignore it or let it change your life . . . I feel intimidated by the men here. (Twombly, 1995: 7)

Reactions to this situation varied from changes in appearance to changes in behaviour. As regards the former, one woman joked that all blond women should dye their hair black, as she deemed being *rubia* (blond) as distinct in Costa Rica and an invitation for local men to say things to her in the street. However, a more serious change of appearance option, and one taken up by some of the women, was to wear different clothes, exchanging shorts for trousers or tight clothes for loose-fitting clothes. As regards changes in behaviour, some women opted for avoidance, simply not going out on their own very much, night or day. However, the reaction of some women to *piropos* was assertive rather than passive. These women fought back, either by answering back or even, in one case, by talking to men before they had a chance to say anything, good or bad.

   Unfortunately, none of these self-conscious changes in appearance or behaviour made the women feel better for very long and what emerged was a mistrust of Costa Rican men and little or no desire to be near them. At the same time, most of the women did not have any Costa Rican female friends away from classes they attended with Costa Rican students at the university. What emerged from this lack of contact was the near impossibility for some of the American women to develop TL-mediated feminine subject positions. Some of the women commented that their lives were very different from the lives of Costa Rican women, and that the latter, in effect, were superficial, overly concerned with their physical appearance and even hostile towards Americans:

> The attitude of women here toward North American women is unfriendly. Even if you try to smile they respond with dirty looks.

(Twombly, 1995: 9)

It is worth noting that not all of the women in Twombly's study reached the point where they had changed their physical appearance and behaviour, and had effectively given up on making their participation in the SA programme in Costa Rica an intercultural experience. Some did manage to gain membership in local communities of practice, such as one woman who played volleyball, and some did have less strained relationships with fellow university students, both male and female.

However, the thrust of Twombly's paper is not about positive experiences, but about sexual harassment and its effect on feminine subjectivities within the SA experience. It is about how, as Susan Ehrlich puts it, 'the degradation and humiliation associated with sexual harassment may restrict women's movements in the target culture, making them less likely to be exposed to target language input, and may create in women negative attitudes toward the target language and culture' (Ehrlich, 1997: 435). Like the female students in Polanyi's study, Twombly's students had trouble developing desirable TL-mediated subject positions, particularly those connected with their relationships with local men. But is it the case that the Costa Ricans, both male and female, are to blame for their plight?

Twombly offers some insight into why matters are not so simple when she discusses several ways in which many of the American students in Costa Rica in effect ensured that they would not establish relationships with Costa Ricans. First, there were meeting places only frequented by Americans, both male and female, and the existence and location of such places became well known both to the American and Costa Rican students. Thus, many of the SA students turned their stay in Costa Rica into an American affair, only spending time with 'their own'. This fairly deliberate move towards isolation from local people and activities is interesting when one considers how some of Twombly's informants referred to Costa Rican women as 'cliquish'.

In essence, some students came to see their fellow SA students as the kind of people they would most like to be around. For these students it was comfortable to experience Costa Rica with people like themselves, with similar backgrounds, points of view and ways of framing and engaging with the new and unknown. This was certainly the case for some of the women who, fed up with *piropos* and the attention they attracted from men in the street, opted to live a kind of feminist existence in the company of fellow female American students. But what kind of feminist existence? Certainly not an international one if one is to judge by the dismissive comments made by these students about Costa Rican women throughout Twombly's article. To my mind, among these students there was a lack of genuine intellectual engagement both with feminism in the US and feminism in Costa Rica and indeed other Latin American countries and beyond. And, as they did not engage with a problematized, nuanced and critical feminism, it was all too easy for them to label Costa Rican women as willingly submissive and to ignore ways of establishing links with these women. From the beginning, there was a strong tendency to frame Costa Rica as relatively backward socially and it is only a short step from such an entry point to position women as backward.

None of this is to take away from the unpleasant experiences reported by some of the women on the programme. However, it is to recognize, as Twombly does, that a part of the problem was the inability or even unwillingness to engage with Costa Rican women as equals. Interestingly, in an article published eight years after Twombly's, Adele Anderson (2003) recounts a very different Costa Rican SA experience. The students are once again American, but this time they are better informed about the host country and most importantly, they are armed with frameworks that convert them into temporary anthropologists or ethnographers (Roberts *et al,* 2001). For example, Anderson reports how students are not just allowed to take observed artefacts, such as how Costa Rican women always seem to be dressed up for even the most mundane of outings, and make assumptions about frivolousness, superficiality or submissiveness, as Twombly's students did. Rather, they must relate the artefact to what Anderson calls 'assumed social knowledge', such as how in the home, women are expected to keep their rooms neat and clean. Anderson relates such social knowledge to cultural logic, which she argues is something deeper and far reaching. In the case of the attention to dress and neatness, this deeper level has to do with *respeto* (respect), both for oneself and one's place in family and society.

For Anderson, it is important for SA students to develop the subject position of critical evaluator of the new social milieu in which they find themselves immersed. On the one hand, a move in this direction makes the experience more proactively about learning as opposed to reactively about feeling secure. And, it opens up the possibility of overcoming the unpleasant experience of receiving bad *piropos* via more active engagement with the local as opposed to a rejection of it. Finally, the result of further engagement with the local would make more likely the emergence of TL-mediated subject positions, especially through participation in specific activities that involve local people (e.g. playing sports, attending dance classes). Nevertheless, analysing and talking about sexual harassment, following Anderson's model, does not guarantee that the SA experience can be positive, as Talburt and Stewart (1999) show.

Sexual harassment in Spain

Susan Talburt and Melissa Stewart (1999) recount the story of Misheila, an African American university student on a five-week study abroad programme in Spain designed to develop her intercultural and communicative competence in Spanish. The programme, divided between Madrid (1 week) and Segovia (four weeks), combined language and culture classes with informal socializing. In the former classes, students studied not only Spanish language, but also history, literature, culture and commentary Spanish politics. Although there is no reference to a model of engagement with local history and sociology, as Anderson (2003; see above) was later to propose, the intention of classes with students was to 'encourage . . . students to draw on the historical background and contemporary culture offered in the course as frameworks for understanding their experiences in Spain' (Talburt and Stewart, 1999: 166). It was in such classes that Misheila first raised the issue of sexual harassment in the form of what Twombly (1995; see above) would term 'bad' *piropos*.

Misheila was a pre-med student in her last year of study. She was from a middle-class background and had grown up in a predominantly European American setting, somewhat isolated from African Americans. She thus had a sense of sticking out when growing up and she said that she had encountered racism during her lifetime in the US. She had been looking forward to her stay in Spain as a colour-free experience, during which she would learn about Spanish history and culture and improve her spoken Spanish. However, after her week in Madrid at the beginning of the SA programme, she stated emphatically in one of her classes: 'I'm not in a hurry to ever get back to Spain' (Talburt and Stewart, 1999: 168). The cause of her unhappiness was the *piropos* she was exposed to in the streets of Madrid, which included *morena* (dark one) *negrita* (little black one), *chocolate* (chocolate) and more elaborate sexual overtures. In Misheila's view, such comments were not only sexist but also racist as they sexualized her as an 'African' woman. She explained her plight as follows:

Mi observación es muy negativa. Para mí mientras estoy en España noto que mujer africana es un símbolo de sexualidad. Cuando camino en las calles siempre recibo comentos sobre piel y comentarios sexuales, especialmente con los viejos y adolescentes entre la edad de 15 y 20. Es muy difícil para mí y no pienso que es algo de cultura, es un mente ignorante. Cuando dicen comentarios a mí me siento que taking advantage que soy extraño y no tengo command de idioma. Y no me gusta.

My observation is very negative. For me, while I've been in Spain, I notice that the African woman is a symbol of sexuality. When I walk in the streets I always receive comments on my skin and sexual commentaries, especially with old men and adolescents between the age of 15 and 20. It's very difficult for me and I don't think it's something cultural, it is an ignorant mind. When they make commentaries to me I feel that they're taking advantage of me being different and not having command of the language. And I don't like it. (Talburt and Stewart, 1999: 168–9) [NB emphasis in original; translation provided by the authors.]

Although they accepted her disgust at the more sexually explicit *piropos,* Misheila's classmates, all of whom were White, initially did not accept outright her framing of her experiences as racialized. There was a tendency to point to Misheila's apparent beauty or the fact that the White female students on the programme also reported hearing such comments when walking in the street. Nevertheless, there was no denying that Misheila stuck out more than her classmates due to her skin colour and therefore that she had to deal with *piropos* not only as gendered phenomenon of retrograde masculinity, but also a racialized phenomenon. Thus, while a tall blond woman or red-headed man might also claim an inability to 'pass' as a Spaniard due to physical appearance, being Black was a step even further from the putative Spanish norm, which is, after all, European. Jacob, a male student on the programme who was surprised and even disturbed by Misheila's plight, put matters as follows:

> I've been very lucky because I've got a bit of camouflage. But Misheila has no camouflage. She is extremely noticeable, so I don't know what to say. I mean you can't say anything until you've experienced what . . . Misheila goes through. (Talburt and Stewart, 1999: 172)

All of this is a reminder of how subject positioning, as was observed in Chapter 2, is not just about '"achieved" or "inhabited" identity – the identity people themselves articulate or claim', but also '"ascribed" or "attributed" identity – the identity given to someone by someone else' (Blommaert, 2006: 238). Misheila clearly stated her wish to inhabit subject positions that were gender-less, race-less and free of overt sexuality. However, she found herself ascribed subject positions of male-objectified femininity, Blackness and hyper-sexuality.

Discussion

Thus far, I have examined the phenomenon of sexual harassment, as reported by American women on SA programmes in three different contexts – Russia, Costa Rica and Spain – and how it came to condition the kinds of subject positions adopted by these women. Examining the stories told by women like Hilda in Russia or Misheila in Spain, there can be little doubt that sexual harassment can be a defining factor of the SA experience and one that, in effect places strong constraints on the prospects of developing new TL-mediated subject positions. These cases of harassment might qualify as TL-mediated critical experiences, but they are critical experiences that push individuals away from the TL rather than moving them towards it. Ultimately, these experiences serve only to strengthen a gender identity grounded in the home (in this case, US) culture. However, as Polanyi, Twombly and Talburt and Stewart note, not all women experience sexual harassment when they go abroad, and perhaps with the exception of Misheila, sexual harassment never defines the entirety of the SA experience. Thus, Hilda and Silvia in Polanyi's study were able to forge relationships with Russian women, and the women in Twombly's study exposed to 'bad' piropos still managed to develop relationships with host family members.

Celeste Kinginger and Kathleen Farrell Whitworth (2005) have suggested that one problem with studies focusing so heavily on sexual harassment is that the phenomenon may come to dominate discussions of emergent gender subject positions in SA contexts. As regards the latter, they state that there is:

> the need for a more subtle account of . . . [gender-related issues] than the emphasis on sexism or harassment in the study abroad literature would allow. It has been established that American women often recount experiences of sexism in the study abroad context. However, when these learners encounter gender-related differences, it is not just a matter of local interactional norms which may or may not sanction the activities known in the US as 'sexual harassment', it is also a matter of how broader and historically-situated ideologies of gender are instantiated in the U.S. and in the study abroad context. (Kinginger and Farrell Whitworth, 2005: 1–2)

Meryl Siegal (1995, 1996) is an example of a relatively early study that did explore gender in terms of historically situated ideologies, specifically discourses of femininity in conflict. For 18 months, Siegal followed four White western professional women who were studying intermediate- to advanced-level Japanese in Japan. She found that despite their desires to achieve the status of valid Japanese interlocutor, her informants resisted politeness and honorific norms to varying degrees. In effect, for these women the available discourses of femininity in Japan constituted unacceptable and demeaning behaviour, what they called speaking 'in a squeaky voice' and being 'too humble' (M. Siegal, 1995: 234; 1997: 356). In interviews with Siegal these women manifested their gender identity dissonance and as if deliberately to flaunt all norms of protocol, one woman, Arina, used a speech she was giving to a group of Japanese businessmen to air her grievances about Japan, criticising the slowness of public services and racism in Japanese society.

Siegal's work is an important move towards more nuanced views of gender. In addition, she does focus in an interesting manner on the development of pragmatic competence and the presentation of self (Goffman, 1959, 1981). However, her study is somewhat limited as regards the presentation of learner stories. In fairness to Siegal, her stated aim in the study was to explore the development of socio-linguistic competence and specifically pragmatic competence. In the next section, I move to a more detailed examination of two recent studies that have managed to delve more deeply into learners' stories and have done so with a view to explore more nuanced gendered subject positions of SA participants. I refer to Pellegrino (2005) and Kinginger and Farrell Whitworth (2005), which focus on SA programmes in Russia and France, respectively.

Gendered subject positions in Russia

Valerie Pellegrino's *Study Abroad and Second Language Use: Constructing the Self* is a detailed account of the experiences of 17 American students, in Moscow and St Petersburg for one or two semesters, during the academic year 1995–96. In this book, sexual harassment is not discussed in depth, although Pellegrino does provide several examples of female students recounting their experiences with Russian men. In one case, a student named Rebeccah recounts her experience of being squeezed and touched by 'a drunk stinky old man' (Pellegrino, 2005: 82) while travelling on a tram, and how she received no assistance from other travellers when she began to yell at him in Russian. Rebeccah explains how she eventually had to push the man down some stairs. Although she seems to have defended herself effectively she was, not surprisingly, shaken by the event.

Echoing the participants in Twombly's (1995) study, some women on the programme wrote and spoke of how it seemed impossible to establish platonic relationships with Russian men and how Russian men had 'unreasonable expectations', always wanting sex before all else. A student named Jill summed up these feelings as follows:

> I haven't met any Russians I could really talk to or feel comfortable with. Mostly just guys who try to hit on me – I've avoided talking to Russian men in general. I'm not interested, and I have a hard time telling who's nice and who isn't. (Pellegrino, 2005: 81)

Another student, Madeline, reported that she often received undue attention from men, although none of these situations is presented as graphically as Rebeccah's or Jill's. Madeline was the only African American in Pellegrino's research sample, and she reported that she was often singled out due to her skin colour. However, in her recounted experiences with men, she did not emphasize race as an important element. Indeed, in her reports she was the one who came across as someone with a propensity to judge people by physical appearance. Like Jill, cited above, she perhaps had 'a hard time telling who's nice and isn't' (Pellegrino, 2005: 81). For example, on one occasion she wrote about how a strange man tried to join a card game that she and her American friends had organized while on a train journey. She described the scene as follows:

> We caught the attention of this stranger whom we assumed to be rude and/or creepy. At first he was seated behind me, but turned around in his seat to look over at our game. Then he actually switched seats in order to sit across from us. I was slightly nervous because an old man had tried to kiss my hand and although I've come to terms with the attention I get I still get on my guard . . . If I hadn't known better I would have pegged him for a mafia bodyguard. I think that his apperence [sic] had a lot to do with how I treated him, how I regarded him. (Pellegrino, 2005: 49)

However, after a while, the man began talking to the group of Americans and eventually he joined their card game. Madeline admitted that she had judged him by his appearance and that she had been wrong, stating that they all 'ended up having a lot of fun' (Pellegrino, 2005: 50).

In another journal entry, written soon after the previous one, Madeline tells of another man who approached her and another American woman, again on a train.

> We had been relaxing and chatting away for some time when a handsome young man approached us and asked us if he could join us. I was slightly dumbstruck because even though I understood the question, I couldn't believe that he would have anything to do with us, the reason being russian [*sic*] women these days are so much deadlier in style, more chic, etc. (Another one of my assumptions) . . . *Yura* in his suave Italian [*sic*] bergandy [*sic*] suit and raw russet loafers was quite cool, charming and odd. (Pellegrino, 2005: 72)

In this case, Madeline treated the man's approach as unthreatening from the beginning, perhaps because he was 'a handsome young man'. Her story is instructive because she turned what could have been seen as an encounter with a pushy man, edging his way into her conversation with her friend, into an experience pleasant enough for her to have remembered his name. It is also of interest because it introduces the notion of Madeline's 'assumption' about Russian women, that they are 'deadlier in style' and 'chic', presumably more so than American women.

Finally, there is the issue of Russian feminine subject positions in contacts with men. On one occasion, a student named Camille related the following anecdote about a conversation with her host mother, Olga, just prior to attending an event organized for a former Yale professor and Japanese businessmen:

> Olga told me in Russian that when I meet these big wigs at the Metropol for lunch I should act shy and open to their words of wisdom. This sickened me. I didn't want to here [sic] how I should act like a blank slate, young, sweet and impressionable, opinion-less, and kiss-ass, because these people are smart. (Pellegrino, 2005: 80)

Here an older woman is telling Camille to act passively, an option that Camille resents. However, in the remainder of Pellegrino's book, there are no other references to women acting passively and on the whole, Pellegrino devotes relatively little space to gender related issues around male-female relationships, feminine subjectivities and the embodiment of femininity. However, in their study of three American university students on a study abroad programme in France in 2003, Kinginger and Farrell Whitworth (2005) do just this.

Gendered subject positions in France

Against the backdrop of the war in Iraq and concerns about idealized versions of femininity, Kinginger and Farrell Whitworth (2005) recount how three students had very different experiences during their semester-long SA programme in France in Spring 2003. One informant, Deirdre, was uneasy about French femininity and she perceived French women as 'snotty', overly concerned with physical appearance and excessively tolerant of French men who approached them with no apparent compunction. In addition, she thought there was 'no respect' for women in French society, citing the ubiquity of naked women in French advertising to make her point. In the following interview excerpt, all of her concerns come together:

> I've noticed that there's <u>no respect</u> to women. I'm not feminist by any means, but I feel like again with guys and the way they talk to girls when they're going down the street, I mean, I just think that there's no respect for them at all. There's naked women pictured in ads everywhere just half naked in their lingerie, um and I guess I mean the French are more comfortable with women being naked. You see it on the beach all the time, but I mean it's just <u>everywhere</u> I go I feel like there's some sort of harassment that I can expect. No matter how I'm dressed, or no matter what I look like that day, no matter how I'm presenting myself, like if I'm coming back from the beach, or I'm coming back from <u>class</u>. I just <u>expect</u> it. (Kinginger and Farrell Whitworth, 2005: 9) (NB: (1) underlined portions indicate emphasis in the original and (2) punctuation has been slightly changed by this author to aid readability.)

As a result of her rejection of this French femininity, nudity and the particular dynamic of heterosexual interaction patterns she observed, Deirdre in essence opted out of the SA programme, avoiding contact with French people and culture, and ultimately the French language. She sought and found refuge from all things French in a self-image of American femininity as 'more athletic', 'laid back' and 'having a good time with whatever they're doing' (Kinginger and Farrell Whitworth, 2005: 9) as well as the opportunities she had for contact with Americans. One such opportunity was access to the computer facilities in the programme's student centre, which in turn allowed her unlimited email contact with her friends and family in the US. Another opportunity was a programme of organized outings and excursions which attempted to 'shelter American students from the atmosphere of sociopolitical tensions that had emerged from French opposition to the US-led invasion of Iraq in the Spring of 2003' (Kinginger and Farrell Whitworth, 2005: 9).

In marked contrast to Deirdre, Jada used her SA experience to meet people, explore as a much of French culture as she could and, as she put it, 'be French'. Jada developed an active social life among the international students in her residence hall and manifested a curiosity that took her beyond merely observing difference to attempting to understand it. She therefore manifested more of what Byram and others (e.g. Byram, 1995; Alred and Byram 2002; see Chapter 5 in this book) term *savoir apprendre,* that is the ability to learn from contact with other cultures. Nevertheless, Jada was similar to Deirdre in her dislike of the way that French men approached and spoke to women they did not know. As she put it, 'the guys are like the *dragueurs* [flirts] and the girls . . . wait to be approached and they enjoy that attention . . .' (Kinginger and Farrell Whitworth, 2005: 12). However, unlike Deirdre, she was able to recount how she dealt with such cases, as the following interview excerpt shows:

When I was at the Internet café the other day some guy heard Liz and I. Um she was speaking to me in English and I was just typing along and the guy started to talking to us and was like: 'Oh you speak English. I would like to speak English with you.' And we were like – I was very like: 'I'm sorry we're actually in the middle of making our plans to go somewhere, so maybe afterwards.' And I was just trying to be very like polite and then like he came up behind us and like he put his arms – like his hands on our back. And I <u>don't</u> like being touched by anyone I don't know. I'm a very affectionate person. Like I'll hug my friends, I don't care. But when I <u>don't</u> know you, do not touch me. And I was like: 'OK, you're disgusting.' And he was like: 'Well, if you need help with your French.' And I was like: 'No, I speak French <u>very</u> well, thank you.' And like told him in French, like I speak ver- and like I don't think I speak ver- speak <u>very</u> well, but like I just felt the need to tell him: . . . *je parle français très très bien merci.* (Kinginger and Farrell Whitworth, 2005: 12) (NB: (1) underlined portions indicate emphasis in the original; (2) punctuation has been slightly changed by this author to aid readability; (3) French portion italicized by this author.)

Such experiences, and Jada's positive way of recounting them to the researchers, suggest that Jada was more immersed in and attuned to the French environment surrounding her than Deirdre was. And in the end, Jada had a far more rewarding and educative experience than Deirdre, coming to terms with the constraints on her original intention to 'be French' while developing a degree of intercultural competence. Thus she was, paraphrasing Byram (1995), able to use her linguistic competence and her sociolinguistic awareness of how language and context interact to manage her French conversations, the misunderstandings caused by differences in values, meanings and beliefs, and the affective and cognitive demands of her ongoing engagement with otherness. Still, there is no indication in Kinginger and Farrell Whitworth that Jada developed new French-mediated feminine subject positions. There is no mention of making friends with French women and if the story above is anything to judge by, her relationships with French men were more about resisting pressure than engagement. It seems that like Deirdre, Jada perhaps did not attain membership in any French mediated communities of practice and she was thus left to spend much of her free time with other Americans on the programme.[1]

Altogether, Jada's SA experience, like Deirdre's, was a far cry from that of Bill, identified by the authors as 'one of the few male participants in . . . [the] study' Kinginger and Farrell Whitworth, 2005: 13). Bill was a business student who had enrolled on a business-oriented programme of study in France. He saw his SA experience as an opportunity to learn about French family values and community spirit. Perhaps the most defining aspect of his experience was the way that he developed contacts with French people via participation in particular activities such as playing video games and playing football. In addition, he embraced cultural differences such as how the French media coverage of the war in Iraq was almost the opposite of that found in the mainstream US media. However, Bill's openness to all things French had its limits, namely in the form of his attitudes towards French men. Like Deirdre and Jada, he found their advances towards women to be lacking in subtlety and qualified them as harassment. He even recounted, with pride, his attempts to repel French men trying to talk to French women with whom he was already talking (the irony of embracing all things French, yet adopting an American form of chivalry, seemed to be lost on Bill). In the following excerpt, Bill explains his dealings with French men:

> I can't say how many times I have like been so forward when like French guys come up to French girls and I have to – with American friends, like they've said 'no' a couple of times, like annoyed them. And I can see it in their face and so I take it upon myself, like: 'Look'. Like first – I'll literally dance with them, literally like. I have no problem. I mean, I would dance with them and if they don't get the point, I'll start yelling at them like: '<u>Go away</u>.' Like: 'You're not wanted here.' And I just don't – like: What's wrong?' Like: 'What don't you understand here?' (Kinginger and Farrell Whitworth, 2005: 14) (NB: (1) underlined portions indicate emphasis in the original and (2) punctuation has been slightly changed by this author to aid readability.)

As regards French women, Bill painted a picture that was both similar to and different from that painted by Deirdre and Jada. Like Deirdre and Jada, he talked about the sense of style that French women exuded. However, unlike the two women, he did not see French women as passive beings waiting for French men to approach them. Rather he denounced American women, who he said 'have absolutely no opinion about anything' (Kinginger and Farrell Whitworth, 2005: 14), and contrasted them with French women whom he saw as 'assertive' with men and willing and able to express their views.

Kinginger and Farrell Whitworth note how the different ways of framing and dealing with French femininities and masculinities impacted directly on the students' French language development while in France, with Bill making far more progress than Jada or Deirdre. However, as regards the emergence of French-mediated subject positions, none of the three seem to have progressed very far. Deirdre, in effect, dropped out early on in the face of feminine subject positions that she could not and would not engage with and masculinities she found intrusive. Jada also rejected French femininities and masculinities, although she did socialize with students living in her residence hall and she reported that she had at least spoken to French men about the rules of the heterosexual market (Eckert, 1989). However, her response to being told that French women are expected to 'make themselves up and dress in tight clothes, so that . . . [men] can look at them' and that the French women effectively 'know that', was to say that the entire situation reminded her of 'the 1950s in America' (Kinginger and Farrell Whitworth, 2005: 11–12). Meanwhile, Bill seemed to engage most with French culture, although the result of his engagement was mixed. On the one hand, he celebrated French femininity – the way French women think and act – while he positioned French men as annoying. Or, as Kinginger and Farrell Whitworth put it:

> Bill . . . celebrates images of French femininity while resisting what he perceives to be normative French masculinity. At the same time, he posits the superiority not only of American masculine practices of avoiding sexual harassment and honoring gender equity, but also his own role as defender of French girls. (Kinginger and Farrell Whitworth, 2005: 14–15)

For Kinginger and Farrell Whitworth, the backdrop to the stories of these three students are discourses of French-ness: of men as effete, sexually obsessed and pleasure-seeking, and women as confident and controlled, as well as naturally elegant. In different ways, the three students have all positioned themselves vis-à-vis these discourses, which in a sense means that they lived their SA experience primarily, if not exclusively, framed by these discourses. One result of this experience filtered by discourses of French-ness is that none of the three students seems to have been transformed by their stay in France, which therefore had served to strengthen their American national identities over all else. In Deirdre and Jada's case, this was because American women presumably have more rights than French women (a highly contentious notion, to be sure). For Bill, it was because everything in his experience affirmed his American masculinity: he positioned himself as a better man than French men, and as able to deal with assertive and elegant French women.

Thus far, I have devoted a good deal of space to sexual harassment, the nuances of male-female heterosexual interaction and images of femininity and masculinity, by focusing on relevant cases presented in selected publications. In literature dealing with sexual harassment (e.g. Polanyi, 1995; Twombly, 1995; Talburt and Stewart, 1999), there is an interest in how negative experiences with men have affected the TL-development of women. However, my interest here has been in how these experiences constrain the potential for the development of TL-mediated subject positions. In the cases reviewed, there is little doubt that women on SA programmes can find their prospects for developing TL-mediated subject positions constrained and curtailed by the self-imposed limitations on their movement that come as a result of having been sexually harassed by strange men in public.

As regards the norms of the heterosexual market, in publications such as Pellegrino (2005) and Kinginger and Farrell (2005), a broader view is provided, one that moves beyond an exclusive focus on sexual harassment. In Pellegrino's study, women did report negative experiences; however, they also reported a whole range of nonthreatening and even positive experiences. In Kinginger and Farrell Whitworth (2005), the authors show how a crucial backdrop to the SA experiences of their informants was the imagery of what French women and men are like.

However, while issues related to gendered subject positions have been a prominent thread in much of the writing about American SA programmes, not all publications have focused on such issues. There are other subject positions arising in SA experiences. It is to these that I now turn.

Teacher–student subject positions in SA experiences

Perhaps because SA programmes begin their lives inside FL contexts, one default subject position for participants, seemingly always waiting in the wings, is that of student. Of course, this student subject position goes through some changes when moved from an exclusively FL context to one that is more complex. Thus, as was observed in Chapter 5, when FL contexts included Internet-mediated exchanges, students mentored each other in English and French, acting alternately as teachers and students. In the SA context, participants still act as students in formal classroom settings. In some cases, this is because they attend classes organized and taught by the universities that have sent them abroad and they know that there will be tests when their sojourn is over. In other cases, it is because they are attending classes at a local university.

Adopting a student subject position in such situations is not particularly surprising and indeed, would seem to be merely a continuation of life at home. However, what is slightly surprising is to see student and teacher roles reprised when SA participants attempt to use the TL with members of their host families or with strangers in the street. On the one hand, there is no reason for host family members or perfect strangers to adopt the subject position of teacher. On the other hand, there is no reason for SA participants to play along by acting as students. However, such transformations of interlocutors, in which communication is mixed with pedagogy, are perhaps more common than one might imagine.

Writing about Americans on an SA summer programme in France, Sharon Wilkinson (2002) explores how members of host families often adopted the subject position of teacher while SA participants acted as students. Thus, in the following two excerpts from Wilkinson's field notes about a student named Heather and an interview with Heather, respectively, the host father and mother act as teachers:

> Sitting outside in the courtyard before dinner, Heather was recounting Saturday evening's adventure *'à le concert de Aerosmith'* to her host parents and me. Her host father smiled, *'Heather, il faut*

faire encore un stage ici – "*à le*" *c'est pas français, ça'* (Heather, you need to do another session here – 'à le', that's not French), referring to the obligatory contraction of *à* and *le* in French to *au*. Heather stopped mid-sentence and paused.

'*Il te faut rester encore un mois'* (You need to stay another month), her host father repeated with the same twinkle in his eye, "'*à le*" *c'est pas français*.'

'Oh,' Heather giggled a little, eyes averted, *'au concert*.' (Wilkinson, 2002: 159)

I remember one time. It was when we had come back from a trip . . . and she said, 'Oh, do you want something to eat?' and I said, 'No, I'm not hungry. I ate on the train.' But I said, 'J'ai mangé sur le train,' instead of 'J'ai mangé dans le train.' And so, you know, it conjugates [sic] the picture of me sitting on top of the train, speeding along, eating the bread . . . She corrected me on a lot of little things like that, which, you know, have totally stuck in my mind. I will always remember them. (Wilkinson, 2002: 160)

Wilkinson notes how on such occasions, host family members were more concerned with the form being used by their lodgers than the meaning they were trying to convey. This behaviour is symptomatic of a generalized metalinguistic awareness among French people as regards the proper way to speak French, what is or is not truly French, as Heather's host father puts it. In my study of French foreign language teachers in London (Block, 2001, 2002b, 2005a, 2006a), I too encountered this discourse of grammar as vital to the French language. For example, one informant, FN, described how French primary school students are imbued with knowledge about how their language works as a system, stating that she had been, 'from the age of six, . . . raised on . . . grammar' (Block, 2001: 303). Meanwhile, another informant, DC, described matters as follows, setting the initiation into grammar slightly later:

Because . . . in France we're even taught this at the age of 8, or 9 or 10 . . . As soon as you know how to write and read, now let's start with grammar . . . And of course, it is really difficult. But then you come to the age of 13 or 14, and we understand . . . (Block, 2001: 303)

Elsewhere, in her study of Americans) on an SA programme in Russia, Pellegrino (2005) also found correction by host family members to be an important part of participants' experiences. Pellegrino categorized such correction as either 'harsh' or 'gentle'. An SA participant named Rebeccah wrote in her diary about an example of the former type of correction as follows:

> Tonight was Russian *Pashka* (Easter). So I was at the dinner table w/ my family. And it happened that I had to talk a lot. I kept screwing up my cases of numbers. Then Irina said, 'I give you *dvoyka* ("D") tonight in Russian. You've been here since Sept. blah blah . . . *You shouldn't be making these mistakes.*' I felt very bad. And after that comment I just shut up. I didn't want to provoke her again w/ my *dvoyka russkii* [sic] ('D' Russian). Was she trying to be mean? Or is that just her nature. (Pellegrino, 2005: 60)

This example of host family correction happened near the end of Rebeccah's stay and it came after she had had similarly humiliating experiences with her economics lecturer at the local university. Just as the French host families' behaviour in Wilkinson's study mirrored French educational culture, so too did Irina's behaviour vis-à-vis Russian educational culture. Pellegrino describes harsh correction in Russian education as follows:

> The Russian educational system . . . values directness and considers poor performance to be a sign of inadequate preparation on the part of the student. In front of their peers, students may be told they are bad or lazy in an effort to encourage them to work harder to avoid such comments in the future. (Pellegrino, 2005: 57)

However, not all host family corrections reported were harsh. Another programme participant, Jim, describes in his diary how his fiancée's host mother corrected his pronunciation in a gentle way:

> Galina would correct my pronunciation or case ending from time to time, but in a non-judgemental way. She would say the word and ask me to repeat it, when she was satisfied, we continued . . . There were occasional times when Galina would lose me, but

we would banter back and forth until I understood, and then we would continue. (Pellegrino, 2005: 61)

In addition, there were corrections by interlocutors in service encounters, as Wilkinson notes in her study. Rebeccah explains how being laughed at by a grocery store cashier became humorous as opposed to face-threatening for her:

> I was in a grocery store today & needed to buy a box of chocolate. So I chose one & brought it to the cashier. I needed to make sure there were more than 11 pieces of candy in the box, so I said, *'mozhno schitat skol'ko shtukov* [sic] *est' v korobke?'* (may I count how many pieces there are in the box?) I knew it had to be genitive plural – but I wasn't sure how to form it. The cashier just started laughing at me! So I knew I made a mistake! Surprisingly though, this did not put me off. I began laughing too. And at the end of the transaction, we were both smiling. And I didn't feel dumb – and I didn't falter or stutter. It was just fun & funny. And once gain I think it was her attitude that made me feel at ease. (Pellegrino, 2005: 64)

Be they harsh, gentle or even lightly ridiculing (as in the latter example), corrections came to signify a reduction of SA participants to the status of children. Throughout the book, there are numerous references by informants to feeling as if they could not be themselves in Russian. Rebeccah, for example, stated on one occasion that:

> In my eyes, my utterances are like ghost towns. They're just sounds, with no color or meaning. People use language to express their unique characteristics and personality. When I use Russian, there is no substance in my sentences. There's no ME in my Russian. I'm surprised that people even understand me at all here. (Pellegrino, 2005: 88)

Julie, another student on the programme, expressed the same sentiment even more graphically:

> The more I think about it, the more I realize that I have the vocabulary of a 5-year-old here! It's a little frustrating to realize that

I really do use mindless constructions like *'ya budu ochen' rada . . .'* (I will be very glad . . .) all the time! There's really nothing I can do about it, aside from working at learning new constructions, but it was interesting when today, as I was brainstorming questions for editors, I realized that even when I speak English now I don't use complex sentences. Argh! Russia has turned me into a monosyllabic *MORON!* (Pellegrino, 2005: 173)

For Pellegrino, there is an issue of low self-esteem, or a lessened sense of self-respect, and a lack of self-efficacy, that is the feeling that one is not fully in control of one's environment and therefore incapable of performing adequately. She expresses a concern at a certain self-fulfilling prophecy at work: in short, SA participants lose faith in themselves and therefore perform to a lower standard. However, beyond Pellegrino's concern with converting the SA programme into a successful language learning experience, there is also an issue of why young American university students in Russia – and indeed young American students in Costa Rica, France, Spain and elsewhere – often seem to enter what might be termed a 'discomfort zone', in which they feel that they have no control over who they are. For if there is one common thread running through accounts of sexual harassment, the difficulty of finding acceptable TL-mediated gendered subject positions and balance as both learner and user of the target language, it is the realization that events, activities and behaviour in the TL environment are well and truly 'foreign' – not just theoretically foreign, but experienced as foreign – and that things back home are different, and perhaps better.

Enhanced national identity

As has been noted by authors writing on the subject (e.g. Billig, 1995; Smith, 2004; Joseph, 2004), national identity is, like other forms of identity, emergent in day-to-day practices. To varying degrees in all of the studies discussed thus far, there has been a reported enhancement of national identity during the SA experience and, indeed, national identity emerges as a subject position trumping all others when a student's individual sense of self is thrown into crisis.

Thus, the women in Polanyi (1995), Twombly (1995) and Talburt and Stewart (1999) all found that their inhabited identities as *American* women became salient as they grappled with how to interpret, make sense of and deal with local men deemed sexually aggressive towards them. Polanyi notes how the women in her study came to frame sexual harassment, not as something that happened to them because of their deficient Russian, but because some of the men they encountered tried to exploit their foreignness. In her study, Twombly mentions the 'Gringo tree', a place where American students would gather every day to talk, a home-like meeting place for students who were tired of dealing with foreignness. Finally, Talburt and Stewart reproduce the following comment, made by a male student named Jacob, about the affinity that American students on the SA programme in Spain felt for each other:

> '[I]t's closed circuit, so to speak. It's a close-knit group, and back home, it's all open . . . You would be much more critical about whether you would be friends with that person or not. Whereas here, you're not, you're all in it together . . . You go out in packs, and make jokes about things because you're comparing this culture with your culture back home.' (Talburt and Stewart, 1999: 171)

Meanwhile, in their studies of SA programmes in Russia and France, Pellegrino (2005) and Kinginger and Farrell Whitworth (2005) also show how when the going gets tough for SA students, the subject position of the American abroad emerges as dominant. In Pellegrino, there are no overtly nationalistic references in the comments of students, for example to a putative superiority of American culture. However, contacts with host families, Russians in the street and the Russian educational system led many students to make reference to how they were more complete human beings in English as they expressed feelings ranging from rejection to disbelief when confronted with different Russian ways and norms. Similarly, in Kinginger and Farrell Whitworth, American gendered subject positions – femininities and masculinities – were framed as superior to their French counterparts, with French masculinities coming in for the most derision.

The idea that SA experiences might lead, not to greater intercultural awareness, but to an enhanced sense of national identity, has been dealt with more explicitly by several authors. For example, in her study of American students on a study abroad programme in France, Wilkinson (1998a) has the following to say:

> The participants in this study experienced a transition in the salience of their American identity in moving from familiar to foreign surroundings. In the predeparture foreign language learning setting of their American classroom, students' first language identities did not seem to be an important issue . . . Upon arrival in France, however, latent home culture and language identities were aroused. Suddenly 'American' became a salient label . . . [T]he formation of American peer groups seemed to serve an important function: it provided the confirmation of native identity necessary to enable the students to face the potentially threatening situations of linguistic and cultural difference. (Wilkinson, 1998a: 32)

In an attempt to chart this and other kinds of socio-affective evolution, authors such as Acton and Walker de Felix (1986), Laubscher (1994), Bacon (1995), Wilkinson (1998b) and Isabelli-García (2006) examine possible stages that SA participants go through. Different authors use different methodologies, but there is a general pattern of movement from initial euphoria to horror before a final stage of balance. This balance might be some degree of intercultural competence or what Isabelli-García (2006), drawing on Bennett (1986), calls 'ethno-relativism'. However, it might also be – and often is – greater ethno-centricism and a strengthened sense of national identity.

In her study, Isabelli-García (2006) charts the extent to which four Americans on an SA programme in Argentina reported in diaries and logs that they were moving towards this ethno-relativism. In particular, Isabelli-García was interested in whether or not the four were able to join established speech communities and build up social networks (Milroy, 1987) in their host environment. However, in three cases, it seems that there remained, to varying degrees, a great deal of ethno-centricism and a tendency to be condescending towards and critical of Argentines, positioning them as inferior to Americans. Thus, when one student, Tom, was unhappy about the lack of resources available in the local university library and his inability to get simple tasks accomplished, he wondered if 'the people will have the training and knowledge to advance as they want' (Isabelli-García, 2006: 245). Meanwhile, another student named Sam turned a comment about corruption in Argentina to a ridiculing of claims by some Argentines (e.g. former president Carlos Menem) that they live in a 'First World' country:

> Corruption here is quite rampant . . . Somebody told me that the police had to take cuts from whores, black market people to even be able to operate. And Menem calls this a First World country . . . Argentines seem to think they are the shit of South America for some reason. I read an article in a newspaper here that made some statement about the fact that God was Argentine. Whatever. (Isabelli-García, 2006: 247)

Another student, Jennifer, made reference to the attitudes of Argentine men towards women, turning her comment into a nationality comparison that favoured the US over Argentina:

> When I am running in the park alone, the men playing soccer often stop and look and yell things at me. That would never happen in the US. I think it stems from arrogance because they think that all women want to impress them. (Isabelli-García, 2006: 250)

Running through these three comments is default American national identity, one which Isabelli-García qualifies as 'patronizing' and 'hegemonic', in that it serves to maintain the premise that the US is superior to all other countries, in particular those lying south of its borders. Clearly, for the students in Isabelli-García's study, as well as for those in the other studies discussed above, the SA experience can mean an enhanced affiliation to one's inherited national identity as opposed to the development of greater intercultural sensitivity.

Of gendered, student and national subject positions: A case study

Thus far, the discussion in this chapter has moved towards a view of the SA context as fertile ground for the emergence of subject positions related to gender, student identity and nationality, albeit subject positions that seem to be more about home culture than TL culture. I have dealt with these subject positions in piecemeal fashion, as I have sewn together the comments of different students, and voices. However, I have not followed one particular student in depth and in longitudinal fashion. In this section, I examine one case study that does just this. My aim is to see how the background and experience of an individual can shape the emergence of gender, student and national identities in the SA context.

Kinginger (2004) charts the trials and tribulations of Alice, 'a highly motivated learner who has overcome significant personal, social, and material obstacles to her learning of French' (Kinginger, 2004: 219), over a period of four years, from 1997 to 2000. One significant obstacle for Alice to overcome was her upbringing by a single mother, an itinerant tree planter who never lived in one place for very long. Growing up whilst moving from one place to another, Alice was home schooled for most of her education and finished high school when she was 16. Unfortunately, she was probably too immature to deal with the responsibility of being a full-time student, financing her studies by working for the same university where she studied. Over the next three years, she dropped out of university, lived with a boyfriend, split up with him, lived a transient existence and ended up pregnant at the age of 19. Faced with the prospect of never being able to study again, Alice decided to change her life. First, she gave her baby up for adoption and second she returned to university to major in French.

She studied and worked for three years before going on an SA programme which would take her first to Quebec for an intensive French course, and then to France. Through face-to-face interviews and Alice's diary entries, Kinginger acts as a witness to Alice's evolution from her university studies to her SA programme and back in the US. During this time, Alice moved from naïve and starry-eyed admirer of all things French to unhappy student in French, before settling into a more stable and balanced orientation to the language.

Kinginger highlights how Alice, once she had gone back to university to study, set up becoming proficient in French as her primary goal. Harbouring an idealized view of French language and culture, during her time in France she wanted – and indeed expected – to be able to join an imagined community of French speakers associated with the lofty ideals of 'equal rights and liberty' as well as 'abstract and universal ideas' (Kinginger, 2004: 228). As she explained in an interview carried after she had completed her SA programme:

> I guess I expected some kind of cultural consciousness, I don't know like everyone would be really cultural . . . I really thought that I was gonna meet a lot of friendly old people and even young people who would think that I was interesting and umm that would invite me into their lives and you know tell me about themselves and teach me about being French, and help with the language and would ask me questions about my country etc. etc. (Interview October 2000) (Kinginger, 2004: 228)

However, when Alice finally did go to France, after an intensive five-week French language course in Quebec, she did not find this welcoming community of French speakers.

In total, Alice spent two years in France. During the first year, she took language courses in Caen and Lille, attending local university courses as well in the latter. During the second year, she attempted, on her own, to study at the University of Lyon. In the studies of SA programmes reviewed thus far, one constant has been the way that students always have the default option of spending time with their compatriots. However, for Alice this option was neither viable nor desirable. First, she was older than most of the students on the programme and, in addition, had lived through experiences (e.g. teenage pregnancy) that they had only read about or seen on television. Second, she was not from a middle-class family and therefore had not had the privileged upbringing of her fellow students. She also had to watch her spending as she had a limited amount of money, the money she had saved while working in various jobs during the year she spent preparing for her SA experience.

Self-exiled from the circle of SA participants and finding it hard to negotiate her contacts with French people, Alice found her two or three months, first in Caen and then in Lille, difficult. Eschewing a social life with her fellow SA participants, she was left to develop contacts with French people. However, when she started attending classes at the University of Lille, she found that not only were the French students not interested in her, but also that she did not like the way that they talked amongst themselves while the professors were lecturing. The refusal to develop a common American-student-abroad subject position coupled with her inability and refusal to develop a French-university-student subject position, left Alice feeling desperate and she claimed that she had considered suicide at one point.

Nevertheless, as the year 1998 was coming to a close, Alice's fortunes improved. She dropped out of her university classes while at the same time developing social networks of fellow French speakers. As she explained:

> I would sit around with my fellow students and we would sit around with our coffee and our cigarettes and we'd have these **long** philosophical conversations using big long French words and I was so French. (Interview October 2000) (Kinginger, 2004: 236; bold in the original)

During this time, Alice also came face to face with French students who wanted to talk about world events, and the political, economic and cultural hegemony of the US in particular. Alice initially tried to avoid such conversations, claiming that she did not 'do politics'. However, she came to discover that if she refused to participate in conversations about politics, she could not be a fully functioning member of the community of practice of French university students that she most desired to belong to. Looking back on this period, some two years later, she describes how an argument with a French student named Cedric had triggered the beginnings of a certain political consciousness, critical of the US's role in the world:

> I had a huge fight with this guy named Cedric because he was like what do you think about this whole bombing thing?[2] I'm like I don't care! I'm not there, I don't know what's going on, I don't care! He's like how can you say that? That's so irresponsible! You know you're dropping bombs on people. I'm like yeah I'm flying the plane. That's right, you're, yeah your right, push the button. And so then you know he actually did in a roundabout indirect way force me into having a political . . . you know . . . having a political consciousness . . . (Interview October 2000) (Kinginger, 2004: 238; NB some punctuation changed)

In broad terms, Kinginger sums up Alice's development over the four years of contact with her as follows:

> For Alice, becoming a speaker of French is a way of reorienting herself in the world – a 'mission' wherein she summons her own strategic use of personal experience, talent and resources to upgrade her access to cultural capital, become a cultured person, and share her knowledge with others. In this sense, Alice's efforts toward French language competence are just as much an 'investment' in social identity as those of the immigrant women in Norton's (2000) study. Alice's stake in language learning is also a bid to break free of the confining circumstances of a peripatetic, working class childhood and to become a person she can admire. Her personal mission is explicitly linked to professional aspirations. Alice insists that she feels no shame about her background, but only frustration at the limited perspectives it offered, and the desire to move beyond them. (Kinginger, 2004: 240)

Unlike so many of the SA participants in the studies cited above, Alice did not end her stay in France with a realization that she could never be taken seriously as a TL speaker. Rather, she seemed to have found a comfortable space in which she changed from a parochial American to an intellectually more sophisticated French speaking person, knowledgeable of and interested in world affairs. And unlike so many female Americans on SA programmes in France, she did not seem to find France upsetting to her established gendered positionings. And while she was a student throughout the study, in the prosaic sense of the word, she was eventually able to join a community of practice of French students that opened up new TL-mediated subject postitionings for her. She therefore managed to do what so many other students so abjectly fail to do, that is, develop deep and meaningful social contacts with TL speakers. As Isabelli-García (2006) suggests, SA participants who manage to become part of TL-mediated speech communities and social networks are more likely to move away from ethnocentricism and towards greater interculturality and ethno-relativity than those who do not. Their experiences therefore become more transformative, as regards their sense of self, something that was surely the case for Alice.

Of course, Alice was different from the university students discussed in the publications cited above. While most of the latter were 19 or 20, Alice was 22 by the time she went to France. She was, therefore, a young adult, as opposed to a late adolescent. More than her age, however, was Alice's socio-economic status. While her life had been one of hardship and – as she saw it – wasted opportunities, the university students discussed above would be classified as distinctly middle class. Indeed, as Kinginger notes, most students who opt for SA programmes are middle class. Finally, while the SA students in the studies cited above were abroad for between two and 12 months, Alice spent some two years away from home. The length, variety and intensity of her contacts with French speakers, coupled with her drive to achieve, meant that she was able to go much deeper, as regards her interculturality, than most SA students.

Thus far in this chapter, I have examined in detail several studies of SA experiences, all of which have been US-based, in order to see how identity manifests itself in contexts combining elements of the immersion experience of the adult migrant context with the formal instruction of the foreign language context. One key question arising from my focus on the US-based publications is the extent to which the experiences of Americans on SA programmes is similar to the SA experiences of individuals from other national and cultural backgrounds. In the next two sections, I examine the experiences of two groups of travelling individuals: Europeans participating in ERASMUS and other European-based SA and work abroad programmes and Japanese women who choose to study English in countries such as Australia, Britain and the US.

The European experience

As I noted in Chapter 1, there is an extensive published literature on ERASMUS programmes. However, most studies have either been questionnaire based, providing surveys of changing attitudes over the SA experience, or dealt with the development of intercultural competence without going too far into identity issues, as framed in Chapter 2. Elizabeth Murphy-Lejeune's (2002) study of students crossing European borders to participate in different types of SA and work abroad programmes is somewhat of an exception because of the sheer amount of data that the author is able to discuss. Thus while she does adopt a portmanteau approach to presenting stories, spreading them across some of the same themes discussed elsewhere (e.g. culture shock, host families, developing friendships), the reader is able to pick out the emergence of TL-mediated subject positions and indeed a kind of embryonic European identity.

In what the book blurb announces as 'the first in-depth qualitative study of student migration within Europe', Murphy-Lejeune (2002) used a combination of questionnaires and in-depth interviews to elicit from young adult Europeans accounts of their experiences on three programmes involving movement across European borders. The first programme was the ERASMUS programme discussed above, which allows for the transfer of credits among European universities and generally means spending one year abroad. The second programme examined by Murphy-Lejeune was that of teaching assistants, that is, individuals who 'teach their own language in a country whose language they are studying' (Murphy-Lejeune, 2002: 47). The third group of interest to Murphy-Lejeune were students on what was known as the EAP (*Ecole des Affaires de Paris*) programme. These students spent one year in Paris, one year in Oxford and one year in either Berlin or Madrid. In total, Murphy-Lejeune had contact with 50 informants: 15 ERASMUS students, 15 assistants and 20 EAP students. In the discussion that follows, I will focus exclusively on the ERASMUS because, as university students on year-long stays abroad, they most resemble the SA participants I have examined thus far in this chapter.

One fairly common characteristic across the ERASMUS students was their previous travel experience and the desire to travel. The majority claimed to have travelled at an early age, these experiences usually being family holidays in other European countries, as well as locations further afield, such as the US. In addition, some informants reported summer sojourns of one or two months in length in the UK, Ireland or even the US, to study English. Murphy-Lejeune notes in several of her informants what she terms 'the travel bug', that is a seemingly insatiable appetite for travel that some of her informants had developed. Maria, a student from Ireland, sums up this feeling as follows:

> I enjoy meeting new people and going new places . . . It's everything about travelling, everything is different, it's not just the people, it's your whole atmosphere, your daily living conditions are different . . . yes, variety, it's variety. (Murphy-Lejeune, 2002: 68)

On the whole, informants seemed to enjoy the experience of expressing themselves in another language, of encountering and living with 'strangeness' and of opening themselves to international relationships. This feeling is exemplified in the following comment made by a student from France named Hélène:

> I was really keen to, eh, dive completely for a very, very long time into English, really . . . I wanted to breathe English, really, so that it would come, that it'd be like a second nature because it's a language I like a lot . . . (Murphy-Lejeune, 2002: 83) (NB translated from the original in French)

As regards living with foreignness, John, a student from Ireland, had the following to say:

> . . . New experiences, enjoyment, adventure. I consider that when you're travelling, especially abroad, you're going to encounter new people, new things, very much new experiences. It's going to be totally new. It's not going to be the same streets, the same people and maybe not the same language. So excitement, ya. I think excitement and adventure of experiencing a whole new culture, new language. (Murphy-Lejeune, 2002: 87–8)

This openness to adventure notwithstanding, there is still the question of whether or not the experiences of living abroad for one year actually transformed these individuals, not only as regards their development as intercultural mediators, but also in terms of new TL-mediated subject positions. As one progresses through Murphy-Lejeune's presentations of comments made by the 15 ERASMUS students, it becomes clear that the year abroad had meant some degree of increased intercultural awareness for all of them. In addition, there were also a few participants in the study who claimed that the experience had transformed their sense of self, even if such a transformation was not necessarily sustainable after the return home. Hugo, a student from Germany who had spent a year in Ireland, sums up his return experience as follows:

> And then I came back and hum. . . . it was a nice experience and on the other hand a very difficult experience because I was talking about this change, you have the feeling that you have changed, all this experience, but then you realize you cannot tell anybody about the experience and they listen about five minutes and then, they say *'ok, come back, you are in Germany no'* and they don't want to hear about it . . . so it's something very personal, you have to keep to yourself. (Murphy-Lejeune, 2002: 142)

One key factor as regards both the initial and lasting impact of the sojourn abroad was the extent to which participants associated with local people, fellow expatriates or fellow ERASMUS students from a long list of third countries. Maria, the Irish student cited above, shared a flat with three Spanish girls of her age, with whom she also socialized. She became, as she described it, the centre of attention as the 'new friend'. Participating in a variety of activities with her Spanish friends, Maria gained a great deal of confidence due to her enhanced cultural capital (her Spanish language skills) and social capital (her connections and overall social know-how). She even helped a fellow Irish participant by teaching her Spanish and introducing her to her Spanish friends.

Meanwhile, Hugo, the German student cited above, comments on the importance of socializing with local people as follows:

> So you suddenly realise that home is strongly related to your social relationships. As soon as you have some social relationships, you can call that home. (Murphy-Lejeune, 2002: 203)

For Hugo and other ERASMUS students, these social relationships meant emergent TL-mediated subject positions related to particular communities of practice. However, as Hugo himself notes in an earlier quotation cited above, such subject positions do not survive the move back to one's home country. What then, does Murphy-Lejeune's study tell us about the prospects of identity work and critical experiences in ERASMUS programmes? And what does it tell us about differences between American SA participants and European ERASMUS students?

In response to the latter, I would say that they ERASMUS students share with American SA students several concerns about spending an extensive period of time aboard. For example, there are worries about TL competence and the ability to fit in with local people. However, in direct contrast to their American counterparts, ERASMUS students seem to approach their experiences abroad with far more awareness of what they might entail. In short, there is little in Murphy-Lejeune's accounts of the kind of awkwardness exhibited by American students. Interestingly there is no mention of conflict, discomfort or confusion related to local norms of heterosexual contact. Although the point is not generally addressed overtly in the US-based literature, there is a sense that on the whole, the American SA participants are relatively unseasoned and even naïve travellers on their first – and quite likely last-ever – extensive sojourn outside the US. By contrast, as was observed above, ERASMUS students generally have previous travel experience, both inside and outside of Europe, and some even have previous SA experiences in the form of one-month or two-month summer English language courses in Ireland or the UK.

In addition, while cultural stereotypes are occasionally drawn on to make sense of experiences, there is nowhere in Murphy-Lejeune's ERASMUS student accounts the kind of nationalism exhibited by so many of the American SA participants.[3] One possible explanation for this lack of nationalistic subject positioning is the aforementioned previous travel experience and SA experience of the ERASMUS students. However, there is also a sense in which these students embody an emergent pan-European identity as participants in a much larger pan-European project that sees ever-greater social, political and economic integration across the European Union and the prospect of living and working across European nation state borders. Their SA experiences, therefore, are not as foreign to them as they would be for American students because while they are crossing nation state, language and cultural borders, they are doing so as Europeans as much as Irish nationals, Spanish nationals, German nationals and so on.

As regards what Murphy-Lejeune's study can tell us about identity work and critical experiences in ERASMUS programmes, my overall assessment is mixed. On the one hand, her informants show to varying degrees that they have gained cross-cultural awareness and intercultural competence. And, in some cases, there is every indication, as Alred and Byram (2002) found in their study following up Youth Abroad programme students ten years after the experience, that these effects will last. However, as Hugo noted above, going home means interruption of identity work done in what he calls 'social relationships'. In summary, ERASMUS students are likely to need more than just a year to move them into more profound and lasting identity work.

Japanese women learning English

In recent years, there has been a series of publications examining the experiences of Japanese women in English-speaking countries such as the US, Britain and Australia. In the work of anthropologists such as Sandra Buckley (1997) and Karen Kelsey (2001), there is in-depth discussion of the lives of Japanese women who, as mature adults, have decided to emigrate from Japan in search of an idealized 'west' where women have more opportunities and, in effect, can live more independent and fulfilling lives. In applied linguistics, there has also been some interest in this phenomenon, although the specific focus has been on the English language and what it means to Japanese women who decide to change their geographical location in search of happiness. For example, in a recent study by Ingrid Piller and Kimie Takahashi (2006), the authors document the experiences of Japanese women aged 20–40 who have moved to Australia on sojourns ranging from a few months to years. In all the cases considered, the official reason for moving to Australia was the opportunity to improve their English. However, Piller and Takahashi note a deeper reason for moving, one related to their informants' need to satisfy their feelings of *akogare,* that is, the idealization or longing for all things western.

The women profiled by Piller and Takahashi seem to know what they want, for example in some cases taking on and rejecting potential boyfriends depending on how close to their ideal of the 'west' they are. Nothing is said about sexual harassment and there is no mention of Japanese women comparing themselves with local women, both dominant themes in US-based publications discussed earlier in this chapter. Rather, the women seem to be in control of the process of satisfying their *akogare* as well as their fantasies about the 'west' and the English language.

Elsewhere, Renae Skarin (2001) discusses the cases of two Japanese women, Haesun and Kyoko, who moved to Hawaii to leave behind their unfulfilling lives in Japan. Haesun found that living in Hawaii, she did not have to deal with her Korean heritage, something about which she was constantly reminded in Japan. In addition, she found that, as a woman, she could be more independent and do more things. Enrolled on an MA course, she related to Skarin her progress from quiet student to active participant in seminars:

> I realize I feel more comfortable in class this semester because almost all the people I know. I have something that I can share with colleagues now. The stuff I know, or form conversation with other colleagues makes me feel more comfortable and confident to speak out. (Skarin, 2001: 40)

Haesun also belonged to a local feminist group and through her participation in activities with members of this group, as well as her university activities, she moved towards new English-mediated subject positions as an independent woman and a good student.

Kyoko's move to Hawaii was, according to Skarin, due to her 'frustration with the social structure in relation to the power of women in the workplace' (Skarin, 2001: 43). Fed up with her lack of career prospects, after 15 years in the same travel agency, she decided to seek a better life in Hawaii. The defining feature of Kyoto's life, both in Japan and in Hawaii, was her strong religious beliefs. A practising Buddhist, she was not interested in changing social structures in Japan, only seeking a place where she could realize her ambitions. The US was such a place for her and in her conversations with Skarin, she manifested a near total affiliation to American culture and the

English language. By contrast, she positioned Japanese culture as sexist, racist, ageist and judgemental.

However, despite her affiliation to the US, Kyoto was not very active in her skills-based English language classes. It seems that unlike Haesun, she was not able to become a fully functioning member of the communities of practice that were her English classes. In addition, she did not have extra-curricular activities, like Haesun's feminist group, which might have led her to develop a more critical stance towards her various life experiences (her religious activities certainly did not push her in this direction). Ultimately, Kyoto was more a passive observer of all around her than the more proactive individual Haesun had become.

Skarin's study effectively shows the two very different self-development trajectories of Haesun and Kyoto. However, it is somewhat limited in the way that she focuses primarily on the development of English-mediated subject positions inside English language classrooms as opposed to providing more information about extra curricular activities. A broader ethnography of these two individuals obviously would have provided the reader with a more nuanced view of the kind of migrant identities the two women were adopting, and above all how they 'did' themselves in Hawaii in ways different from how they 'did' themselves in Japan. Still, the study is interesting in how, along with Piller and Takahashi (2006), it shows a very different perspective on SA. In contrast to the US and European-based studies – where increased linguistic and intercultural competence were the most commonly expressed goals – here the desire for more liberated gender subject positions overshadows all else.

In my own research focusing on female Japanese graduate students as middling transmigrants (Block, 2006a), I have also found a similar story of SA as a liberating experience. One informant, Kimi, spent several weeks in Australia at the age of 17 and then two years later, went to the US for six weeks. In the following interview excerpt, she describes how she changed as a result of her second SA experience:

> . . . I think that when I was in the States, I can express every – not everything – I don't have to be, I would say, obedient in the States.

I kind of – I felt I had at the time even if I had some of my own opinions inside me, I felt I shouldn't express everything in front of the people when I was in Japan. But when I was in the States, I started to express more and more, not the daily things, but the opinions. I think that's because in Japan, maybe as you know, females . . . there is a notion the female should behave like 'a female' so I think I felt the pressure in Japan. This is because – not mainly, but partially – because I was raised in the female school, so there were only female students so I didn't have to think about this so much. But then when I was in the university – again it was a women's university – but we had more contact with university students, also male students . . . we discussed some things. And I realized that I am not a very typical Japanese female because I tend to have a strong opinion. I tend to express that kind of thing overtly. And some people didn't like that. So I felt sometimes very . . . unhappy with that. But in the States, I felt like I can say what I think and the people take it in a very natural way. So I think in that sense I felt comfortable with that. (Kimi, 11/6/02)

Within a year of her American experience, Kimi was in Britain for a Youth Abroad programme at a British university. During this year, she socialized with fellow overseas students, some of whom were Japanese, but very few British nationals. Nevertheless, she further developed an assertiveness that she identified with becoming 'westernized'. When she returned to Japan, she encountered gender bias when job hunting, experiencing what she termed a 'very big reverse cultural shock', which led her to develop what she called an 'anti-Japanese' attitude. She explains the situation as follows:

My crisis was after going to Japan, I think after one year in Britain I had to do the Japan thing. That was the most difficult part because I kind of became, kind of became westernized . . . so I expect, you know, my way of thinking and what I think abruptly, not strongly but strongly for a Japanese, I think. And then Japanese men, especially older men, don't like that. So I still remember that I went to a kind of job interview and they asked me some questions like this. And he kind of asked, 'What is most important for you in the job?' And I said something like, 'First of all, I need to be brave enough to challenge or try out new things'. And he started to laugh. And he said to me, 'Oh, I think all I expect from female students is just smiling every day . . .' or something like that. (Kimi, 11/6/02)

By the time she was in her late 20s, which is when I came in contact with her, Kimi had had several more SA experiences in English-speaking countries, ranging in length from one month to one year. These repeated experiences had allowed her to develop a good level of communicative competence in English. But more importantly, she had developed new feminine subject positions – more assertive in both talk and behaviour – which, as she explains above, were not the norm in Japan.

In their accounts of SA experiences, Kimi, Haesun, Kyoto and the women in Piller and Takahashi all adopt a discourse of English-mediated liberated gendered subject positions linked to their sojourns away from Japan. This dominant discourse is significant in that it suggests that what the Japanese women are doing while on SA programmes is much different from what has been observed in the Americans and the Europeans. In addition, these women do not seem to cling to any strong sense of Japanese nationalism, as was the case with the US informants discussed in this chapter, and while they do talk about becoming more interculturally aware, this development is more about their immersion in local culture, as opposed to a knowledge or an ability that they would take back home with them. However, it is worth noting that in all of the cases cited, there has been a longer period away from home than is normally the case in SA. And, there is a need for more detailed ethnographies of the experiences of Japanese women – and, indeed, Japanese men – as well as other East Asians. Such studies would allow the exploration of very different ways of experiencing SA and most importantly, the examination of very different ways that SA impacts on a participant's sense of self.

Conclusion

SA is the SLL context of a growing number of students (university undergraduate and postgraduate) who seek to complement their FL context learning with something more similar to what migrants experience when they cross borders and are immersed in new languages and cultures. However, there is no simple formula for qualifying SA as halfway in between the adult migrant and the FL contexts discussed in Chapters 4 and 5 respectively. On the one hand, although all SA either begins in or has strong connections to an FL context, it is not FL in nature for the simple reason that learners are resident in environments where the TL is the normal linguistic means of communication. At the same time, SA is very different from the adult migrant context as represented by the studies discussed in Chapter 4: SA participants are usually of a certain age (18–22), enrolled in university studies and they are overwhelmingly from middle-class backgrounds. Thus in terms of age, activity, education, social class and so on, they have little in common with the kinds of migrants in studies such as Broeder *et al* (1996), Goldstein (1996) and Norton (2000).

In this chapter, I hope to have shown that the SA context is indeed varied: as varied as the different nationalities enrolled on SA programmes and as varied as the countries receiving them. In my view, the US-based research effectively suggests that SA can lead to critical experiences, even if these critical experiences are sometimes reactive, causing the individual to become less, as opposed to more, interculturally aware. It also shows that there is not a monochrome American abroad experience; rather individual circumstances and host environments vary considerably. Nevertheless, there are generalizations to be made about the way that American students orient to and experience SA, most notably how SA is often their first and last lengthy sojourn abroad and how encountering difference leads not to active engagement with the local but to a recoiling into a discourse of American superiority. It is especially when one examines studies such as Murphy-Lejeune (2002), in a pan-European context, and Piller and Takahashi (2006) and Skarin (2001), focusing on Japanese women in English-speaking countries, that this general difference becomes clear.

With this difference in mind, I think that there is a need for an opening up of SA studies. On the one hand, there needs to be a broadening of what identity means and the range of subject positions explored in research. There is a clear inclusion of race in Talburt and Stewart (1999) and social class in Kinginger (2004). However, more could be done on these all-important perspectives on identity and how they play out in SA contexts. But most crucially, there simply need to be more studies, and more involving different nationality combinations as regards sending and receiving countries. Thus, there need to be more ethnographies of ERASMUS students in different European contexts and Japanese women (and men) in different countries around the world, following up what I have briefly covered here. However, more importantly, there is a need for ethnographies of Latin Americans on SA programmes in the US, of East Asians in Australia, of Africans in Europe and so on. Only then will it be possible to see the full potential of SA experiences as contexts replete with emerging TL-mediated subject positions.

Notes

1 However, Kinginger (personal communication, January 2006) informs me that although they did not discuss the matter in their paper, the authors did have data indicating that this situation might have changed as the SA programme came to an end. It seems that at this time, Jada became friends with a French woman of her age and that she was able to learn something about how to do acceptable French-mediated femininities.

2 In December 1998, the US and British governments began a bombing campaign in Iraq that was to last some five months, causing hundreds of civilian casualties (US bombing watch: www.ccmep.org/usbombingwatch/2003.htm).

3 But see Bacon (2002) and Tusting, Crawshaw and Callen (2002) for accounts of British Year Abroad students taking nationalistic stances towards their host countries.

7

Second language identities: Future directions

Introduction

Chapter 2 provided a review of the key constructs associated with a poststructuralism-inspired approach to identity that in recent years has become popular among many social scientists and theorists, including applied linguists. From there, I moved in Chapter 3 to a consideration of past SLL research focusing on sociopsychological variables. I argued that in this research identity was an issue waiting in the wings, which never quite came to the fore. These two chapters opened the way for Chapters 4–6, in which research on three specific contexts – the adult migrant, the FL and the SA – was discussed. My aim was to examine how identity is an issue in each of these contexts. I concluded that while the adult migrant context affords multiple and varied opportunities for TL-mediated identity work, the FL context presents an altogether more limited scenario. In the latter context, identity work relates to the immediate sociohistorical context, which is not necessarily mediated to a significant degree by the TL or the target culture. Still, where such contexts include Internet-based communication with TL users or membership in international communities of TL users, there does appear to be some potential for TL-mediated identity work. The third context discussed in this book, study abroad, sits somewhere between the adult migrant and FL contexts. On the one hand, there is the link with the

FL context and above all home, which effectively is a constraint on TL-mediated identity work. However, where SA students manage to 'sneak backstage', to use Hannerz's (1996) term, the prospects of TL-mediated identity work are enhanced.

As I argued in Chapter 2, identity is a multilayered phenomenon and it is well-nigh impossible to arrive at a definition or list of perspectives that will hold up for very long. As individuals make their way through the world around them, they are forever inhabiting and having attributed to them new and emergent subject positions that call into question constructs commonly used by researchers, such as gendered identity or national identity. Looking back over the different discussions taking place in Chapters 3–6, I can see many different perspectives on identity and new directions for identity research arising. In some case, these perspectives and new directions were mentioned explicitly and in some cases, they were not. In this chapter, I briefly outline five perspectives on identity that I think might fruitfully be explored and taken up in the future by researchers interested in second language identities.

A greater emphasis on social class

Social class, in particular Beverley Skegg's Bourdieu-inspired take on it described in Chapter 2, has received limited attention in SLL research. This applies to the three contexts which I have discussed in this book as well as those that I have not discussed. For example, in order to understand types of identity work taking place in adult migrant contexts, one needs to keep a keen eye on the symbolic capital that these migrants bring with them to their new environments. In this regard, it is useful to draw on recent work on migration and in particular research that has focused on different types of migrants. As I noted in Chapter 2, there has been a move in recent years away from a conceptualization of migrants as classic immigrants, that is individuals who move to a location, assimilate to local norms and proceed to live the rest of their lives isolated from their home language and culture. Transnationalism and diaspora have emerged as key terms to understand how the dispersal of people around the world today does not usually mean the severing of roots; rather, it means the development of new hybrid and third place migrant identities constructed around economic, social, familial and political ties to both the new home environment and the environment of origin.

However, within transnationalism there is inequality and there is little doubt that the experiences of unskilled labour migrants differ markedly from the experiences of middle-class or 'middling' transmigrants that I discussed in Chapter 3 (see also Block 2006a, Chapters 5 and 6). For example, the migrants in Broeder *et al*'s (1996) study do not possess the symbolic capital necessary to create transnational spaces that would allow them to lead fulfilling lives in their new European homes. Their relatively low economic capital, their lack of language skills and local *savoir faire* and their marginalization from key social and political networks all act as constraints on their attempts to better their lives. The Portuguese women in Goldstein's (1996) study also bring with them to their Canadian experiences relatively low levels of economic and cultural capital. However, they have managed to develop a strong sense of community, which carries with it social networks that allow community members to live rewarding lives, even if the price to be paid is the acceptance of a diminished status in Canadian society, economically, culturally and socially.

As regards middle-class migrants, the issue of economic, cultural and social capital is turned around. In Norton's (2000) study, the older women – Katarina, Martina and Felicia – all found that they lost considerable economic, cultural and social capital in their moves to Canada. However, just one – Felicia – seemed to be coping badly with the declassing that this loss of capital meant. Frustrated at her husband's inability to find a job comparable to the one that he had had in Peru, and unhappy because she could not position herself as a well-educated middle-class woman in Canada, Felicia's prospects for overcoming her declassing did not look promising. Elsewhere, in my study of Spanish-speaking Latinos, I found that Carlos, the university lecturer from Colombia, was also unhappy about the declassing that his move from Colombia to Britain had meant. However, he had managed to develop a personal narrative of membership in a transnational community of educated Spanish speakers, something that allowed him to inhabit a space linked to his cultural capital. He had also benefited from the fact that he is married to a British national, something that gives him a degree of social capital. These two capitals together will ultimately allow Carlos to prosper economically whilst living his life on his own terms, maintaining Spanish as his primary language and resisting assimilation to British society to a great degree.

It is not only in the adult migrant context that social class is a factor; indeed, in FL and, in particular, SA, contexts, it is important to explore how the symbolic capital of language learners mediates language learning activity and ultimately the kind of identity work that takes place. In FL contexts, long-term expectations as regards academic achievement might differ considerably along social class lines, with high expectations being inclusive of a positive disposition towards the study of an FL and low expectations framing such study as of little use. Of course, this is a very stark contrast, indeed a *classist* one, that needs to be teased out. But my point here is that precisely because it does need to be teased out, there is a need for research examining identity work in foreign language learning from a social class perspective.

In SA contexts, there is also such a need, as I can only cite Kinginger's (2004) study of Alice as an example in which social class is a construct explicitly brought to the fore. From a background affording very little in the way of economic, cultural or social capital, Alice nonetheless developed an 'imagined' sense of self in French. This imagined self was indeed a hyper-romanticized one, including scenes of drinking coffee, smoking cigarettes and discussing philosophy in Parisian cafés; importantly, however, it was not ephemeral and indeed was powerful enough to catalyse her move away from the US to France, where she would spend nearly two years.

One interesting aspect of Alice's case is how her low symbolic capital in the context of the US affords her opportunities to gain symbolic capital in the French context. Lacking in funds, she could not afford to take trips with her fellow SA students, and this meant that she had to find things to do locally with local people. In addition, her previous life of hardship meant that she had little in common with other students and this lack of middle-class cultural and social capital likely facilitated her move to seek contact with French students who would be more attentive to her American-ness than to her position in American society as poor. Finally, through her contacts with French students, Alice moves from an adopted position of ignorance and indifference about US foreign policy to an altogether more informed, engaged and critical position.

As I noted in Chapter 6, SA experiences might serve to enhance one's sense of national identity far more than to facilitate the development of intercultural competence. My question here would be the extent to which this is the case when individuals feel that they have a strong stake in the society and culture of their home country. Perhaps Alice's membership in a family unit that had failed to realize the American dream of prosperity and material possessions, meant that the relative strength of her stakeholder status in American society was weaker than it would be for the children of middle-class families. In a sense, the latter always have something to go back to. Alice, by contrast, did not.

Expanding the ambit of the 'First Language' (L1)

Throughout this book, I have made reference to TL-mediated identities, but I have said little to problematize the linguistic resources that learners bring with them to the language-learning task. In Block (2003), I make the point that in much SLL research, 'L1' is all too often a very crude identity marker for individuals learning a second, third, fourth or fifth language. Many second language learners come to the task as users of two or more linguistic repertoires officially recognized as languages. These learners generally are identified as bi or multilingual, although it would be useful to question what these terms actually mean as regards their competence in languages attributed to them. In addition, those who are classified in this way often manifest competence in a multitude of varieties of the languages that putatively make them bi or multilingual. Two examples suffice to make this point.

In his study of Spanish/English bilingual adolescents in an urban secondary school in the US, Benjamin Bailey (2000, 2003) counted as many as five varieties of English and Spanish used by his main informant Wilson in just six turns in a conversation lasting just over a minute and a half. These varieties were standard or general Spanish, distinctively Dominican Spanish, African American Vernacular English, Dominican English, general American English and Hispanicized English (the English spoken by Spanish-speaking migrants in the US). Thus, more than bilingual, Wilson was a user of multiple varieties of English and Spanish. Significantly, through his use of these varieties, Wilson was able to slip in and out of racially and ethnically defined subject positions. The fact that he was phenotypically Black meant that in the context of a secondary school in the US, his variable uses of general American English, African American Vernacular English and Spanish inflected Englishes were linked to very different inhabited and ascribed positions. Thus, American English indexed a general race-free American identity, African American Vernacular English indexed membership in the African American community and Spanish inflected Englishes indexed membership in a broad Hispanic or Latino community. As regards the latter, his use of either general or Dominican Spanish further refined his self-presentation on a moment-to-moment basis.

Elsewhere, Jürgen Jaspers shows how adolescent boys of Moroccan descent in Flanders, the Dutch-speaking northern part of Belgium, creatively draw on Arabic, Berber and Dutch as they position themselves as subversive elements in school. They achieve the latter by *'doing ridiculous'*, which is activity 'involving play acting in class, pretending not to understand, simulating enthusiasm or giving confusing or inappropriate answers in class as well as in interviews in order to slow things down or cause teachers to digress and pay attention to non-school subjects' (Jaspers, 2005: 285). For Jaspers, these students from a Moroccan background have a greater command of Dutch than they are generally given credit for, but they choose to use the language in such variable ways that this competence is not perceived by educational authorities, who persist in classifying them as deficient in what is the linguistic medium of education.

In the context of SLL research and specifically the focus on second language identities, such cases move researchers away from a monolingual learner bias and L1–L2 dichotomies to something more akin to L1s–L2 or even Ls–AL (Languages-Additional Language). In doing so, they lead researchers to different sets of questions regarding TL development and TL-mediated identities. Regarding the latter, one key question is if multilinguals, in any kind of patterned or generalizable sense, orient to TLs in a substantially different way from monolinguals and if the nature of their identity work is somehow greater, lesser, richer or poorer. For example, if Wilson or the boys in Jaspers's study were to migrate to Germany, would their respective Spanish-English bilingualism and Arabic-Berber-Dutch trilingualism be determinant in their engagement with German language and culture? Or would their sociohistories, as regards race, ethnicity, nationality, gender and so on, prove to be more important shapers of their experiences? In contexts where multiculturalism and multilingualism have become the norm more than the exception, there is a need to problematize the linguistic and cultural baggage that individuals bring to SLL experiences.

The emergence of local *lingua francas*

An issue related to the multiple linguistic resources of second language learners is the emergence in ethnolinguistically diverse environments of *lingua francas*, that is, languages that are mutually accessible to individuals from other language backgrounds and that are not the predominant language of the host community. For example, in Goldstein's (1996) study of Portuguese factory workers in Toronto, discussed in Chapter 4, the author found that Portuguese was not only the principle medium of communication for Portuguese workers; it was also adopted by some Spanish-speaking and Italian-speaking co-workers who thought that they needed it for effective communication at work. In her study of five female immigrants in Toronto, Norton (2000) found two cases in which her informants used Italian on the job as opposed to English and therefore were in a situation of improving their Italian as opposed to English whilst living in a predominantly Anglophone city. Mai, the young Vietnamese woman, came under pressure at the small garment factory where she worked to learn Italian because the latter was the dominant language of her co-workers. Meanwhile, Eva, the young Polish woman, worked for period of time in what she called 'the Italian store', a small store run by an Italian family in an Italian neighbourhood in Toronto. Already proficient in Italian when she arrived in Canada, Eva found that during her time working in this establishment, she was developing Italian-mediated subject positions and that she was not living very much of her life in English.

In my study of Spanish-speaking Latinos (see Chapter 4; Block, 2005b, 2006a), I found a similar phenomenon taking place with Spanish emerging as a *lingua franca* in some workplace and social environments in London. This was confirmed by Carlos when he told me that the Spanish speakers he knew:

> . . . *siempre quieren enseñar español pero no quieren aprender inglés o otras lenguas, sinó que esperan que la gente con que nos relacionamos empiezen a entendernos en español. (Carlos, 12/9/03)*

> . . . always want to teach Spanish but they don't want to learn English or other languages; rather, they expect the people that we associate with to start understanding us in Spanish. (Carlos, 12/9/03)

Elaborating on the same theme, he explained the dominance of Colombians in London as follows:

> *Los colombianos han organizado, por ejemplo, festivales, muchos salones de club o muchos torneos deportivos. Entonces eso hace que quienes quieran participar, como los portugueses, por ejemplo . . . tienen que [hablar español] . . . Africanos que son cercanos a la comunidad latina empiezan a soltar frases en español básicas. Y eso es porqué la comunidad es fuerte en cuanto a número y en cuanto a actividades. Y para estar para participar de ella se necesita hablar bien español. Aquí se reciben gentes de otras nacionalidades pero la persona debe de ir acediendo al español. (Carlos, 12/9/03)*

The Colombians have organized, for example, festivals, a lot of nightclubs or a lot of sports tournaments. So that means that whoever wants to participate, like the Portuguese, for example . . . have to [speak Spanish]. . . . Africans who are near the Latin community are starting to come out with basic Spanish phrases. And that is because the community is strong as regards numbers and activities. And in order to be ready to participate in it, you need to speak Spanish well. Here people from other nationalities are welcome but the person has to go along with Spanish. (Carlos, 12/9/03)

An example of a non-SSL 'going along' with Spanish was Ricardo, a young Brazilian man taking part in my study. Ricardo grew up in a middle-class family in Porto Alegre, in the southern part of Brazil, and he had learned Spanish whilst living in Argentina for two years. Upon his arrival in London, where he planned to live in order to improve his English, he took a job working for a catering company in the same building as Carlos, and he soon realized that many of his co-workers were from South America. On the one hand, there were numerous Brazilians with whom, not surprisingly, he communicated in Portuguese. However, there were also many SSLs working in various low-level service jobs, such as portering and cleaning, with whom he also had contact. As a general rule, he spoke to Spanish speakers he encountered in London in Spanish. Ricardo, with whom I always spoke in Spanish, described his relationship with different languages in London as follows:

> Puedo hablar en un dia creo que puedo hablar los tres idiomas que sé: Portugués, Español y Inglés. Con certeza, dos, y cuando encuentro Carlos o te encuentro, hablo español también . . . Este punto es fantástico en Londres porqué tienes gente de todas partes del mundo. Puedo hablar con personas de España, Suramerica, en Español, Portugués . . . (Ricardo, 5/2/04)

> In a single day, I can speak, I think I can speak the three languages that I know: Portuguese, Spanish and English. Surely two, and when I run into Carlos or I run into you, I speak Spanish as well . . . This is a fantastic thing in London because you have people from everywhere in the world. I can speak with people from Spain, South America, in Spanish, Portuguese . . . (Ricardo, 5/2/04)

Thus, London offered Ricardo the prospect of developing as a multilingual transnational during his time in London, able not only to relate to Brazilians in Portuguese but to engage with different communities of practice in English and Spanish. In a sense, he occupied the subject position mediated by three different languages, a third place existence *par excellence*, beyond the traditional immigrant learning the language of the host community and the transnational maintaining a balance between the language of the host community and the language 'back home'. The emergence of *lingua franca*-mediated subject positions, such as Ricardo's London life lived in Spanish, is a phenomenon in need of further exploration because of the identity issues which it raises.

Electronically mediated SLL experiences

In recent years, there has been a boom in publications focusing on how information technology mediates our lives (e.g. Turkle, 1995; Cherny, 1999; Thurlow, Lengel and Tomic, 2004; Dutton, 2004) and this boom extends to authors interested in SLL. There are now two major journals devoted to SLL and technology – *Language Learning and Technology* and *CALICO Journal* – and there have been several key books on the topic over the past ten years (e.g. Warschauer, 1999, 2003; Chapelle, 2001; White, 2003; Egbert and Petrie, 2005; Belz and Thorne, 2006). Among the many SLL and technology publications, there are instances where authors focus on identity specifically. Thus, in Chapter 5, I discussed Steve Thorne's (2003) work with FL learners in the US. Elsewhere, Mark Warschauer (2003) touches on identity issues in his discussion of Internet access. One area in particular where the prospects for identity work are very promising is the participation in chat rooms where the language of communication is either the TL or a heritage language. I discuss one such example.

Wan Shun Eva Lam (2004) documents the case of two young Hong Kong Chinese immigrants living in California, who were able to develop new English-mediated Chinese identities via their participation in chat-room exchanges in which their interlocutors were members of an international Chinese community. The two women, Yu Qing and Tsu Ying, were 18 and 17, respectively, at the time of the study, and both had been living in California for three years when Lam first contacted them. Over a period of eight months in 2001 (January– August), Lam conducted eight interviews with each of the girls and analysed some 20 hours of chat-room exchanges.

From her contacts with the two girls, Lam learned that while Yu Qing and Tsu Ying expressed an interest in interacting with English speakers both at school and outside of school, they also reported numerous barriers to such contact. Outside of school, the girls found few opportunities to speak English as their families were living in a predominantly Chinese neighbourhood. Inside school, they felt marginalized and indeed stigmatized by their inability to speak perfect American English. While their schoolmates from non-Chinese backgrounds tended to ignore them, they found no comfort associating with students who were from Chinese backgrounds, the American Born Chinese (ABCs). For example, Tsu Ying reported that ABCs would sometimes laugh at her English and Yu Qing described ABCs as 'like white people', explaining that 'even though they have a Chinese face, we don't feel like they are Chinese' (Lam, 2004: 50).

It was against this backdrop that the two girls discovered the 'Hong Kong chat-room', a website designed and hosted by a Hong Kong resident, which attracts Chinese people from all over the world. Although interactions were in both Chinese and English, Yu Qing and Tsu Ying logged on when they knew that exchanges would be in English. Lam describes the English used as a 'mixed code', predominantly English but with some Cantonese discourse markers such as *ar*, described by Lam as 'a softener or down-toner, to signal a question or to seek a confirmation', or *la*, described as 'a suggestion or plea for a course of action' (Lam, 2004: 55). Though such features were used with slightly different meanings when code mixed with English, the point is that they formed part of the unique emergent English that served as the medium of communication for members of an emergent international community of like-minded people, what Lam calls 'bilingual Chinese immigrants' (Lam, 2004: 59). Participation in the chat-room exchanges thus afforded Yu Qing and Tsu Ying the opportunity to develop new third place identities drawing on resources related to their Hong Kong Chinese past and their English- mediated American present.

Among other things, Lam's findings suggest that studies of migrants which focus exclusively on face-to-face interactions may be missing a big part of the identity work being done. For example, while I can claim to know something about Carlos's transnational Spanish-speaking identity through my interviews with him and the conversations that he recorded for me, I do not have access to his Internet-mediated communications using both Spanish and English. I know from informal contacts with him that he was a habitual user of the Internet and I know that he was in contact with people not only in Colombia but also in Spain and other countries using this technology.

Ultimately, this corner of his existence represents a substantial part of the identity work he was doing in London, a part that I did not explore because my research focused more narrowly on face-to-face communication. My point, then, is that in second language identity research, there is a need to examine how information technology-mediated communication either reinforces identity work done face to face or offers an alternative to it.

The psychoanalytic perspective[1]

At the start of the book, I made reference to Mervyn Bendle's (2002) discussion of identity, citing his five reasons for its rise to prominence in the social sciences. Here I aim to explore another part of this argument, namely, how the rise of identity is 'indicative of crisis' in the social sciences, a crisis born from contradiction:

> There is an inherent contradiction between a valuing of identity as something so fundamental that it is crucial to personal well-being and collective action, and a theorization of 'identity' that sees it as something constructed, fluid, multiple, impermanent and fragmentary. The contemporary crisis of identity thus expresses itself as both a crisis of society, and a crisis of theory. The crisis of identity involves a crisis of 'identity'. (Bendle, 2002: 1–2)

This crisis of identity is most pronounced in sociology, in particular among those who examine current globalizing forces and flows related to the movement of peoples, money and culture around the world. And the crisis arises no doubt because of the newness of the ontology which has become the focus. However, the crisis also results from having borrowed the concept of identity from an already established field, which many (including Bendle) see as its rightful home: psychology. Bendle critiques the work of Anthony Giddens and Manuel Castells, two of the better-known globalization and identity theorists in recent years. He makes the point that they have, in effect, superficialized identity, focusing on surface malleability and change in the self in response to an ever more complex set of stimuli served up by the environment. And, he asks '[u]pon what psychological substrate such a transient construction rests and how it mobilizes the energies that are observably necessary to maintain an integrated personality in dynamic conditions of social change . . .' (Bendle, 2002: 8).

Bendle argues that there is a need to move from 'surface' models of analysis, put forth by so many today, to more 'depth' models, and from overly optimistic and romanticized approaches, to more pessimistic and 'dark' ones. For Bendle, such a move means looking more carefully at ego psychology and so-called 'left' psychoanalytic theories of identity, based on the work of Jacques Lacan (1977). It would mean an examination of the inner core self, not entirely stable and surely conflicted, which acts as a constraint on human development. Including such a perspective, there would be more to the fluid and unstable identity than a response to the environment. In addition, the notions of multiple identities and fragmentation, so important to poststructuralists, would be seen by psychoanalysts as something to be treated. While the former seem to put conflict out there as emergent in interaction, the latter see it as evasively retiring into the inner recesses of the mind.

For Bendle, Giddens is one of the few social theorists interested in identity who has tried to engage with psychoanalysis. In his 1991 book, *Modernity and Self-Identity*, there are references to Freud, Lacan and others. Unfortunately, Bendle thinks that Giddens has either not fully understood the work of these authors, and therefore has misrepresented it, or that he simply has not been able to convey his understandings to readers in a coherent fashion. While Giddens brings in terminology such as 'ontological security' and 'existential anxiety', he soon takes the more optimistic tack that human beings manage to adapt to social change around them leaving to the side the inner self of paranoia, schizophrenia and so on. He therefore does not address how all of these inner-self phenomena might hold individuals back and act as a check on their self-realization, self-identity projects. Indeed, the very term self-identity seems to be at the crossroads of psychological and sociologically informed versions of who people are. However, Giddens, and many others who hold similar views on identity, have systematically failed to address the psychological while emphasizing the social.

Bendle seems to think that sociologists can take psychoanalytical theory on board in their analyses, and indeed that they are duty bound to do so, writing that 'an adequate response requires that critical and uncompromising analysis be conducted at the interface of sociology with the key underlying models of identity derived from constructionism, psychoanalysis and psychology' (Bendle, 2002: 17). To date, there has been very little movement in applied linguistics along the lines of what Bendle suggests for sociology, a notable exception being Colette Granger.[2] Focusing on the phenomenon of silence in SLL, Granger laments that it has traditionally been seen either as a sign that language learners do not comprehend or as a period during which they gather the linguistic knowledge necessary to be able to speak. For Granger, such interpretations of silence ignore a third possibility, namely that silence is a part of an internal identity struggle as individuals sort out feelings of loss (of the L1) and anxiety at the prospects of an uncertain future in a new language. She selectively mines the psychoanalytic theories of Sigmund Freud, Donald Winnicott, Adam Philips and Jacques Lacan and develops a theory of identity that seems to be, at first glance, somewhat in line with what Bendle has in mind. She then draws on this theory of identity to make sense of two databases: published memoirs written by individuals who have experienced language and culture border crossings in their lifetimes and diary studies of language learners, produced by applied linguistics.

Granger employs the Freudian construct of ego, which she somewhat elliptically defines as 'a kind of overseeing intermediary, negotiating relations between internal and external worlds' (Granger, 2004: 42), where the medium of this negotiation is language.[3] She also employs constructs such as anxiety, conflict, projection and avoidance, all of which arise in relation to experiences of destabilization and loss. Parallels are drawn between what the infant experiences and what child, adolescent and adult L2 learners experience. Above all, ambivalence and liminality (i.e. existing at the threshold) are the emotional and physical metaphors, respectively, that arise from destabilization and the loss of the 'love object', in this case what Granger calls 'the first language self, that is the self that could make itself known, to the world and to itself, in its first language' (Granger, 2004: 56). Thus, in Granger there is a discourse of psychoanalysis which the author aims to draw on in her attempt to make sense of silence in SLL.

Granger revisits Marjorie Walsleben's diary study, discussed both in Bailey (1983) and Chapter 5 of this book. In particular, she questions Bailey's analysis of Walsleben's relationship with her teacher, presented as a struggle over control of her language learning. For Granger, Bailey might be right in her interpretation of Walsleben's experience; however, she thinks that there is another way of framing Walsleben's experience based on psychoanalysis. Thus, she suggests that Walsleben is involved in a struggle between the inside and outside, between Freud's' 'I should like to eat this' and 'I should like to spit it out' (Freud, 1925: 439). She sums up Walsleben's conflictive relationship with her teachers as follows:

> This conflict between 'taking in' a second language and rejecting it is rooted in the ambivalence of the learner's desire both to learn and to refuse learning that accompanies learning's perpetual state of emergency . . . It is articulated . . . in frequent analogies that the diarists make between the relationships of teachers and students and those of aprons and children. These analogies also call to mind once again the Freudian concept of family romance . . . entailing, in part, motives of sibling rivalry, among which is a sense in which the child may imagine herself as the product of a clandestine love affair between her mother and a man other than her actual father, or alternatively as the only 'legitimate' child among her siblings. (Granger, 2004: 99)

The kind of ambivalence described by Granger can be found in learners in all types of SLL contexts. For example, Silvia's ambivalence about her teacher and her classmate Rosa (see Chapter 5), might easily be seen as a conflict with a parent and sibling, respectively. (See Block, 2006b, for further discussion).

Granger's book provides food for thought regarding the application of key concepts from psychoanalysis to interview, diary and memoir data focusing on language learning experiences, even if it does not delve too deeply into psychoanalytic theory. Indeed, Granger seems to rely rather too heavily on one source in particular – Fink (1995). However, within applied linguistics, her book does represent a somewhat daring move towards the reclaiming of identity for psychology that Bendle envisages. Overall, I find Bendle's comments and suggestions about integrating psychoanalytical frameworks and constructs into social science research, and Granger's attempt to do just this in applied linguistics, thought-provoking. However, I think that before rushing to balance an overwhelmingly social view of identity with a more introspective psychoanalytically inspired one, theorists and researchers should consider that such a change in orientation is not a simple move and that there are some potential pitfalls to bear in mind.

First, there is the perhaps obvious point that psychoanalysis is not to be taken lightly. It is not an area of inquiry and/or applied discipline that an individual can take up after attending a short course covering the essentials of Freud and Lacan; rather, it is both diachronically and synchronically rich and involves years of study and practice if one wishes to theorize about identity drawing on key psychoanalytic frameworks and concepts. Thus, any applied linguists considering a sideways move, with a view to taking on board psychoanalytically inspired frameworks, should do so with both caution and respect for the field.

There is also the question of whether or not psychoanalysis is appropriate in the kind of research carried out by Goldstein, Norton, Lantolf and Genung, Kinginger and others. Perhaps psychoanalysis is not for social scientists who are exclusively oriented by social theory and sociology and who are interested in developing understandings of the identity work done by people living what Bauman (2005) has called 'liquid lives'. Liquid lives are lives in the fast lane, where 'the conditions under which . . . [people] act change faster than it takes the ways of acting to consolidate into habits and routines' (Bauman, 2005: 1). When researching the fast and furious world that Bauman describes, the right analytical framework may well be something that Bendle would find 'superficial', but which many – Bauman included – would find appropriate.

In addition, as I explained in Chapter 2, the poststructuralism-inspired model of identity that has been taken up in applied linguistics frames the construct in terms of what Gee calls 'Discourses', that is 'ways of being in the world, or forms of life which integrate words, acts, values, beliefs, attitudes and social identities, as well as gestures, glances, body positions, and clothes' (Gee, 1996: 127). This view of identities, as emergent in ongoing semiotic behaviour, is eminently social and does not move into the realm of the psychological. Indeed, it is firmly based on a social constructionist tradition going back a century, based on the early work of scholars such as George Mead (1934) and succinctly summed up by Peter Berger (1963) many years ago, when he wrote that 'identity is socially bestowed, socially sustained, and socially transformed' (Berger, 1963: 98).

Another reason for being circumspect about Bendle's call to take psychoanalysis on board is the fact that he is making reference to what is a huge discipline, including under one general heading important historical changes – from Freud to the present – and a fragmentation of different schools in the present. Thus, when Bendle suggests a psychoanalytical perspective on identity, the question arises as to whether this will be neo-Freudian, Kleinian, Lacanian and so on. In addition, if cherry-picking constructs and frameworks is the alternative to adopting an entire school of psychoanalysis, then one runs the risk of being theoretically and empirically superficial.

Finally, as Margaret Wetherell notes, there are the problematic ethics of diagnosing 'character' and 'the potential voyeuristic violence of research as diagnosis' (Wetherell, 2003: 113) which comes with the importation of frameworks from psychoanalysis into research which in principle examines the discursive. Indeed, away from its institutional habitat, a psychoanalytically inspired examination of life story interviews may seem inappropriately intrusive to those being studied, in that it focuses on individuals' intimacies.[4]

Conclusion

In this chapter, I have suggested five directions for future second language identity research carried out in adult migrant, FL, SA and other contexts. These directions require greater attention to: (1) social class as a key analytical construct; (2) more expanded and expansive conceptualizations of the second language learner's 'first language'; (3) the emergence of local *lingua francas,* such as Italian in Toronto or English in London; (4) how SLL experiences are electronically mediated in different ways; and (5) psychoanalysis as a source of analytical frameworks and constructs. No doubt, there are other directions for future research that will have occurred to the reader of this book and indeed, as this book goes to press, more will surely occur to me. However, the five directions which I have glossed here seem to be the most salient, in my view, given the current state of second language identity research.

I opened this book with three quotations, one of which was Bonny Norton's call for SLL researchers to incorporate identity in their work. With reference to the social sciences in general, Zygmunt Bauman has written that identity has become 'today's talk of the town and the most commonly played game in town' (Bauman, 2001: 16). While applied linguists have not embraced the construct to this extreme, I think that it is safe to say that many have heeded Norton's call. In Chapter 1, I cited a long list of recent books that point to this development and in Chapters 4–6, I have shown how identity is used more and more as a key construct in research.

This current interest in identity in the social sciences in general, and in applied linguistics in particular, looks likely to continue into the foreseeable future. In this book, I have taken a selective pulse of the enterprise, focusing on three specific SLL contexts. My main aim has been to show how second language identity work varies considerably across these contexts. First, it varies as regards the extent to which it actually takes place. Thus, while the formal classroom setting of FL contexts does not afford many opportunities for second-language-mediated identity work to take place, the naturalistic setting, which comes with the adult migrant context, does. Second, when second language identity work does take place, there is a good deal of variability as regards the aspects of identity that emerge as salient. Thus, in some situations, gender emerges as the single most significant aspect of identity, while in other situations, it is race or social class that is most significant. Third and finally, second language identity work varies according to highly localized social factors, shaped by the forces and flows of globalization, and the sociohistorical baggage of the individuals involved. Thus, beyond the immediate context – be this adult migrant, FL or SA – there are macro-level forces, such as the world economic order, and micro-level forces, such as moment-to-moment experiences, that impinge on and shape opportunities for second language identity work to take place.

To conclude, second language identities are variable, multifaceted and multi-levelled across different SLL contexts. In this book, I have reviewed and critiqued research which has, to varying degrees, taken on board the complexity of the construct. However, as I have made clear throughout, there is still a need for research that not only problematizes contexts – documenting the constellations of sociohistorical and sociocultural elements that form and define them – but also draws on multiple sources of data: interviews, diaries, recorded interactions and so on. Adopting such a broad approach, both conceptually and empirically, is an ambitious proposition, though not an impossible one. Above all, I think it imperative if future second language identities research is to do justice to its object of inquiry.

Notes

1 An expanded version of this section can be found in Block (2006a).

2 Although it is worth noting that Guiora, Beit-Hallahmi, Brannon, Dull and Scovel (1972) carried out research around concepts like 'language ego' some 35 years ago (see Chapter 3).

3 A more formal definition of ego is provided by Stephen Frosh, author of several books on psychoanalysis:

> [The ego is] that part of the mental apparatus in which consciousness and perception reside and which has the phenomenological status of self. Freud's word for ego was 'das Ich', the 'I'. However, as well as housing consciousness it also contains unconscious elements; these are the defence mechanisms whose role is to place the boundaries of ego and id and to ensure that troubling unconscious material is kept repressed. (Frosh, 2002: 106)

4 Still, it is worth noting that some theorists and researchers, working under the umbrella of discursive psychology, have incorporated psychoanalytical constructs and frameworks into conversation analysis (e.g. Billig, 1999, Wetherell, 2003). For example, in his book *Freud's Repression,* Michael Billig (1999) moves Freud's concept of repression – the debarring of impulses and thoughts from consciousness – from the purely unconscious to the surface. Billig is critical of Freud's treatment of repression in the different cases he discusses in his writings, stating that: 'His interest is in the causes and effects of repression rather than in the repression itself' (Billig, 1999: 27). Examining Freud's accounts, Billig sees not only how Freud's patients managed to 'do' repression, but also how Freud himself repressed certain topics and events, perhaps because they would have been shocking, embarrassing or even painful for him had he incorporated them into his accounts.

References

Acton, W. (1979) 'Second language learning and perception of difference in Attitude'. Unpublished PhD dissertation, University of Michigan.

Acton, W. and Walker de Felix, J. (1986) 'Acculturation and mind', in J. M. Valdes (ed.), *Culture Bound: Bridging the Cultural Gap in Language Teaching*. Cambridge: Cambridge University Press, pp. 20–32.

Adler, P. (1972) 'Culture shock and the cross cultural learning experience', in D. S. Hoopes (ed.), *Readings in Intercultural Education*, vol. 2. Pittsburgh, PA: Intercultural Communication. Network, pp. 6–22.

ADMIT (2000) *Higher Education Admissions and Student Mobility within the EU: Work Package 3 Students who Study Abroad: Perspectives on Mobility*. London: London School of Economics, Centre for Educational Research (and European Commission Research Directorate-General).

Ali, S. (2004) *Mixed-Race, Post-Race: Gender, New Ethnicities and Cultural Practices*. London: Berg.

Alred, G. and Byram, M. (2002) 'Becoming an intercultural mediator: a longitudinal study of residence abroad', *Journal of Multilingual and Multicultural Development* 23 (5), 339–52.

Alsop, R., Fitzsimons, A. and Lennon, K. (2002) *Theorizing Gender*. Cambridge: Polity.

Anderson, A. (2003) 'Women and cultural learning in Costa Rica: reading the contexts', *Frontiers: The Interdisciplinary Journal of Study Abroad*, 9, 21–55.

Anderson, B. (1983) *Imagined Communities: Reflections on the Origins and Spread of Nationalism*. London: Verso.

— (1991) *Imagined Communities: Reflections on the Origins and Spread of Nationalism*, 2nd edn. London: Verso.

Antonio, R. (2000) 'Karl Marx', in G. Ritzer (ed.), *The Blackwell Companion to Major Social Theorists*. Oxford: Blackwell, pp. 105–43.

Atkinson, D. (2002) 'Toward a sociocognitive approach to second language acquisition', *Modern Language Journal*, 86 (4), 524–45.

Austin, J. L. (1962) *How to Do Things With Words*. Oxford: Oxford University Press.

Baars, B. (1986) *The Cognitive Revolution in Psychology*. New York: The Guildford Press.

Bacon, S. (1995) 'Coming to grips with the culture: another use of dialogue journals in teacher education', *Foreign Language Annals,* 28 (2), 193–207.

— (2002) 'Learning the rules: language development and cultural adjustment during study abroad', *Foreign Language Annals,* 35 (6), 637–46.

Bailey, B. (2000) 'Language and negotiation of ethnic/racial identity among Dominican Americans', *Language in Society,* 29 (4), 555–82.

— (2003) *Language, Race, and Negotiation of Identity: A Study of Dominican Americans.* New York: LFB Scholarly Publishing.

Bailey, K. (1978) 'Mon journal de la classe de Français: an introspective analysis of an individual's language learning experience'. Unpublished manuscript, English Department (ESL Section), University of California, Los Angeles.

— (1983) 'Competitiveness and anxiety in adult second language learning: looking at and through the diary studies', in H. Seliger and M. Long (eds), *Classroom-oriented Research in Second Language Acquisition.* Rowley, MA: Newbury House, pp. 67–103.

Baker, P. and Eversley, J. (eds) (2001) *Multilingual Capital.* London: Battle-bridge Publications.

Bardovi-Harlig, K. (1999) 'Exploring the interlanguage of interlanguage pragmatics. A research agenda for acquisitional pragmatics', *Language Learning,* 49 (4), 677–713.

Baron-Cohen, S. (2003) *The Essential Difference: Men, Women and the Extreme Male Brain.* London: Allen Lane.

Basch, L., Glick Schiller, N. and Blanc-Szanton, C. (1994) *Nations Unbound: Transnational Projects, Postcolonial Predicaments, and Deterritorialized Nation States.* Langhorne, PA: Gordon and Breach.

Bauman, Z. (1991) *Modernity and Ambivalance.* Cambridge: Polity.

— (1992) *Intimations of Postmodernity.* London: Routledge.

— (1999) *Culture as Praxis,* new edn. London: Sage.

— (2001) *Identity.* Cambridge: Polity.

— (2005) *Liquid Life.* Cambridge: Polity.

Bayley, R. and Schechter, S. R. (eds) (2003) *Language Socialization in Bilingual and Multilingual Societies.* Clevedon, UK: Multilingual Matters.

Béal, C. (1992) 'It's all in the asking: a perspective in cross-cultural communication between native speakers of French and native speakers of Australian English in the workplace', in A. Pauwels (ed.) *Cross-cultural Communication in the Professions in Australia.* Melbourne: Applied Linguistics Association of Australia, pp. 23–52.

Beck, U. (1992) *Risk Society: Towards a New Modernity.* London: Sage.

Belz, J. (2002) 'Second language play as representation of the multicompetent self in foreign language study', *Journal of Language Identity and Education,* 1 (1), 13–39.

— and S. Thorne (eds) (2006) *Internet-mediated Intercultural Foreign Language Education*. Boston, MA: Heinle & Heinle.

Bendle, M. (2002) 'The crisis of identity in high modernity', *British Journal of Sociology*, 53 (1), 1–18.

Bennett, M. J. (1986) 'Towards ethnorelativism: a developmental model of intercultural sensitivity', in R. M. Paige (ed.), *Cross-cultural Orientation: New Conceptualizations and Applications*. New York: University Press of America, pp. 27–69.

Benson, P. and Nunan, D. (eds) (2005) *Learners' Stories: Difference and Diversity in Language Learning*. Cambridge: Cambridge University Press.

Benwell, B. (ed.) (2003) *Men's Lifestyle Magazines*. Edinburgh: Edinburgh University Press.

— and Stokoe, L. (2006) *Discourse and Identity*. Edinburgh: Edinburgh University Press.

Berger, P. (1963) *Invitation to Sociology*. Garden City, NY: Doubleday.

— and Luckmann, T. (1966) *The Social Construction of Reality*. Harmondsworth: Penguin.

Bhabha, H. (1994) *The Location of Culture*. London: Routledge.

Billig, M. (1995) *Banal Nationalism*. London: Sage.

— (1999) *Freud's Repression: Conversation Creating the Unconscious*. Cambridge: Cambridge University Press.

Block, D. (1995) 'Exploring learners' worlds: two studies'. Unpublished PhD dissertation, University of Lancaster.

— (2000) 'Learners and their meta-pedagogical awareness', *International Journal of Applied Linguistics*, 10 (1), 97–123.

— (2001) 'Foreign nationals on PGCE in Modern Languages Course: issues in national identity construction. *European Journal of Teacher Education*, 24 (3), 291–312.

— (2002a) 'Destabilized identities across language and cultural borders: Japanese and Taiwanese experiences', *Hong Kong Journal of Applied Linguistics*, 7 (2), 1–19.

— (2002b) 'Communicative language teaching revisited: discourses in conflict and foreign national teachers', *Language Learning Journal*, 26, 19–26.

— (2003) *The Social Turn in Second Language Acquisition*. Edinburgh: Edinburgh University Press.

— (2004) 'Globalisation, transnational communication and the internet', *International Journal on Multicultural Societies*, 6 (1), 13–28.

— (2005a) 'Convergence and resistance in the construction of personal and professional identities: four French Modern Language teachers in London', in S. A. Canagarajah (ed.), *Reclaiming the Local in Language Policy and Practice*. Mahwah, NJ: Lawrence Erlbaum Associates, pp. 167–96.

— (2005b) 'Introducing Spanish-speaking Latino London: some numbers and the life of an individual', *Language Issues: The Journal of NATECLA,* 17 (2), 9–15.

— (2006a) *Multilingual Identities in a Global City: London Stories.* London: Palgrave.

— (2006b) 'Identity in applied linguistics: where are we?', in T. Omoniyi and G. White (eds), *The Sociolinguistics of Identity.* London: Continuum, pp. 34–59.

Blommaert, J. (2005) *Discourse.* Cambridge: Cambridge University Press.

— (2006) 'Language policy and national identity', in T. Ricento (ed.), *Language Policy: Theory and Method.* Oxford: Blackwell, pp. 238–54.

Bourdieu, P. (1977) 'The economics of linguistic exchanges', *Social Science Information,* 16 (6), 645–68.

— (1984) *Distinction: A Social Critique of the Judgement of Taste.* London: Routledge.

— (1991) *Language and Symbolic Power.* Oxford: Polity.

Bouton, L. (ed.) (1996) *Pragmatics and Language Learning,* monograph series vol. 7. Urbana-Champaign: Division of English as an International Language, University of Illinois, Urbana-Champaign.

— (ed.) (1999) *Pragmatics and Language Learning,* monograph series vol. 9. Urbana-Champaign: Division of English as an International Language, University of Illinois, Urbana-Champaign.

Breen, M. (1987) 'Learner contributions to task design', in C. Candlin and D. Murphy (eds), *Language Learning Tasks, Lancaster Working Papers in English Language Education,* vol. 7. London: Prentice Hall, pp. 23–46.

Broeder, P., Bremer, K., Roberts, C., Vasseur, M. T. and Simonot, M. (1996) *Achieving Understanding: Discourse in Intercultural Encounters.* Longman: London.

Broner, M. and Tarone, E. (2001) '"Is it fun?" Language play in a fifth grade Spanish immersion classroom', *Modern Language Journal,* 85 (3), 363–79.

Brown, H. D. (1973) 'Affective variables in second language acquisition', *Language Learning,* 23 (2), 231–44.

— (1980) *Principles of Language Learning and Teaching.* Englewood Cliffs, NJ: Prentice Hall.

Bucholtz, M. (2003) 'Sociolinguistic nostalgia and authentification of identity', *Journal of Sociolinguistics,* 7 (3), 398–416.

Bucholtz, M. and Hall, K. (2004) 'Theorizing identity in language and sexuality research', *Language in Society,* 33 (4), 469–515.

Buckley, S. (1997) *Broken Silence: Voices of Japanese Feminism.* Berkeley, CA: University of California Press.

Butler, J. (1990) *Gender Trouble: Feminism and the Subversion of Identity*. London: Routledge.

— (1993) *Bodies That Matter: On the Discursive Limits of 'Sex'*. London: Routledge.

— (1999) *Gender Trouble: Feminism and the Subversion of Identity* (10th anniversary edn). London: Routledge.

— (2004) *Undoing Gender*. London: Routledge.

Byram, M. (1990) 'Intercultural education and foreign language teaching', *World Studies Journal*, 1 (7), 4–7.

— (1995) 'Intercultural competence and mobility in multinational contexts: a European view'. in M. Tikoo (ed.), *Language and Culture in Multilingual Societies*. Singapore: SEAMEO, pp. 21–36.

— (ed.) (1997) *Face to Face: Learning Language-and-Culture Through Visits and Exchanges*. Clevedon, UK: Multilingual Matters.

— and Alred, G. (1993) *L'Assistant(e) Français(e) in the British School*. Durham, UK: School of Education.

— and Fleming, M. (eds) (1998) *Language Learning in Intercultural Perspectives*. Cambridge: Cambridge University Press.

— and Grundy, P. (eds) (2002) *Context and Culture in Language Teaching and Learning*. Clevedon, UK: Multilingual Matters.

—, Nichols, A. and Stevens, D. (eds) (2003) *Developing Intercultural Competence in Practice*. Clevedon, UK: Multilingual Matters.

Cameron, D. (1995) 'Rethinking language and gender studies: some issues for the 1990s', in S. Mills (ed.), *Language and Gender: Interdisciplinary Perspectives*. London: Routledge, pp. 31–44.

— (1996) 'The language-gender interface: challenging co-optation', in Bergvall, V. Bing, J. and Freed, A. (eds), *Rethinking Language and Gender Research*. London: Longman, pp. 31–53.

— (2005) 'Language, gender, and sexuality: current issues and new directions', *Applied Linguistics*, 26 (4), 482–502.

— and Kulick, D. (2003) *Language and Sexuality*. Cambridge: Cambridge University Press.

— and Kulick, D. (2005) Identity Crisis? *Language & Communication*, 25 (2), 107–25.

Canagarajah, S. N. (1999) *Resisting Linguistic Imperialism in English Teaching*. Oxford: Oxford University Press.

Canale, M. and Swain, M. (1980) 'Theoretical bases of communicative approaches to second language teaching and testing', *Applied Linguistics*, 1 (1), 1–47.

Castles, S. and Miller, M. (2003) *The Age of Migration*, 3rd edn. London: Palgrave.

Cazden, C., Cancino, H., Rosanksy, E. and Schumann, J. (1975) *Second Language Acquisition in Children, Adolescents, and Adults, Final Report*. Washington DC: National Institute of Education.

Chapelle, C. (2001) *Computer Applications in Second Language Acquisition.* Cambridge: Cambridge University Press.

Cherny, L. (1999) *Conversations and Community: Chat in the Virtual World.* Stanford, CA: CSLI Publications.

Childs, I. L. (1943) *Italian or American? The Second Generation in Conflict.* New Haven, CO: Yale University Press.

Coates, J. (2003) *Men Talk.* Oxford: Blackwell.

Cohen, R. (1997) *Global Diasporas. An Introduction.* London: UCL Press.

Coleman, J. (1998) 'Language learning and study abroad: the European perspective', *Frontiers: The Interdisciplinary Journal of Study Abroad,* 9, 167–203.

Collentine, J. and Freed, B. (eds) (2004) *Learning Context and Its Effects on Second Language Acquisition,* Special Issue of *Studies in Second Language Acquisition,* 26 (2).

Collins, J. and Slembrouck, S. (eds) (2005) *Multilingualism and Diasporic Populations: Spacializing Practices, Institutional Processes, and Social Hierarchies,* Special Issue of *Language and Communication,* 25 (2).

Conradson, D. and Latham, A. (2005) 'Friendship, networks and transnationality in a world city: Antipodean transmigrants in London', *Journal of Ethnic and Migration Studies,* 31 (2), 287–305.

Cook, G. (1997) 'Language play, language learning', *English Language Teaching Journal,* 51 (2), 224–31.

— (2000) *Language Play.* Oxford: Oxford University Press.

Cook, V. (1996) 'Competence and multi-competence', in G. Brown, K. Malmkjaer and J. Williams (eds), *Performance and Competence in Second Language Acquisition.* Cambridge: Cambridge University Press, pp. 57–69.

Corder, S. P. (1981) *Error Analysis and Interlanguage.* Oxford: Oxford University Press.

Cordero-Guzmán, H. R., Smith, R. C. and Grosfoguel, R. (eds) (2001) *Migration, Transnationalization, and Race in a Changing New York.* Philadelphia: Temple University Press.

Creese, A. (2005) *Teacher Collaboration and Talk in Multilingual Classrooms.* Clevedon, UK: Multilingual Matters.

Cummins, J. (1996) *Negotiating Identities: Education for Empowerment in a Diverse Society.* Los Angeles: California Association for Bilingual Education.

— (2000) *Language, Power and Pedagogy: Bilingual Children in the Crossfire.* Clevedon, UK: Multilingual Matters.

Davies, B. and Harré, R. (1999) 'Positioning and personhood', in R. Harré and L. van Langenhove (eds), *Positioning Theory.* London: Sage, pp. 32–52.

Day, E. M. (2002) *Identity and the Young English Language Learner.* Clevedon, UK: Multilingual Matters.

Delanty, G. (2003) *Community.* London: Routledge.

Dewaele, J. M. (2005) 'Investigating the psychological and the emotional dimensions in instructed language learning: óbstacles and possibilities', *The Modern Language Journal,* 89 (3), 367–80.

Doughty, C. and Long, M. (eds) (2003) *The Handbook of Second Language Acquisition.* Oxford: Blackwell.

Dörnyei, Z. (2001) *Teaching and Researching Motivation.* London: Longman.

— (2005) *The Psychology of the Language Learner: Individual Differences in Second Language Acquisition.* Mahwah, NJ: Lawrence Erlbaum.

Dufon, M. and Churchill, E. (eds) (2006) *Language Learners in Study Abroad Contexts.* Clevedon, UK: Multilingual Matters.

Du Gay, P. (1996) *Consumption and Identity at Work.* London: Sage.

Durkheim, E. ([1893] 1964) *The Division of Labor in Society.* New York: Free Press.

— ([1895] 1964) *The Rules of Sociological Method.* New York: Free Press.

Dutton, W. H. (2004) *Social Transformation in an Information Society: Rethinking Access to You and the World.* Paris: UNESCO.

Eckert, P. (1989) *Jocks and Burnouts: Social Categories and Identity in the High School.* New York: Teachers College Press.

— (2000) *Linguistic Variation as Social Practice.* Oxford: Blackwell.

— and S. McConnell-Ginet (1992) 'Think practically and act locally: language and gender as community-based practice', *Annual Review of Anthropology,* 21, 461–90.

— and (2003) *Language and Gender.* Cambridge: Cambridge University Press.

Egbert, J. L. and Petrie, G. M. (eds) (2005) *CALL Research Perspectives.* Mahwah, NJ: Lawrence Erlbaum Associates.

Ehrlich, S. (1997) 'Gender as social practice: implications for second language acquisition', *Studies in Second Language Acquisition,* 19 (4), 421–46.

Ekeh, P. (1982) 'Structuralism: the principle of elementarism, and the theory of civilization', in I. Rossi (ed.), *Structural Sociology.* New York: Columbia University Press, pp. 122–48.

Ellig, J. R. and Morin, W. (2001) *What Every Successful Woman Knows.* New York: McGraw-Hill.

Elliot, A. (1996) *Subject to Ourselves.* Cambridge: Polity.

Ellis, R. (1985) *Understanding Second Language Acquisition.* Oxford: Oxford University Press.

— (2007) *The Study of Second Language Acquisition,* 2nd edn. Oxford: Oxford University Press.

Faist, T. (2000) *The Volume and Dynamics of International Migration.* Oxford: Oxford University Press.

Fetzer, J. S. and Soper, J. C. (2005) *Muslims and the State in Britain, France, and Germany*. Cambridge: Cambridge University Press.

Fink, B. (1995) *The Lacanian Subject: Between Language and Jouissance*. Princeton, NJ: Princeton University Press.

Fishman, P. (1980) 'Conversational insecurity', in H. Giles, P. Robinson and P. Smith (eds), *Language: Social Psychological Perspectives*. New York: Pergamon Press, pp. 127–32.

Foner, N. (2001) 'Transnationalism then and now: New York immigrants today and at the turn of the twentieth century', in H. R. Cordero-Guzmán, R. C. Smith and R. Grosfoguel (eds), *Migration, Transnationalization, and Race in a Changing New York*. Philadelphia: Temple University Press, pp. 35–57.

Foucault, M. (1981) *The History of Sexuality. Vol. 1: An Introduction*. Harmondsworth: Pelican.

— (1986) *The History of Sexuality. Vol. 2: The Use of Pleasure*. Harmondsworth: Viking.

— (1988) *The History of Sexuality. Vol. 3: The Care of the Self*. Harmondsworth: Viking.

Fouron, G. E. and Glick Schiller, N. (2001) 'The generation of identity: redefining the second generation within a transnational social field', in H. R. Cordero-Guzmán, R. C. Smith and R. Grosfoguel (eds), *Migration, Transnationalization, and Race in a Changing New York*. Philadelphia: Temple University Press, pp. 58–86.

Freed, B. (ed.) (1995) *Second Language Acquisition in Study Abroad Context*. Amsterdam: John Benjamins.

Freud, S. ([1923] 1990) *The Ego and the Id*. New York: Norton.

— (1925) *The Penguin Freud Library*, vol. 11. London: Penguin Books.

Frosh, S. (2002) *Key Concepts in Psychoanalysis*. London: The British Library.

Fuchs Ebaugh, H. R. (1988) *Becoming an Ex: The Process of Role Exit*. Chicago: University of Chicago Press.

Gardner, R. and Lambert, W. (1972) *Attitudes and Motivation in Second Language Learning*. Rowley, MA: Newbury House.

Gass, S. (1988) 'Integrating research areas: a framework for second language studies', *Applied Linguistics,* 9 (2), 198–217.

Gee, J. P. (1996) *Social Linguistics and Literacies: Ideology in Discourses*, 2nd edn. London: Falmer.

— (2004) *Situated Language and Learning: A Critique of Traditional Schooling*. London: Routledge.

—, Hull, G. and Lankshear, C. (1996) *The New Work Order: Behind the Language of the New Capitalism*. Boulder, CO: Westview Press.

Gellner, E. (1983) *Nations and Nationalism*. Oxford: Blackwell.

Giddens, A. (1991) *Modernity and Self-Identity: Self and Society in the Late Modern Age*. Cambridge: Polity.

Giles, H. and Byrne, J. (1982) 'An intergroup approach to second language acquisition', *Journal of Language and Social Psychology*, 5, 291–302.

— and Coupland, N. (1991) *Language: Contexts and Consequences*, Pacific Grove, CA: Brook/Cole.

Gilroy, P. (2000) *Between Camps: Nations, Culture and the Allure of Race*. London: Allen Lane.

— (2004) *After Empire*. London: Routledge.

Glick Schiller, N., Basch, L. and Blanc-Szanton, C. (1992) *Towards a Transnational Perspective on Migration: Race, Class, Ethnicity, and Nationalism Reconsidered*. New York: New York Academy of Sciences.

Goffman, E. (1959) *The Presentation of Self in Everyday Life*. New York: Anchor.

— (1981) *Forms of Talk*. Oxford: Blackwell.

Goldstein, T. (1996) *Two Languages at Work: Bilingual Life on the Production Floor*. New York: Mouton de Gruyter.

Granger, C. A. (2004) *Silence in Second Language Acquisition: A Psychoanalytic Reading*. Clevedon, UK: Multilingual Matters.

Gray, J. (1992) *Men are from Mars, Women are from Venus*. New York: Harper Collins.

Guiora, A. (1972) 'Construct validity and transpositional research: towards an empirical study of psychoanalytic concepts', *Comprehensive Psychiatry*, 13, 139–50.

—, Lane, H. and Bosworth, L. (1967) 'An explanation of some personality variables in authentic pronunciation of a second language', in H. Lane and E. Zale (eds), *Studies in Language and Language Behavior*, vol. 4.

—, Acton, W., Erard, R. and Strickland, F. (1980) 'The effects of benzodiazephine (valium) on permeability of language ego boundaries', *Language Learning*, 30, 351–63.

—, Brannon, R. and Dull, C. (1972) 'Empathy and second language learning', *Language Learning*, 22 (1), 111–30.

—, Beit-Hallahmi, B., Brannon, R., Dull, C. and Scovel, T. (1972) 'The effects of experimentally induced changes in ego states on pronunciation ability in a second language: an exploratory study', *Comprehensive Psychiatry*, 13, 421–8.

Gumperz, J. (1992) 'Contextualization revisited', in P. Auer and A. DiLuzio (eds), *The Contextualization of Language*. Amsterdam: John Benjamins, pp. 39–53.

Hadi-Tabussen, S. (2006) *Language, Space and Power: A Critical Look at Bilingual Education*. Clevedon, UK: Multilingual Matters.

Hall, D. (2004) *Subjectivity*. London: Routledge.

Hall, J. K. (2002) *Teaching and Researching Language and Culture.*
London: Longman.

Hall, K. (1997) '"Go suck your husband's sugarcane!" Hijras and the
use of sexual insult', in A. Livia and K. Hall (eds), *Queerly Phrased:
Language, Gender, and Sexuality.* Oxford: Oxford University Press,
pp. 430–60.

Hall, S. (1996) 'Introduction: Who needs "identity"?' in S. Hall
and P. du Gay (eds), *Questions of Cultural Identity.* London: Sage,
pp. 1–17.

Han, Z. H. (2004) *Fossilization in Adult Second Language Acquisition.*
Clevedon, UK: Multilingual Matters.

Hannerz, U. (1996) *Transnational Connections.* London: Routledge.

Harris, R. (2006) *New Ethnicities and Language Use: The Emergence of
Brasian Identities.* London: Palgrave.

— and Rampton, B. (2002) 'Creole metaphors in cultural analysis: on the
limits and possibilities of (socio-)linguistics', *Critique of Anthropology,*
22 (1), 31–51.

Harvey, D. (1989) *The Condition of Postmodernity.* Oxford: Blackwell.

Hegel, G. W. F. ([1806] 1977) *Phenomenology of Spirit.* Oxford:
Clarendon Press.

Held, D., McGrew, A., Goldblatt, D. and Perraton, J. (1999) *Global
Transformations: Politics, Economics and Culture.* Cambridge: Polity.

Hobsbaum, E. (1990) *Nations and Nationalism Since 1780: Programme,
Myth, Reality.* Cambridge: Cambridge University Press.

Holmes, J. (2000) 'Doing collegiality and keeping control at work: small
talk in government departments', in J. Coupland (ed.), *Small Talk.*
London: Longman, pp. 32–61.

— and Meyerhoff, M. (eds) (2003) *The Handbook of Language and
Gender.* Oxford: Blackwell.

Holstein, J. and Gubrium, J. (2000) *The Self We Live By.* Oxford: Oxford
University Press.

hooks, b. (1996) *Bone Black: Memories of Girlhood.* New York: Henry
Holt and Company.

Hutnyk, J. (2005) 'Hybridity', *Ethnic and Racial Studies,* 28 (1), 9–102.

International Studies Abroad website: www.studiesabroad.com.

Isabelli-García, C. (2006) 'Study abroad and social networks,
motivation and attitudes: implications for second language
acquisition', in M. DuFon and E. Churchill (eds), *Language Learners
in Study Abroad Contexts.* Clevedon, UK: Multilingual Matters,
pp. 231–58.

James, W. ([1890] 1961) *Psychology: The Briefer Course.* New York:
Harper and Brothers.

Jaspers, J. (2005) 'Linguistic sabotage in a context of monolingualism
and standardization', *Language and Communication,* 25 (2), 279–97.

Jensen, A., Jaeger, K. and Lorentsen, A. (eds) (1995) *Intercultural Competence: A New Challenge for Language Teachers and Trainers in Europe. Vol. II: The Adult Learner.* Aalborg: Aalborg University Press.

Johnson, S. and Meinhof, U. (eds) (1997) *Language and Masculinity.* Oxford: Blackwell.

Jordan, B. and Düvell, F. (2003) *Migration: The Boundaries of Equality and Justice.* Cambridge: Polity.

Joseph, J. (2004) *Language and Identity.* London: Palgrave.

Kanno, Y. (2003) *Negotiating Bilingual and Bicultural Identities: Japanese Returnees Betwixt Two Worlds.* Mahwah, NJ: Lawrence Erlbaum Associates.

Kasper, G., and Rose, K. (2002) *Pragmatic Development in a Second Language.* Oxford: Blackwell.

Kelsky, K. (2001) *Women on the Verge.* Durham, NC: Duke University Press.

Kinginger, C. (2004) 'Alice doesn't live here anymore: foreign language learning and identity construction', in A. Pavlenko and A. Blackledge (eds) *Negotiation of Identities in Multilingual Contexts.* Clevedon, UK: Multilingual Matters, pp. 219–42.

— and Farrell Whitworth, K. (2005) 'Gender and emotional investment in language learning during study abroad'. CALPER Working Papers, Series No. 2. The Pennsylvania State University, Center for Advanced Language Proficiency Education and Research.

Kramsch, C. (1993) *Context and Culture in Language Teaching.* Oxford: Oxford University Press.

— (1998) *Culture.* Oxford: Oxford University Press.

— (2000) 'Social discursive constructions of self in L2 learning', in J. Lantolf (ed.), *Sociocultural Theory and Second Language Learning.* Oxford: Oxford University Press, pp. 133–53.

— (2003) 'Identity, role and voice in cross-cultural (mis)communication', in J. House, G. Kasper and S. Ross (eds), *Misunderstanding in Social Life.* London: Longman, pp. 129–53.

— and Lam, W. S. E. (1999) 'Textual identities: the importance of being non-native', in G. Braine (ed.), *Non-Native Educators in English Language Teaching.* Mahwah, NJ: Lawrence Erlbaum Associates, pp. 57–75.

Krashen, S. (1981) *Second Language Acquisition and Second Language Learning.* Oxford: Pergamon.

Kress, G. and van Leeuwen, T. (2001) *Multimodal Discourse.* London: Edward Arnold.

Kulick, D. (1998) *Travesti: Sex, Gender and Culture among Brazilian Trans-gendered Prostitutes.* Chicago: University of Chicago Press.

Labov, W. (1966) *The Social Stratification of English in New York City.* Washington DC: The Center for Applied Linguistics.

— Labov, W. (2001) *Principles of Linguistic Change, Vol. 2: Social Factors*. Oxford: Blackwell.

— and Fanshel, D. (1977) *Therapeutic Discourse*. New York: Academic Press.

Lacan, J. (1977) *Écrits: A Selection*. New York: Norton.

Lachman, R., Lachman, J. and Butterfield, E. (1979) *Cognitive Psychology and Information Processing*. Hillsdale, NJ: Lawrence Elrbaum.

Lakoff, R. (1975) *Language and Woman's Place*. New York: Harper & Row.

Lam, W. S. E. (2004) 'Second language socialization in a bilingual chat room', *Language Learning and Technology*, 8 (3), 44–65.

Lambert, W. (1972) 'A social psychology of bilingualism', in A. S. Dil (ed.), *Language, Psychology, and Culture. Essays by Wallace E. Lambert*. Stanford, CA: Stanford University Press, pp. 212–35. Originally published in 1967 in *The Journal of Social Issues*, 23 (2), 91–109.

—, Gardner, R., Barik, H. and Tunstall, K. (1963) 'Attitudinal and cognitive aspects of intensive study of a second language', *Journal of Abnormal and Social Psychology*, 66, 358–68.

Lantolf, J. (1997) 'The function of language play in the acquisition of L2 Spanish', in A. Pérez-Leroux and W. R. Glass (eds), *Contemporary Perspectives on the Acquisition of Spanish*. Somerville, MA: Cascadilla Press, pp. 3–24.

— and Genung, P. (2003) '"I'd rather switch than fight": an activity theoretic study of power, success, and failure in a foreign language classroom', in C. Kramsch (ed.), *Language Acquisition and Language Socialization*. London: Continuum, pp. 175–96.

Laubscher, M. R. (1994) *Encounters with Difference: Student Perceptions of the Role of Out-of-class Experiences in Education Abroad*. Westport, CO: Greenwood Press.

Lave, J. and Wenger, E. (1991) *Situated Learning: Legitimate Peripheral Participation*. Cambridge: Cambridge University Press.

Layder, D. (1993) *Sociological Practice*. London: Sage.

— (1997) *Modern Social Theory*. London: UCL Press.

Leech, G. (1983) *The Principles of Pragmatics*. London: Longman.

LePage, R.B. and Tabouret-Keller, A. (1985) *Acts of Identity: Creole-based Approaches to Language and Ethnicity*. Cambridge: Cambridge University Press.

Leung, C., Harris, R. and Rampton, B. (1997) 'The idealised native speaker, reified ethnicities and classroom realities', *TESOL Quarterly*, 31 (3), 543–60.

Levi-Strauss, C. (1972) *Structural Anthropology*. Harmondsworth, UK: Penguin.

Liddicoat, A. and Crozet, C. (2001) 'Acquiring French interactional norms through instruction', in K. Rose and G. Kasper (eds), *Pragmatics in Language Teaching*. Cambridge: Cambridge University Press.

Long, M. (1985) 'Input and second-language acquisition theory', in
S. Gass and C. Madden (eds), *Input in Second Language Acquisition.*
Rowley, MA: Newbury House, pp. 377–93.

McLaughlin, B. (1987) *Theories of Second Language Learning.* London:
Edward Arnold.

McMahill, C. (1997) 'Communities of resistance: a case study of two
feminist English classes in Japan', *TESOL Quarterly,* 31 (4),
612–22.

— (2001) 'Self-expression gender, and community: a Japanese feminist
English class', in A. Pavlenko, A. Blackledge, I. Piller and M. Teutsch-
Dwyer (eds), *Multilingualism, Second Language Acquisition,*
pp. 307–44.

MacMaster, N. (2001) *Racism in Europe.* London: Palgrave.

Maiworm, F., Steube, W. and Teichler, U. (1991) *Learning Europe: The
ERASMUS Experience.* London: Jessica Kingsley Publishers.

— (1993) *Experiences of ERASMUS Students 1990/91.* Kassel:
ERASMUS Monographs.

— (1996) *Studying Abroad and Early Career: Experiences of Former
ERASMUS Students.* London: Jessica Kingsley Publishers.

Mathews, G. (2000) *Global Culture/Individual Identity: Searching for a
Home in the Cultural Supermarket.* London: Routledge.

May, S. (2001) *Language and Minority Rights.* London: Longman.

Mead, G. H. (1934) *Mind, Self and Society.* Chicago: Chicago University
Press.

Mercer, K. (1990) 'Welcome to the jungle: identity and diversity
in postmodern politics', in J. Rutherford (ed.), *Identity: Culture,
Community, Difference.* London: Lawrence and Wishart,
pp. 43–71.

Miller, J. (2003) *Audible Differences: ESL and Social Identity in Schools.*
Clevedon, UK: Multilingual Matters.

Milroy, L. (1987) *Language and Social Networks.* Oxford: Blackwell.

Mitchell, R. and Myles, F. (2004) *Second Language Leaning Theories,*
2nd edn. London: Arnold.

Modood, T. (2005) *Multicultural Politics: Racism, Ethnicity and Muslims
in Britain.* Edinburgh: Edinburgh University Press.

Mohan, B., Leung, C. and Davison, C. (2001) *English as a Second
Language in the Mainstream: Teaching, Learning, and Identity.*
London: Longman.

Moyer, A. (2004) *Age, Accent and Experience in Second Language
Acquisition: An Integrated Approach to Critical Period Inquiry.*
Clevedon, UK: Multilingual Matters.

Mübig-Trapp, P. and Schnitzer, K. (1997) *Gearing up for Europe via
Student Mobility and Internationalization of Study.* Hanover,
Germany: Higher Education Information System.

Murphey, T., Jin, C. and Li-Chi, C. (2005) 'Learners' constructions of identities and imagined communities', in P. Benson and D. Nunan (eds), *Learners' Stories: Difference and Diversity in Language Learning.* Cambridge: Cambridge University Press, pp. 83–101.

Murphy-Lejeune, E. (2002) *Student Mobility and Narrative in Europe: The New Strangers.* London: Routledge.

Naiman, N., Frohlich, M. Stern, D. and Todesco, A. (1978) *The Good Language Learner.* Toronto: Ontario Institute for Studies in Education.

Nederveen Pieterse, J. (2004) *Globalization and Culture. Global Mélange.* Oxford: Rowman and Littlefield.

Norton (Pierce), B. (1995) 'Social identity, investment, and language learning', *TESOL Quarterly,* 29 (1), 9–31.

Norton, B. (2000) *Identity and Language Learning.* London: Longman.

— (2001) 'Non-participation, imagined communities and the language classroom', in M. Breen (ed.), *Learner Contributions to Language Learning.* London: Longman, pp. 159–71.

Omoniyi, T. (2004) *The Sociolinguistics of Borderlands: Two Nations, One Community.* Trenton, NJ: Africa World Press.

ONS (Office for National Statistics) (2001) Census. London: ONS. www.statistics.gov.uk/census2001.

Ortner, S. (2005) 'Subjectivity and cultural critique', *Anthropological Theory,* 5(1), 31–52.

Papastergiadis, N. (2000) *The Turbulence of Migration.* Cambridge: Polity.

Parker, G. and Rouxeville, A. (eds) (1995) *The Year Abroad: Preparation, Monitoring, Evaluation.* London: AFLS/CILT.

Parsons, T. (1937) *The Structure of Social Action.* New York: McGraw Hill.

Pavlenko, A. (2002) 'Poststructuralist approaches to the study of social factors in second language learning and use', in V. Cook (ed.), *Portraits of the L2 User.* Clevedon, UK: Multilingual Matters, pp. 277–302.

— (2006) *Emotions and Multilingualism.* Cambridge: Cambridge University Press.

— (ed.) (2006) *Bilingual Minds: Emotional Experience, Expression and Representation.* Clevedon, UK: Multilingual Matters.

— and Blackledge, A. (eds) (2004) *Negotiation of Identities in Multilingual Settings.* Clevedon, UK: Multilingual Matters.

—, Blackledge, A., Piller, I. and Teutsch-Dwyer, M. (eds) (2001) *Multilingualism, Second Language Learning, and Gender.* New York: Mouton De Gruyter.

Payne, P. and Smith, B. (eds) (1998) *Research Issues in the Year Abroad.* Lancaster: Centre for Research in Language Education.

Pellegrino, V. (2005) *Study Abroad and Second Language Use: Constructing the Self.* Cambridge: Cambridge University Press.

Perdue, C. (ed.) (1993a) *Adult Language Acquisition: Crosslinguistic Perspectives. Volume 1: Field Methods.* Cambridge: Cambridge University Press.

— (ed.) (1993b) *Adult Language Acquisition: Crosslinguistic Perspectives. Volume 2: The Results.* Cambridge: Cambridge University Press.

Perlmutter, H. V. (1991) 'On the rocky road to the first global civilization', *Human Relations,* 44 (9), 897–920.

Pierce, C. S. ([1902] 1955) 'Logic as semiotic', in J. Buchler (ed.), *Philosophical Writings of Peirce.* New York: Dover Books.

Pilkington, A. (2003) *Racial Disadvantage and Ethnic Diversity in Britain.* London: Palgrave.

Piller, I. and Takahashi, K. (2006) 'A passion for English: desire and the language market', in A. Pavlenko (ed.), *Bilingual Minds: Emotional Experience, Expression and Representation.* Clevedon, UK: Multilingual Matters, pp. 59–83.

Polanyi, L. (1995) 'Language learning and living aboard: stories from the field', in B. Freed (ed.), *Second Language Acquisition in Study Abroad Context.* Amsterdam: John Benjamins, pp. 271–91.

Portes, A., Guarnizo, L. E. and Landolt, P. (1999) 'The study of transnationalism: pitfalls and promise of an emergent research field', *Ethnic and Racial Studies,* 22 (2), 217–37.

Puri, J. (2004) *Encountering Nationalism.* Oxford: Blackwell.

Ramanathan, V. (2005) *The English-Vernacular Divide: Postcolonial Language Politics and Practice.* Clevedon, UK: Multilingual Matters.

Rampton, B. (1990) 'Displacing the "native speaker": expertise, affiliation and inheritance', *ELT Journal,* 44 (2), 97–101.

— (1995) *Crossing: Language and Ethnicity among Adolescents.* London: Longman.

— (2005) *Crossing: Language and Ethnicity Among Adolescents,* 2nd edn. Manchester: St Jerome Press.

— (2006) *Language in Late Modernity: Interaction in an Urban School.* Cambridge: Cambridge University Press.

Reich, R. (1991) *The Work of Nations.* New York: Vintage.

Reicher, S. and Hopkins, N. (2001) *Self and Nation.* London: Sage.

Renan, E. ([1882] 1990) 'What is a nation?', in H. K. Bhabha (ed.), *Nation and Narration.* London: Routledge, pp. 8–22.

Ribé, R. (1997) *Tramas creativas y aprendizaje de lenguas: prototipos de tareas de tercera generación.* Barcelona: Universitat de Barcelona.

—, and Vidal, N. (1993) *Project Work: Step by Step.* Oxford: Heinemann.

Ritzer, G. (1992) *Sociological Theory,* 3rd edn. New York: McGraw Hill.

Roberts, C., Byram, M., Barro, A., Jordan, S. and Street, B. (2001) *Language Learners as Ethnographers.* Clevedon, UK: Multilingual Matters.

Rose, K. and Kasper, G. (eds) (2001) *Pragmatics in Language Teaching.* Cambridge: Cambridge University Press.

Sarangi, S. and Slembrouck, S. (1992) 'Non-cooperation in communication: a reassessment of Gricean pragmatics', *Journal of Pragmatics,* 17 (2), 117–54.

Sardar, Z. (2004) *Desperately Seeking Paradise.* London: Granta.

Schechter, S. R. and Bayley, R. (2002) *Language as Cultural Practice: Mexicanos en el Norte.* Clevedon, UK: Multilingual Matters.

Schmidt, R. (1983) 'Interaction, acculturation, the acquisition of communicative competence', in N. Wolfson and E. Judd (eds), *Sociolinguistics and TESOL.* Rowley, MA: Newbury House, pp. 137–74.

—, and Frota, S. (1986) 'Developing basic conversational ability in a second language: a case study of an adult learner of Portuguese', in R. R. Day (ed.), *Talking to Learn: Conversation in Second Language Acquisition.* Rowley, MA: Newbury House, pp. 237–326.

Schumann, J. (1974) 'The implications of interlanguage, pidginization and creolization for the study of adult second language acquisition', *TESOL Quarterly,* 8 (1), 145–52.

— (1976a) 'Social distance as a factor in second language acquisition', *Language Learning,* 26 (2), 135–43.

— (1976b) Second language acquisition: the pidginization hypothesis, *Language Learning,* 26 (4), 391–408.

— (1978) *The Pidginization Process: A Model for Second Language Acquisition.* Rowley, MA: Newbury House.

— (1986) 'Research on the acculturation model for second language acquisition', *Journal of Multilingual and Multicultural Development,* 7 (5), 379–92.

Scovel, T. (1978) 'The effect of affect on second language learning: a review of anxiety research', *Language Learning,* 28, 129–42.

Scollon, R. (2001) *Mediated Discourse: The Nexus of Practice.* London: Routledge.

— and Scollon, S. W. (2003) *Discourses in Place: Language in the Material World.* London: Routledge.

Selinker, L. (1992) *Rediscovering Interlanguage.* London: Longman.

Siegal, M. (1995) 'Individual differences and study abroad: women learning Japanese in Japan', in B. Freed (ed.), *Second Language Acquisition in a Study Abroad Context.* Amsterdam: John Benjamins, pp. 225–44.

— (1996) 'The role of learner subjectivity in second language sociolinguistic competency: Western women learning Japanese'. *Applied Linguistics,* 17 (3), 356–82.

Silverstein, M. (1998) 'Contemporary transformations of local linguistic communities', *Annual Review of Anthropology,* 27, 401–26.

Simmel, G. (1950) 'The Stranger', in K. Wolff (ed.), *The Sociology of Georg Simmel.* New York: Free Press, pp. 401–8.

Singleton, D., and Ryan, L. (2004) *Language Acquisition: The Age Factor,* 2nd edn. Clevedon, UK: Multilingual Matters.

Skarin, R. (2001) 'Gender, ethnicity, class and social identity: a case study of two Japanese women in US universities', in E. Churchill and J. McLaughlin (eds), *Qualitative Research in Applied Linguistics: Japanese Learners and Contexts.* Tokyo: Temple University, Japan, pp. 26–55.

Skeggs, B. (1997) *Formations of Class and Gender: Becoming Respectable.* London: Sage.

— (2004) *Class, Self, Culture.* London: Routledge.

Smart, B. (1999) *Facing Modernity.* London: Sage.

Smith, A. (1991) *National Identity.* Harmondsworth, UK: Penguin.

— (2003) *Chosen Peoples: Sacred Sources of National Identity.* Oxford: Oxford University Press.

— (2004) *The Antiquity of Nations.* Cambridge: Polity.

Snow, D. and Byram, M. (1997) *Crossing Frontiers: The School Study Visit Abroad.* London: CILT.

Solomos, J. (2003) *Race and Racism in Britain,* 3rd edn. London: Palgrave.

Spivak, G. (1990) *The Post-Colonial Critic: Interviews, Strategies, Dialogues.* London: Routledge.

Talburt, S. and Stewart, M. (1999) 'What's the subject of study abroad?: race, gender, and "living culture"', *Modern Language Journal,* 83 (2), 163–75.

Tannen, D. (1990) *You Just Don't Understand: Men and Women in Conversation.* New York: William Morrow.

Taylor, C. (1989) *Sources of Self: The Making of the Modern Identity.* Cambridge, MA: Harvard University Press.

Teutsch-Dwyer, M. (2002) '(Re)constructing masculinity in a new linguistic reality', in A. Pavlenko, A. Blackledge, I. Piller and M. Teutsch-Dwyer (eds), *Multilingualism, Second Language Acquisition, and Gender.* New York: Mouton de Gruyter, pp. 175–98.

Teichler, U. and Maiworm, F. (1997) *The ERASMUS Experience: Major Findings of the ERASMUS Evaluation Research Project.* Kassel: ERASMUS Monographs.

Thomas, J. (1983) 'Cross-cultural pragmatic failure', *Applied Linguistics,* 4 (1), 91–112.

Thorne, S. (2003) 'Artifacts and cultures-of-use in intercultural communication', *Language Learning and Technology,* 7 (2): 38–67.

Thurlow, C., Lengel, L. and Tomic, A. (2004) *Computer Mediated Communication: Social Interaction and the Internet.* London: Sage.

Toohey, K. (2000) *Learning English at School: Identity, Social Relations and Classroom Practice*. Clevedon: Multilingual Matters.

Turkle, S. (1995) *Life on the Screen: Identity in the Age of the Internet*. New York: Simon and Schuster.

Tusting, K., Crawshaw, R. and Callen, B. (2002) '"I know, 'cos I was there": how residence abroad students use personal experience to legitimate cultural generalizations', *Discourse and Society*, 13 (5), 651–72.

Twombly, S. (1995) 'Piropos and friendships: gender and culture clash in study abroad', *Frontiers: The Interdisciplinary Journal of Study Abroad*, 1, 1–27.

van Langenhove, L. and Harré, R. (1999) 'Introducing positioning theory', in R. Harré and L. van Langenhove (eds), *Positioning Theory*. London: Sage, pp. 14–31.

Walsleben, M. (1976) 'Cognitive and affective factors influencing a learner of Persian (Farsi) including a journal of second language acquisition'. Unpublished manuscript, English Department (ESL Section), University of California, Los Angeles.

Warschauer, M. (1999) *Electronic Literacies: Language, Culture, and Power in Online Education*. Mahwah, NJ: Lawrence Erlbaum Associates.

— (2003) *Technology and Social Inclusion: Rethinking the Digital Divide*. Cambridge, MA: MIT Press.

Watson-Gegeo, K. (2004) 'Mind, language, and epistemology: toward a language socialization paradigm for SLA', *The Modern Language Journal*, 88 (3), 331–50.

Weedon, C. (1987) *Feminist Practice and Poststructuralist Theory*. Oxford: Blackwell.

— (1997) *Feminist Practice and Poststructuralist Theory* 2nd edn. Oxford: Blackwell.

Wenger, E. (1998) *Communities of Practice*. Cambridge: Cambridge University Press.

West, C. (1984) 'When the doctor is a "lady"', *Symbolic Interaction*, 7 (1), 87–106.

Wetherell, M. (2003) 'Paranoia, ambivalence, and discursive practices: concepts of position and positioning in psychoanalysis and discursive psychology', in R. Harré and F. Moghaddam (eds), *The Self and Others*. London: Praeger, pp. 99–120.

White, C. (2003) *Language Learning in Distance Education*. Cambridge: Cambridge University Press.

Whyte, W. F. (1943) *Street Corner Society*. Chicago: University of Chicago Press.

Widdowson, H. G. (1978) *Teaching Language as Communication.*
Oxford: Oxford University Press.

Wilkinson, S. (1998a) 'Study abroad from the participants' perspective:
a challenge to common beliefs', *Foreign Language Annals,* 31 (1),
23–39.

— (1998b) 'On the nature of immersion during study abroad: some
participant perspectives', *Frontiers: The Interdisciplinary Journal of
Study Abroad,* 4, 121–38.

— (2002) 'The omnipresent classroom during summer study abroad:
American students in conversation with their French hosts', *Modern
Language Journal,* 86 (2), 157–73.

Winder, R. (2004) *Bloody Foreigners.* London: Little, Brown.

Wodak, R., de Cillia, R., Reisigl, M. and Liebhart, K. (1999) *The
Discursive Construction of National Identity.* Edinburgh: Edinburgh
University Press.

Woodward, K. (2002) *Understanding Identity.* London: Arnold.

Zuengler, J. and Miller, E. (2006) 'Cognitive and sociocultural
perspectives: two parallel SLA worlds?', *TESOL Quarterly,* 40 (1),
35–58.

Index

Printed in Great Britain
by Amazon

16349784R00165